Close the Deal

Other Books by the Authors

Smart Moves: 140 Checklists to Bring Out the Best from You and Your Team

Smart Moves for People in Charge: 130 Checklists to Help You Be a Better Leader

Yes, You Can! 1,200 Inspiring Ideas for Work, Home, and Happiness

Power Tools: 33 Management Inventions You Can Use Today

What to Say to Get What You Want: Strong Words for 44 Challenging Bosses, Employees, Coworkers, and Customers

What to Ask When You Don't Know What to Say: 555 Powerful Questions to Use for Getting Your Way at Work

COMEX: The Communication Experience in Human Relations

Speaking Skills for Bankers

By Sam Deep

Human Relations in Management

A Program of Exercises for Management and Human Behavior (with James A. Vaughan)

Introduction to Business: A Systems Approach (with William D. Brinkloe)

Studies in Organizational Psychology (with Bernard M. Bass)

Current Perspectives for Managing Organizations (with Bernard M. Bass)

By Lyle Sussman

Communication for Supervisors and Managers

Increasing Supervisory Effectiveness

Contents

Acknowledgments   xi
Introduction: Less Pain, More Gain   xiii

☑ **Chapter 1: Prepare for Success**   1

1. Eleven Advantages of a Selling Career   1
2. Fourteen Tips for Presenting a Professional Image   3
3. Nine Steps to a Positive First Impression   6
4. Nineteen Steps to Get Value from a Sales Meeting   8
5. Seven Ways to See Yourself as Others Do   11
6. Fifteen Affirmations to Get Through a Tough Day   13
7. Eleven Actions That Increase Your Energy   14
8. Ten Hints to Beat Procrastination   16
9. Twenty Areas of Life Where Your Actions Need to Match Core Values   18
10. Ten Communication Strategies of Successful Sales Professionals   20
11. Ten Tips for Avoiding Common Communication Errors   22
12. Ten Ways to Keep Your Selling Skills Sharp   25

☑ **Chapter 2: Master TIPPS (Time, Information, People, Place, and Stress)**   28

13. Thirteen Tips for Time Management   28
14. Nine Ways to Maximize "Pay Time" and Minimize "No Pay Time"   31
15. Eleven Qualities of a Successful Sales Plan   33
16. Thirteen Strategies for Serving Large Territories   35
17. Ten Guidelines for Phoning across Time Zones   37
18. Thirteen Ways to Make Valuable Contributions to a Meeting   39

19. Thirteen Guidelines for Working with Tough
    Coworkers   41
20. Seventeen Guidelines for Working with Tough Bosses   46
21. Seventeen Questions to Help You Sell with Integrity   50
22. Thirteen Tips for Maintaining Personal Balance   52
23. Thirteen Empowering Responses to Adversity   55
24. Fourteen Antidotes for Stress   57
25. Sixteen Goals That Successful Salespeople Achieve   60

☑ **Chapter 3: Know Your Market**   63

26. Ten Methods to Track Market Trends   63
27. Ten Techniques for Conducting a Competitor
    Analysis   65
28. Fourteen Sources of Market and Customer
    Information   67
29. Ten Dimensions That Define Your Market   70
30. Eleven Guidelines for Creating a Customer
    Advisory Group   72
31. Thirteen Smart Price-Setting Strategies   75
32. Thirteen Qualities of Attractive Premiums   77
33. Six Methods to Create a Sales Forecast   80
34. Twenty-Five Strategic Questions to Improve the
    Impact of Sales and Marketing Campaigns   81
35. Fifty Business Terms to Master   83

☑ **Chapter 4: Find Buyers**   88

36. Forty Sources for Leads   88
37. Thirteen Tips for Increasing Your Net Worth Through
    Networking   90
38. Nine Strategies for Getting Past the Receptionist
    on the Phone   93
39. Sixteen Strategies for Getting More Appointments with
    Buyers over the Phone   96
40. Nine Creative Ways to Get the Appointment   101
41. Seven Steps for Remembering a Person's Name   103
42. Fifteen Ways to Warm Up to Cold Calling   105
43. Fourteen Methods for Rejecting Rejection   107
44. Ten Ways to Get the Most Out of a Booth
    at a Trade Show   110

45. Twenty-One Ways You and Your Company Can Make a Splash at a Trade Show   114
46. Ten Tips for Working a Trade Show   116
47. Seventeen Ingredients of a Successful Direct Mail Marketing Campaign   118
48. Sixteen Tips for Getting Your Letters Read   122

☑ Chapter 5: Analyze Buyers   125

49. Ten Psychological Principles You Need to Know   125
50. Four Ways to Categorize Personality Types   128
51. Ten Signs of Interpersonal Style   129
52. Twelve Ways to Tailor Your Sales Presentation to How Buyers Screen the World   131
53. Seven Fears All Buyers Have   134
54. Eleven Negative Assumptions Most Buyers Have about You and the Sales Process   136
55. Seven Ways You Don't Want to Enable Buyers to Abuse You   138
56. Ten Steps for Discovering the Buyer's Budget   139
57. Twenty-Seven Facts to Learn about Your Buyer   142
58. Twenty-One Questions to Ask about the Buyer's Decision-Making Process   143

☑ Chapter 6: Bond and Build Rapport   146

59. Eleven Reasons Up-Front Contracts Help You and the Buyer   146
60. Ten Ways to Increase Sales Effectiveness Through Vocals   150
61. Fifteen Ways to Increase Sales Effectiveness Through Body Language   152
62. Fourteen Statements That Help Buyers Maintain Their Self-Esteem   155
63. Ten Suggestions for Selling to a "Dominant" Type   157
64. Eight Suggestions for Selling to an "Influencer" Type   159
65. Six Suggestions for Selling to a "Steady Relater" Type   161
66. Eight Suggestions for Selling to a "Compliant" Type   162
67. Twelve Ways to Identify and Sell to a Visual Buyer   164
68. Twelve Ways to Identify and Sell to an Auditory Buyer   166
69. Twelve Ways to Identify and Sell to a Kinesthetic Buyer   168

☑ Chapter 7: Determine the Pain 172

70. Seven Motives Your Buyer May Have 172
71. Nine Reasons Why Questions Are Your Most
    Powerful Sales Tools 174
72. Eight Types of Questions and When to Ask Them 175
73. Nine Ways to Ask Questions Without Sounding
    Alienating or Manipulative 177
74. Fifteen Steps to Better Listening 179
75. Thirty-Four Pains Your Product or Service
    Might Reduce 183
76. Thirty Questions That Probe for Pain 184
77. Nineteen Reverses That Clarify the Buyer's Position 186
78. Fifteen Dummy-up Reverses That Keep You in Charge 190
79. Nine Ways to Remain Third-Party During a Sales Call 192
80. Fourteen Intangibles Buyers Will Buy 194

☑ Chapter 8: Get the Sale 198

81. Thirteen Uses of Negative Reverse Selling 198
82. Sixteen Tough Questions to Build Your Product
    Knowledge 202
83. Eight Ways to Communicate Product Knowledge 204
84. Seven Tips for Translating Your Jargon 205
85. Fourteen Ingredients of a Winning Proposal 207
86. Fourteen Steps to Ensure Successful Sales Presentations
    to Groups and Committees 210
87. Twenty Steps to a Successful Presentation to a Large
    Audience 214
88. Eight Questions to Ask When the Buyer Is Considering
    Someone Else's Offer 218
89. Eight Questions to Ask When Pressured to Respond to
    an Unreasonable Deadline or Price Offer 220
90. Eleven Questions to Ask When the Buyer Says, "Take
    It or Leave It" 221
91. Fourteen Strategies for Creating Win-Win Negotiations 224
92. Eight Times to Walk Away from a Sale 227

☑ Chapter 9: Manage the Post-Sell 229

93. Twenty Questions That Help You Debrief Your
    Sales Call 229

94. Six Ways to Add Value to a Client's Business   230
95. Five Ways Customers Want Your Product or Service   232
96. Fifteen Questions to Answer to Ensure Major Account
Penetration   234
97. Fifteen Customer Service Visions   236
98. Eighteen Categories of Questions to Focus Your
Customer Service   238
99. Ten Commandments of Exceptional Customer Service   241
100. Fourteen Steps to a Customer Satisfaction Survey   243
101. Seventeen Customer Encounters That Call for Gracious
Responses   245
102. Nine Strategies for Preventing Buyer's Remorse   248
103. Eleven Responses to Heal the Customer Who
Feels Betrayed   250
104. Twelve Strategies for Hanging on to Your Customers   254
105. Six Steps to Ensure You Don't Lose an Endangered
Customer   257

☑ **Chapter 10: Selling in the New Millennium**   259

106. Ten Personal Characteristics Required of Sellers
in the New Millennium   259
107. Nine Ways to Become More Resilient in Times
of Change   261
108. Fifteen Ideas for Better Use of Information Technology   264
109. Eleven Hints for Using Presentation Software   267
110. Eighteen Tips for Selling on the Internet   269
111. Eleven Principles of E-mail Etiquette   273
112. Fourteen Tips for Successful Team Sales   276
113. Thirteen Rules for Selling Across Cultures   279
114. Nine Tips for Selling Through an Interpreter   282
115. Ten Ways to Increase Customer Share   284
116. Fourteen Areas in Which to Become a Complete
Sales Team Leader   286
117. Nine Guidelines for Sales Force Compensation   289
118. Ten Expectations to Have When Your Company
Is Merged   291
119. Ten Prescriptions for Staying Out of Legal Trouble   294

☑ **Chapter 11: A Day in the Life of Wally Weakcloser**   296

120. Forty-Four Things Wally Did Wrong   296

About the Authors   307
Does Your Sales Team Need Help?   309
Do You Have Sales Smarts?   311

Acknowledgments

We owe much to many people for the roles they played in the writing of this book.

The success that *180 franchisees* of the Sandler Sales Institute have had with the Sandler Selling System convinced us that it was a perfect complement to the material we were putting into a book on sales.

Also from the Sandler Sales Institute, *Edna Sandler* and *Jim Martin* helped us to envision the *Smart Moves*–SSI blend on a foggy and rainy day in the Laurel Mountains. As writing proceeded, *Bruce Seidman* and *Al Lucco* joined the team to draft occasional lists and ensure that our rendition of David Sandler's ideas remained faithful to the original. Special thanks to Bruce for his insistence that we find a place for Wally Weakcloser (list #120).

Mark Elfstrand wrote list #32.

Raymond "Buddy" LaForge provided the foundation for list #34.

Lisa Ivancic advised us on what to include and exclude in list #119. We got a confirming second opinion from *Dick Joseph*, who also wordsmithed our attempt to stay out of trouble on a list on staying out of trouble.

Lloyd Corder helped us look at the book through the eyes of its readers.

The finest editor any authors ever had, *John Bell*, was right in believing that there was yet another *Smart Moves* book to be written. And, as usual, John's final contribution makes him as much a co-author as an editor.

Our loving wives, *Di* and *Suzy*, put up with our absent minds and long nights at the keyboard over the months of manuscript preparation.

Introduction:
Less Pain, More Gain

*If you don't have a selling system of your own
when you are face to face with a buyer, you will
unknowingly default to his system.*
                                        —David Sandler

Let's face facts. If selling were easy, every sales professional would meet or surpass sales goals, turnover would be nonexistent, and sales managers would want their children and grandchildren to follow in their footsteps.

But it's not easy. Trying to get leads and then trying even harder to get those buyers to return your call is enough to make anyone disheartened, frustrated, and sick. Fighting to keep existing customers constantly wooed by competitors makes even the most upbeat salesperson wonder if maybe there isn't an easier to way to make a buck. But you don't have to succumb to the frustration and heartache. You don't have to wish for success and carry lucky charms. You *can* reduce your pain and increase your sales. You can do it because David Sandler did it and created a renowned sales training program that has helped thousands achieve financial success.

Sandler's quote begins our book and provides our first tip for reducing your pain. Even though buyers never attend training programs entitled "How to Deal with Salespeople," they nonetheless all seem to follow the same system. Your buyer feels little if any remorse about ignoring your calls, soliciting free market information, controlling your agenda, and draining your energy. Without your own set of proven principles and rules, you will "unknowingly default to his system," a system guaranteed to make you feel overworked, unappreciated, and underpaid.

Masterful sales professionals are neither lucky nor gifted. They do not dream, wish, or hope for victory. They go out and make it happen. The wannabe salesperson hopes for luck, the professional relies on a proven system. You can be that professional by applying the Sandler sales principles set forth in this book.

The *Smart Moves* Format

In our more than fifty years' combined experience as consultants, trainers, executive coaches, and speakers, we discovered a fundamental truth: The most insightful principles in the world are meaningless if they aren't read, aren't understood, or can't be applied. This truth provides the foundation for the simple yet powerful *Smart Moves* format: cross-referenced lists containing practical, proven advice. It has served as the foundation for two of our most popular books: the original *Smart Moves* and *Smart Moves for People in Charge*. These two books combined have more than 250,000 copies in print in 13 languages.

Why the *Smart Moves* Format Works

The popularity and usefulness of the *Smart Moves* books stem from their construction. They are built from lists (like this one). These lists do five things for you, the reader.

1. They yield nuggets of information with little verbiage.

2. They provide comprehensive coverage with little verbiage.

3. They give you options to read sequentially, randomly, or purposively.

4. They appeal to our need for order, logic, and structure.

5. They bring simplicity and practicality to complex and theoretical issues.

The Sandler Selling System

The two earlier *Smart Moves* books relied on our personal knowledge and experience. The advice was based on our primary expertise: communication and management. We knew that in writing *Close the Deal: Smart Moves for Selling* we would want to tap the expertise of sales training professionals. We found that expertise at the Sandler Sales Institute. The partnership with SSI exists for a simple reason: its system works. Thirty years in the marketplace, thousands of satisfied corporate clients, and endorsements from some of the top companies around the world attest to the system's power.

Why the Sandler Selling System Works

The Sandler System is based on two simple tenets. First, if you are feeling abused and pressured, you're doing something wrong. After reading *Close the Deal* you will wonder why you worked so hard on leads that were destined to fail. Through the use of up-front contracts, candor, and reverses, you can regain control without coming across as hungry, pushy, or arrogant.

Second, the buyer will close the sale. You need not guess, hope, or manipulate. You simply have to probe the buyer's pain, budget, and decision process. When you probe these three key elements you will hear the buyer magically composing the script that contains the exact words the buyer wants to hear. That's right. With the Sandler Selling System you simply help buyers sell themselves.

These tenets are reflected in eight characteristics that differentiate this system from other sales training programs.

1. It is a *system* as opposed to a collection of scripts, gambits, techniques, and one-liners. Other sales training programs rely on specific tactics, such as memorizing specific closers. The Sandler approach views selling as a process that begins with bonding and concludes with servicing the sale.

2. The principles and strategies are designed to achieve a fundamental goal: reducing the buyer's pain, the barrier blocks, and the frustrations that prevent personal and organizational success.

3. Unlike other sales training programs, the Sandler Selling System does not require you to memorize scripts, hooks, or closers. Probing the buyer's needs provides the script.

4. The buyer does not feel manipulated or "psyched out," because your goal is to match the buyer's pain to your proposed solution.

5. Thanks to up-front contracting, both you and the buyer develop a clear understanding of expectations and commitments; neither feels threatened, confused, or abused.

6. Most buyers bring assumptions, prejudices, and potentially devious tactics to their meetings with salespeople; this system candidly addresses those issues.

7. The principles and strategies are based on the essential compo-

nents of effective communication: empathy, listening, and adaptation.

8. The system ultimately creates win-win outcomes: both you and the buyer develop a mutually beneficial relationship built on candor and trust.

We are excited that 40 of the 120 lists in this book directly teach the Sandler Selling System. These lists are concentrated mostly in chapters 4 through 8. From "Finding the Buyer" to "Getting the Sale," you'll learn how to maintain control while leading the buyer to the decision you want the buyer to make.

How to Get the Most Value from This Book

Turn your investment in this book into life-long dividends.

Use the reading strategy best for you. Read it cover to cover, "cherry-pick" the best from lists you choose at random, or focus on those chapters and lists of greatest use to you right now.

Keep this book handy. A book like this can't help you while sitting on your bookshelf. Keep it on your desk when you're in your office and in your briefcase when you're on the road. Use it to review your options at each stage of the selling process.

Take advantage of the cross-references. A number in parentheses following certain items in the lists indicates another list with supporting information. Use these cross-references each time they appear to strengthen the advice you read.

Build in your own reinforcement. One of David Sandler's favorite lines was that you can't teach a kid to ride a bicycle at a seminar. He might have said the same for books. You can't learn to sell effectively just by reading *Close the Deal*. You need to go over it repeatedly, apply its prescriptions, learn from the results, apply them again, learn again from the results, and keep going.

Take plenty of notes. We hope you're not afraid to write in books, because this one is a perfect candidate for lots of scribble. Record the successes and failures you have with each list. Write in your own scripts to apply the ideas in the face-to-face selling chapters. Add your own actions to the ones we suggest.

Share it. Don't be stingy. You have colleagues and friends who can benefit from these lists. Turn them on to the book, but if you loan it out, prepare never to get it back. When you believe you have achieved a real breakthrough in one of the areas covered by a list or two, lead a brown bag seminar for your colleagues to share your new insights.

Test everything you read. Don't take our word for anything in this book. If anything we suggest doesn't feel right to you, ignore it. Use what fits your style and the buyer you're meeting with.

Pick and choose from the best of Sandler to create your personal selling system. The Sandler Selling System really works. Just ask the thousands of sales professionals who use it to make more sales and more money than they ever thought possible. But those same thousands have their own stories of how they tailored the approach to their personalities, their products, and their buyers. You'll understand the options you have for customization after you get into the lists. Before you do that, experience the character of the system by scanning through David Sandler's tantalizing one-liners. Many are at the root of the concrete advice presented throughout the book.

The Best of David Sandler's One-Liners

As a sales trainer, David Sandler was a combination therapist, teacher, comedian, and coach. Although no printed text could capture the energy and spontaneity of his style, we can capture the essence of his wit and his sales training approach. We conclude this introduction with 22 David Sandler quips that provide a glimpse into the Sandler Selling System and set the stage for the 120 lists that follow.

1. **Selling is no place to get your needs met—only a place to go to the bank.**

The purpose of selling is to make money. You'll achieve that purpose when you put your ego aside and focus your energy on what it takes to close the deal.

2. **If you're not having fun, get out of the business.**

When you use the Sandler Selling System, there will be times that the hardest thing for you to do will be to keep a straight face.

3. **Selling is a Broadway show played by a psychiatrist.**

Buying is an emotional experience for the prospect, but shouldn't be one for the salesperson. Becoming emotionally involved in a sales call makes it harder for you to close. Keep your composure and objectivity, as a psychiatrist does. The buyer and the seller (you) are the players. You as psychiatrist also need to be the director.

4. You must be invited in. No begging.

Use the system to get the buyer to ask you for an appointment.

5. No planning on the first call.

Just show up and work off the buyer's responses.

6. You have to be a third party at the selling event.

The clearest perspective is the view from the ceiling, where you are detached—observing the seller (you) and the buyer.

7. The problem the buyer brings you is *never* the problem.

Your buyers have learned over the years to protect their vulnerabilities by not voluntarily revealing their real problems.

8. The way to get rid of a bomb is to defuse it before it blows.

You have a recurring problem with your service or product. Rather than wondering when your buyer will "lower the boom," bring it up yourself in order to defuse it on your own terms. The first rule of "avalanche prevention" is to trigger smaller, planned avalanches, thereby eliminating any possibility of a major, unexpected downslide.

9. If your competition does it, stop doing it right away.

If you do what your competition is doing, where is the edge? Be unique in how you present your product and yourself.

10. When your foot hurts—you're probably standing on your own toe.

Take responsibility for the way your buyer is or isn't behaving by setting firm, up-front contracts about what is supposed to happen next.

11. You can't sell anything to anybody—they must discover they want it.

Try to convince people and they become defensive. Instead, help them feel their pain vividly. Let them discover how you can eliminate that pain.

12. Don't spill your candy in the lobby.

Don't reveal product knowledge too soon. Wait until you learn the buyer's pain. And then reveal only that which relieves the pain. Don't talk yourself out of the sale by saying too much.

13. Salespeople don't get thrown out, they bail out.

Under pressure from the buyer, most traditional salespeople end the sales interview on their own, without any help from the buyer. Take one more crack at uncovering the buyer's pain before you walk out.

14. Get an IOU for everything you do.

Be of service. Go the extra mile. Do whatever it takes to satisfy your customers. Let them dump on you. Just get an IOU for it. Otherwise, you'll train customers to expect it.

15. Always let a buyer preserve his or her dignity.

Even when a buyer takes a shot at himself (knowingly or not), bail him out. Help people feel OK about themselves.

16. You are earning exactly what you believe you're worth—not a penny more, and not a penny less.

Sales represents the classic case of the self-fulfilling prophecy.

17. You don't learn how to win in sales by getting a yes; you learn how to win every time you get a no.

Rejoice in the "no's." Learn from your lessons.

18. Don't look professional: struggle, struggle, struggle.

The way to make people feel comfortable being around you is not to come across like the "Shell Answer Man"—too polished, with all the answers. Learn to struggle naturally and people will want to bail you out. Be not-OK on purpose.

19. People buy for their reasons, not yours.

Don't get excited about the features and benefits of your product. Get excited by getting to the root of the buyer's pain.

20. Don't paint seagulls in your buyer's picture.

Every feature and benefit you add to the list of reasons your buyer should buy adds one more possibility for an objection. The buyer may be allergic to birds.

21. It's OK to be depressed.

You don't need a positive mental attitude to be a great sales professional. People who jump up and down and reply, "Great!" when you ask them, "How are you doing?" scare people. It's not the real world to be in a profession where you stick your arm in a meat grinder every day and shout, "I love it, I love it, I love it!"

22. The moment you get angry is the moment you'll become more successful in sales.

There's a point most people reach in sales—a point from which there's no turning back—a point when you're angry enough not to put up with the baloney buyers have been throwing at you for years. This is the point where you decide that you will gain control of the sales process with the Sandler Selling System.

Prepare for Success

Without a solid foundation a house could not weather storms and would eventually crumble. Similarly, the sales profession is built on a foundation. That foundation is composed of values reflecting family, integrity, work ethic, and personal accountability. These values are also reflected in skills and behaviors that help you weather personal and professional storms. In this chapter you'll learn to build a personal and professional foundation and fix any cracks that might appear in it.

— — —

1 Eleven Advantages of a Selling Career

> My father always told me, "Find a job you love and you'll never have to work a day in your life."
> — Jim Fox

Rodney Dangerfield built his comic career on a signature tag line: "I get no respect." Unfortunately, there are far too many salespeople who suffer from the Dangerfield syndrome—either they feel they get no respect or, worse, they act that way. They walk around with sullen expressions and a woe-is-me outlook. They are selling sympathy rather than solutions. If we are describing you, study this list carefully. Hold your head high and reflect the pride of your profession. Selling really is a great field. It has advantages that few other careers can claim.

1. Selling solves problems and fulfills needs.

What you're selling will either relieve pain or provide pleasure. Depending on what you sell, customers will be better able to solve problems, make more money, serve others better, enhance their self-esteem, improve their knowledge, or fulfill a heart's desire. When you do your job, you help people get what they want out of life.

2. Only your efforts and creativity limit your potential.

Selling is the classic example of pay for performance. This explains why so many high-energy, focused people are attracted to sales. Their level of achievement, and therefore their income, has no ceiling.

3. Selling provides an opportunity to work with people.

Are people exasperating? Absolutely. Will they give you heartaches, headaches, and stomachaches? Without question. But they are also fun, exciting, and challenging. As a salesperson you experience this exhilarating challenge every time you go to work. (19, 20)

4. Selling may be the purest form of empowerment.

When you sell, you have to solve problems on the spot. You are accountable for solving a customer's problem then and there. While everyone else in your company may be debating the pros and cons of empowerment, you are living it.

5. Selling is a psychological high.

Stand outside any factory and study the faces of the workers leaving their shift. Are you witnessing the "joy of victory" or the "agony of defeat"? Now look at any salesperson who has just closed an important deal, landed a new customer, or solved a current customer's problem. You're watching a winner.

6. Selling makes you test your mettle every day.

Every time athletes step onto the playing field they have to prove themselves. They're only as good as their next performance. Sales provides you the same opportunity to show your stuff.

7. Selling provides immediate feedback on your performance.

It's also unmistakable. The reactions you get from buyers and customers leave no doubt of how you're doing. You can use that feedback to constantly improve. Every time you present yourself and your product, you have a chance to sharpen your skills.

8. Selling generates revenue.

A company makes money only when a customer decides to buy its product. You help the customer make that decision. As long as you're generating sales, you have little reason to worry about job security.

9. **Selling is the direct communication link between the customer and the company.**

Salespeople are in the best position to monitor market trends. Your customers tell you exactly what's right and wrong with your product, what to improve, and what to leave alone. You hear about their pains and frustrations, and you hear about their dreams and aspirations. You are the eyes and ears of the company. When you speak, you describe the future of the company.

10. **Selling provides a path for upward mobility.**

Sales is a highly visible office in most companies. When you succeed, everyone in your company as well as your competitors knows it. Your chances for advancement increase in direct proportion to your sales success.

11. **Sales prepares you for other careers.**

The on-the-job training you get in sales is unparalleled. You succeed in sales only by being an effective presenter, psychologist, sociologist, planner, peacemaker, negotiator, consultant, leader, follower, financier, and deliverer.

▬ ▬ ▬

2 Fourteen Tips for Projecting a Professional Image

Nothing succeeds like the appearance of success.
— Christopher Lasch

It's one thing to lose a sale because you can't solve the buyer's problem. It's quite another to fail because the buyer chose not to deal with someone who didn't fit the image of a professional salesperson. What is the correct image? You don't have to look like a professional model, wear Ermenegildo Zegna suits, or get plastic surgery. Just follow these steps to help make buyers happy to deal with you.

1. **Select clothes that enhance your coloring, shape, and height.**

Although clothes come in standard sizes, no two people are exactly alike. Some look better in solid muted colors, others in bold patterns. If you have doubts about what looks best on you, confer with a professional fashion consultant, an image counselor, or a friend with obvious fashion sense.

2. Develop a relationship with a single store and if possible with a single salesperson.

Find someone just like you: a professional committed to solving a customer's problem. Make sure that professional knows what apparel you need, knows what's available to meet that need, and will sell you only those garments that are best for you and the buyers you call on.

3. Don't *buy* clothes, *invest* in them.

View your wardrobe as part of your tool chest. A professional doesn't skimp on the tools that provide a livelihood. But remember, you want the best tool chest for your needs, not necessarily the most expensive one. As with any investment, look for top value for your dollar.

4. Maintain your wardrobe.

Keep your clothing clean and protected. Take care to avoid food stains. Regularly dry-clean those garments requiring it. Wear raincoats and use umbrellas in inclement weather. Store your wardrobe away from dust and sunlight.

5. Match your daily outfits with taste.

As you dress for each day, combine and accessorize the clothing you've bought in order to look good, feel comfortable, and be relaxed.

6. Take care of your shoes.

As many as one out of four buyers will intentionally take note of the condition of your shoes during the sales call. What will they see? Worn heels and soles? Only ancient evidence of shoe polish? Dust or dirt? Worn or broken shoelaces? Cracks in the leather? Salt stains from walking in slush? If they see such things, they may lose confidence that you'll pay proper attention to the details of their order. (61)

7. Dress for the season and the climate.

Depending on where you work and the respective seasons, you may need different wardrobes for different times of the year. If you travel around the country, dress for the people at the destination, not the departure.

8. Dress for the place.

Choose a wardrobe and make daily selections according to the city you are in and the buyer you're calling on. You might not choose to call on a hands-on plant manager in a double-breasted suit, or call on a Fortune 500 CEO in a sports jacket.

9. For long plane flights (or waits in airports) choose wrinkle-resistant fabrics.

You can look like fifty million bucks walking into an airport and a buck fifty walking out of it. Plan your daily wardrobe for the wear and tear it will receive.

10. Pack your clothes carefully for travel.

Buy garment bags and suitcases that will enable your clothes to arrive looking as good as when you packed them. Experiment with various ways of packing shirts, blouses, dresses, or suits until you learn the secrets of wrinkle-free travel. Pack a travel iron.

11. Always maintain proper hygiene.

You can't sell quality and excellence if your personal appearance contradicts those values. Check with trusted friends about personal hygiene predicaments such as halitosis, dandruff, or body odor. If any of these problems exist, change your brand of mouthwash, shampoo, or bath soap. If they persist, check with a physician.

12. Consult a makeup specialist.

This is more often an issue for women, but men may also benefit from hints to help disguise weaknesses and accentuate attributes.

13. Project confidence.

You can't lead a cavalry charge if you think you look funny on a horse. The confidence you have in yourself, the faith you have in your product, and the assurance you have in your problem-solving ability will go a long way toward helping you make a positive impression. If you feel good inside, you are more likely to look good outside. Everything about your persona should communicate a clear and consistent message: I am the person who will help you solve your problem. (6, 43)

14. Don't . . .

- Wear too much fragrance or use perfumed hair spray.
- Stroke or play with your hair.
- Wear clothes that are too tight or too loose.
- Think you can get away with wearing black running shoes.
- Brag about your designer labels, your Rolex, or your Mercedes.
- Wear socks that allow your calf to show (men).
- Wear outfits or makeup more suitable for evening wear (women).
- Unbutton a double-breasted suit.
- Wear short-sleeved shirts under jackets.
- Let your nails grow too long or get dirty.
- Leave the house without checking yourself out in a full-length mirror.

3 Nine Steps to a Positive First Impression

Wear a smile and have friends; wear a scowl and have wrinkles. — George Eliot

Regardless of what you sell, you are competing for the buyer's business. Why make it harder on yourself by having to overcome a negative first impression? Why give your competitors the advantage because you fail to present yourself in the best light? Remember, as the saying goes, you never get a second chance at a first impression. Get it right the first time.

1. Make sure any letters you send before your first meeting are grammatically perfect.

Anything with your name or your company's name on it is a billboard. What does your billboard say? Run your letters through the grammar checker of your software program. Make absolutely certain you spell the buyer's name correctly. (11)

2. If the buyer has an unusual name, learn the correct pronunciation before the meeting.

You should be able to obtain the correct pronunciation from someone at your buyer's company or from the buyer directly. Don't be afraid to ask the buyer, who will be impressed by your desire to be courteous and respectful. If the name is difficult, practice it a few times. (41)

3. Arrive early.

Plan for road construction, traffic patterns, and inclement weather. Arrive about 15 minutes prior to your appointment. When you announce yourself to the receptionist, say something like, "My name is [. . .]; I am [. . .] minutes early for an appointment with [. . .]."

4. If the first meeting requires a flight, ask your travel agent to allow for delays and cancellations.

Make sure there's a later plane you can take if your planned flight is canceled. Arrive at your airport at least one hour before departure; add a half hour to check baggage. Schedule layovers of no less than one hour at connecting airports; add a half hour if connecting planes are not from the same airline. Give yourself double the time you're told you'll need to get from the airport to the buyer's office. You don't want to arrive feeling stressed or huffing, puffing, and looking disheveled.

5. Check yourself out in a mirror before you meet a buyer.

Full-length mirrors are best. When pressed for time, store windows will do the trick. Fix what you can.

6. Check your teeth, clean your breath.

Using mouthwash, mints, or sprays about 30 minutes prior can make a meeting more pleasant for the buyer. Be sure you can smile and speak without offending.

7. Greet the client with a smile and direct eye contact.

Sam Walton taught his Wal-Mart associates the "10-foot rule." Whenever they were within 10 feet of a customer they were expected to smile, engage in eye contact, and prepare to greet warmly. Convey the message to your buyer that you are truly glad to be there.

8. Extend your hand for a bonding handshake.

The handshake is one of your first opportunities to connect with the buyer. Don't blow it. Slide your hand completely into that of the buyer and make *full palm contact*—do not cup your hand. Once you've made this critical connection, one or two pumps, six inches up and down, will suffice. Don't crush the hand or rotate the wrist. You're introducing yourself, not taking a blood pressure reading or proving you lift weights.

9. **Make sure any information you bring to show the client is easily retrieved, attractive, and functional.**

Shuffling though a briefcase for brochures, pulling out an unexpectedly tattered file, or turning on a laptop that takes too long to load will be a true test of both the buyer's patience and the effectiveness of your deodorant.

---

4 Nineteen Steps to Get Value from a Sales Meeting

> *Education costs money, but then so does ignorance.* —Sir Claus Moser

As a professional salesperson you continually look for ways to add value to your clients and your company. It is equally important to seize every opportunity to add value to *yourself*. One way to do this is to attend a sales conference, which may be put on by your employer or, more typically, by a trade association or other sponsoring organization. Don't take the decision to attend a sales conference lightly. There can be a hefty registration fee, along with other out-of-pocket costs. Even more important are the opportunity costs of attending—every hour you spend listening to a speaker or strolling the exhibits is an hour in which you'll not be calling on buyers. Use this list to ensure that you make good choices among sales conferences and that you get the most out of the ones you attend.

Choose the Right Meeting for You

1. **What do you want to get out of a meeting?**

What makes a sales meeting valuable to you? What kind of learning are you looking for? Whom do you hope to network with? What competitive intelligence do you need?

2. What do you think of the sponsoring organization?

Do you respect it? Are you confident it can pull off the kind of meeting you value? Is it experienced with this sort of thing, or is this its first time out?

3. What does the brochure tell you?

Do you sense a commitment to quality, integrity, and professionalism? You can't always judge a book by its cover, but program brochures have a way of telling reliable tales.

4. Whom is the program aimed at?

Does it look appropriate for your level, organization, industry, interests, values, experience, and client base? The brochure will often give answers. The location chosen for the program will also give you clues to its appropriateness to your station in sales.

5. Who are the speakers and their topics?

Do you recognize names or their organizations? Is their experience relevant to your needs? Are the learning objectives of their presentations meaningful to you?

6. What's the format of the program?

How many plenary sessions will there be? How many concurrent sessions are scheduled, and are they lecture or workshop? What's happening at lunchtime? Are receptions planned? Does the schedule look either too full or too sparse?

7. Who's likely to attend?

Will enough people be there to make networking valuable? Will too many people be present at breakout sessions to allow for personal attention to your needs and your questions? Do typical attendees have the same interests as you?

8. What materials are provided?

Will you receive a comprehensive conference workbook? How extensive are each speaker's handouts? Are audiotapes or videotapes of sessions available? Will you receive a copy of the proceedings? Is any form of follow-up made available after the program?

9. What about the fee?

How does the fee relate to your perception of program quality? Does it appear to be either too high or too low? Are discounts offered for registering in advance? Is there a money-back guarantee for dissatisfaction? Can you get a full refund at the last minute if you can't attend?

Once You Choose a Meeting

10. Set goals.

Depending on the length and breadth of the conference, establish from three to six goals. In what areas of sales do you need to grow? Which educational sessions will you attend to achieve your goals? Make a list of 20 pointed questions you intend to have answered at the meeting.

11. Create an action-plan notebook.

Prepare a loose-leaf notebook that contains plenty of blank paper. One sheet should list your 20 questions. Dedicate a blank sheet to each of your growth goals. Draw a line down the center of each goal sheet. In the left half of each goal sheet write the forces that you believe have been blocking that goal. Some of these forces will be constraints imposed on you by your employer, your clients, or the environment; most of the forces are constraints you impose on yourself. List them all.

12. Contact selected speakers.

Get the names and addresses of speakers at sessions that look good to you. Write, call, or send e-mail to them to learn what you can expect from their sessions. These communications will help you create a bond with speakers that you can reinforce at the meeting.

Once You Get to the Meeting

13. Network.

Ask speakers out to breakfast, lunch, or dinner. Meet everyone at the meeting; talk to as many of them as you can. Collect business cards and make notes about people's expertise, interests, and referral potential on the back. (37)

14. Participate actively in sessions.

Ask questions, make contributions, and be visible. This will energize your mind and increase your learning. But be careful to remain relevant to the current focus of the discussion and not to hog time.

15. Take detailed notes.

Use the blank sheets in your notebook. Whenever you get an insight that relates to one of your goals, record it on the appropriate goal sheet directly next to the constraining force it counteracts. (If it doesn't counteract a negative force on the sheet, either it's not really helpful or you haven't yet listed all the constraining forces.) Aggressive note taking helps you organize your thoughts and keeps you involved in your learning.

16. Study your action-plan notebook.

Within 48 hours after the meeting, sit down with your notebook. Examine it for the most important insights you received. In your notebook, write three actions you'll take immediately to increase your sales effectiveness.

17. Brief your boss.

Share your notebook and your three actions with your manager. Get a commitment for whatever support you need in order to profit from your learning experience.

18. Write a report.

Prepare a one- to three-page paper summarizing the primary value you found at the meeting. Circulate it to your manager, to coworkers, and to anyone else who might be interested.

19. Brief the staff.

Share whatever value you received from the meeting with your coworkers—perhaps over a brown-bag lunch.

■■■ ■■■ ■■■

5   Seven Ways to See Yourself as Others Do

> *People who shut their eyes to reality simply invite*
> *their own destruction.*   —James Baldwin

In *The Scarlet Letter*, Hester Prynne was forced to wear the letter *A* across her bosom to signify adultery. We know many salespeople who should sport the letter *D*—for denial. These salespeople have yet to get a reality check. They look at themselves through their own eyes, not their boss's, coworkers', buyers', or customers' eyes. Only when they see themselves as others do will they be empowered to make those changes that will cause others to feel better about working with them.

1. Study yourself on videotape.

Make a sale to the camera. Try to be as natural as possible, doing exactly what you would do if the camera were an actual customer. Play the tape and study it carefully. As a result, make three commitments to improve your presentations.

2. Ask a trusted colleague to view your videotape with you and offer coaching tips.

An objective third party will see things on the tape you may not. You may also discover that what you think is a problem is nothing of the sort. If your colleague hesitates to be honest with criticisms, pose this question: "What *three* things can I do to improve the next presentation I make?"

3. If you can afford a personal coach, hire one.

A professional sales coach is trained to detect subtleties and nuances in your performance that others may overlook or be reluctant to bring to your attention.

4. When you receive performance evaluations, listen carefully before you deny or defend.

Although some observations should be taken with a grain of salt, look for the kernel of truth. Even if the evaluator's perceptions are distorted, *those are the perceptions.* Make sure you understand the perceptions before either defending your behavior or attempting to correct it.

5. Ask for and study feedback from customers.

Use written or phone surveys to learn what your customers like best and least about your image, presentation style, and persona. (100)

6. Ask for and study feedback from buyers who rejected your proposals.

You may obtain more honest information from buyers who turned you down than from current customers. They're not prone to respond to a written survey, and they may be tough to get on the telephone, but their feedback is worth a king's ransom. Get it.

7. Ask for feedback using the word *one*.

How did you respond to the last restaurant cashier who asked, "How was everything?" You probably said, "Fine" even if the bread was a bit stale. Why weren't you more truthful and more helpful? You were asked the wrong question! It was too easy for you to politely wriggle off the hook. Had the restaurant cashier asked, "What's *one* thing we could have done to make your meal more enjoyable?" you would have said, "Serve fresher bread." In the same way, get honest performance feedback by asking, "What's *one thing* I could do to improve my . . . ?"

▬ ▬ ▬

6 Fifteen Affirmations to Get Through a Tough Day

> *You will never stub your toe by standing still. The faster you go, the more chance there is of stubbing your toe, but the more chance you have of getting somewhere.* — Charles Kettering

There are going to be days when your tooth aches, your car won't start, and your last sales call was a disaster. You'll need a shot in the arm, a pat on the back, or a kick in the pants. One of the following thoughts may be just what you need in order to make the next sales call the best of your career.

1. Success is a choice. — *Rick Pitino*

2. Success in life comes not from holding a good hand, but in playing a poor hand well. — *Warren Lester*

3. I shall tell you a great secret, my friend. Do not wait for the last judgment; it takes place every day. — *Albert Camus*

4. If you're not fired up with enthusiasm, you'll be fired with enthusiasm. — *Vince Lombardi*

5. There is no security on this earth; there is only opportunity. — *Douglas MacArthur*

6. Yesterday's the past and tomorrow's the future. Today is a gift, which is why they call it the present. —*Bill Keane*

7. Show me a thoroughly satisfied man and I will show you a failure. —*Thomas Edison*

8. When you get to the end of your rope tie a knot and hang on. —*Franklin D. Roosevelt*

9. The best way to predict your future is to create it. —*Author unknown*

10. I always remember an epitaph which is in the cemetery at Tombstone, Arizona. It says, "Here lies Jack Williams. He done his damnedest." I think that is the greatest epitaph a man can have. —*Harry S Truman*

11. Triumph? Try Umph! —*Author unknown*

12. You hit home runs not by chance but by preparation. —*Roger Maris*

13. If you don't have enough pride, you're going to get your butt beat every play. —*Gale Sayers*

14. My mother taught me very early to believe I could achieve any accomplishment I wanted to. The first was to walk without braces. —*Wilma Rudolph*

15. You may have to fight a battle more than once to win it. —*Margaret Thatcher*

— — —

7 Eleven Actions That Increase Your Energy

I want to be remembered as the ballplayer who gave all he had to give. —Roberto Clemente

Selling is a stressful occupation. It challenges your physical strength. It calls for every ounce of stamina, endurance, and vitality you can muster. Here's how to meet the challenge.

1. Eat right.

High-fat foods, high-protein foods, and foods high in sugar are hard to digest and tire you. Favor the complex carbohydrates found in grains, fruits, and vegetables. Sweets may help in midafternoon when sugar levels in the body drop sharply.

2. Exercise regularly.

Moderate exercise opens blood vessels, strengthens the heart, delivers more oxygen to the brain, and deepens your sleep. Walk, run, climb, swim, ride a bicycle, ski cross-country, or work out on an exercise machine.

3. Breathe deeply.

When you're feeling run down, take several deep breaths through your nose, holding the air in for a few seconds before releasing it slowly through your mouth. Help your breathing with good posture; elevate your collarbones about one inch.

4. Get enough sleep.

You may be sleep deprived, having conditioned your body to accept five or six hours when it needs closer to eight. To lengthen your sleep, get to bed 15 minutes earlier each night for the next week. Increase that by another 15 minutes each succeeding week until you feel rested when you arise. To deepen your sleep, avoid alcohol, nicotine, caffeine, and heavy eating within four hours of bedtime. Don't exercise or get mentally keyed up within an hour of bedtime. Keep your bedroom cooler than the rest of your home.

5. Drink plenty of water.

Even mild dehydration causes fatigue. Drink a full glass of water in the morning, with every meal, and in the evening. Avoid highly caffeinated beverages; they dry you out.

6. Remain positive and upbeat.

Stay away from negative people; don't allow them to drag you down to their lethargic and depressed states. Focus on the blessings and successes in your life. Unexplained fatigue, drowsiness, and a need for extraordinary amounts of sleep are potential signs of depression. If there's any chance you suffer clinical depression, see a professional right away. If you live in a northern climate, make a point of getting sun in the winter months to avoid seasonal affective disorder. (23, 43)

7. Get a complete physical.

Rule out disease or illness as energy robbers.

8. Manage your stress.

Poorly managed stress can rob you of energy and vitality. Eradicate some of the sources of stress in your life to increase your power to deal with what remains. Unsettled resentments, unresolved anger, and long-standing grudges dampen your zest for life. Talk to the people involved and fix your troubled relationships. (19, 20, 23, 24)

9. Monitor your medications.

Many prescription and over-the-counter medications cause drowsiness. Talk to your doctor and read labels for side effects. Ask your pharmacist for alternatives to favorite antihistamines, pain relievers, and cough suppressants that may be slowing you down.

10. Go easy on legal drugs.

Caffeine, nicotine, and alcohol all sap your energy. Coffee may jump-start you in the morning, but drinking too much may rob you of deep evening sleep. Cigarette smoke impairs lung function, deprives you of oxygen, and constricts blood vessels, slowing down the flow of energy-building blood. As a depressant, alcohol in more than moderation slows down the speed of the central nervous system.

11. Get others to do their share.

Don't wear yourself out by being everything to everyone. You can't do it all, either at home or at work. Learn how to delegate and how to get others to accept more responsibility and do more of their share of the work. (19, 112, 116)

▬ ▬ ▬

8 Ten Hints to Beat Procrastination

> *The truth of the matter is that you always know the right thing to do. The hard part is doing it.*
> — General H. Norman Schwarzkopf

The work you do as a sales professional can be divided into two categories: what's fun and what isn't. The tasks that are fun get done right away, even sooner than needed. The drudgery gets put on the back burner, and too often we forget to turn the gas on. In other words, we procrastinate—sometimes endlessly. How do you beat procrastination?

1. Do what you hate first.

Start your workday by first doing the task you most dread. Schedule the least enjoyable tasks to be done during the time of day when you are most energetic. Never put them at the end of the day; it's too easy at five o'clock to say, "Oh well, I can always do that tomorrow." On your call schedule, put at the top of the list the buyer you'd rather not call. Then, reward yourself for your discipline by getting on with the fun part of your schedule. (13)

2. Make an accountability contract.

Find a friend who'll do this with you until you're both cured of procrastination. Every morning one of you calls the other. You each name the one thing you least want to do that day. Before the end of the day each of you must report back that you have accomplished that task.

3. Follow the 24-hour rule.

Within one day of receiving any new communication requiring action—mail, e-mail, phone calls, requests, and so on—take at least one step toward responding to it. Better yet, do one thing on each new task the minute you learn of it. This will keep dreaded tasks from looming larger than life.

4. Visualize completion.

Instead of thinking about how bad you feel that you have to do something, think about how great you'll feel when you get it done. The more real you can make the feeling of accomplishment, the quicker you'll start making it happen.

5. Announce your deadlines.

Make public commitments to starting and finishing unpleasant tasks. You're less likely to accept embarrassment in front of others than you are to let yourself down. For instance, tell your boss each morning how many cold calls you plan.

6. Divide and conquer.

Break especially difficult or complex jobs into manageable pieces. Work on one piece each day.

7. Ask for clarification.

If you're putting off a task for your boss or a client, a lack of information may be your major stumbling block. Do you need more explanation of the nature of the assignment or the purpose behind it? Ask.

8. Face your fears.

Another reason for delay is that you may be afraid of the task ahead. For example, you may be reluctant to get back to a customer with the truth about a mistake you made. Know that every time you act in the face of fear you strengthen your character. In this case you may also strengthen your relationship with the customer, who will admire your honesty. (6, 23, 102)

9. Turn it into a game.

Imagine you have to make cold calls. Give yourself one, two, or three points for each call you make; the toughest calls earn the most points. Set a goal. If you need to make 50 calls, you should expect to earn 100 points on an average day. Give yourself a reward that you really like—for instance, a new putter—every day on which you exceed 110 points.

10. Stop reading this book.

Put it down right now. Don't pick it up again until you make significant progress on the most nagging task in your backlog.

▬ ▬ ▬

9 Twenty Areas of Life Where Your Actions Need to Match Core Values

> *There is only one success—to be able to spend life in your own way.* —Christopher Morley

Your core values and beliefs are unique. No one shares them with you. If you live your life in such a way that your daily actions and priorities reflect those core values and beliefs, you'll achieve an uncommon measure of satisfaction and success. Here's how to do it. First, write down what's important to you—your core values, beliefs, and desires—in those areas of life most meaningful for you. (You may need to combine similar values and beliefs into single statements in order to achieve a workable list of from 10 to 20 items.) Second, prioritize the list. Third, compare the prioritized list (your "talk") to how you live your life (your "walk"). Fourth, respond to the comparison. Change your priorities—where you spend your time and energies—to match your core values and beliefs. You'll get even greater value from this exercise by bringing your significant other into the process at step four, when you respond to the comparison between your talk and your walk. Here are the life categories people find helpful to consider when writing their core values, beliefs, and desires.

1. Faith/worship/religion/spirituality

2. Spouse/significant other

3. Family/children/parents

4. Friends/relationships

5. Alliances/teamwork/partnerships

6. Finances/wealth/possessions

7. Health/fitness/energy

8. Hobbies/recreation/pleasure/relaxation

9. Achievement/creativity/career/work

10. Excellence/beauty/perfection/accuracy

11. Persistence/commitment/follow-through

12. Courage/risk taking/standing up for beliefs

13. Thoughtfulness/consideration of others

14. Service/generosity/charity/sacrifice

15. Integrity/honesty/ethics/law

16. Learning/education/wisdom/intellect

17. Responsibility/reliability/loyalty

18. Leading/developing others/role modeling

19. Happiness/contentment/positive outlook

20. Tolerance/forgiveness/acceptance

10 Ten Communication Strategies of Successful Sales Professionals

Man does not live by words alone, despite the fact that sometimes he has to eat them.

— Adlai Stevenson

You don't need a silver tongue to be successful in sales. Neither should you be a poor speaker who can't get your points across well enough to show the buyer that you know what you're talking about. Great salespeople accept that their upbringing and their education have given them a certain level of communication skills that they can continue to sharpen. They take several steps to make this happen.

1. Picture your communication goal.

What do you want to achieve with this person you are about to speak with? What do you want the person to look like, feel like, and do as a result of what you say? Set a clear goal for the new state you want this person to be in at the end of the conversation. You'll be more likely to achieve it.

2. Focus less on being clear, more on being understood.

When you worry about being clear, you are centered on yourself. Communicators who focus on themselves and *their* need to speak often fail. When you concern yourself with being understood, your attention is directed to your audience, where it belongs.

3. Know your audience. (49, 53, 70)

Before you speak, ask yourself how others will listen to you.

- How do they feel about you?
- What do they expect of you?
- What do they expect you to say?
- How much do they already know?
- What is their level of education?
- What are their occupations and professional standing?
- What are their core values and beliefs?
- Where do they hurt?
- What are their ambitions, aspirations, hopes, and dreams?

- How do they feel about themselves?
- What language do they use?
- How much time do they have to listen to you?

4. Know yourself.

What are your communication foibles? What words do you tend to mispronounce or misuse? What are your communication strengths and weaknesses? What is the unique impact you make when you speak because of who you are and how you come across? If you don't know the answers to these questions, find out. Ask others for feedback; watch and listen to yourself communicating on videotape. (5)

5. Create pictures with your words.

Someone once said that the most effective orators are those who make people see with their ears. Choose words that are specific, visual, colorful, memorable, or picturesque. For example, don't ask, "Can your employees use a product that will make them more efficient and effective?" when you can say, "Could your accounting staff use an accounts payable package that would cut their processing time in half and reduce errors by 70%?"

6. Rid your language of clichés.

Few buyers will be impressed by such expressions as "You can lead a horse to water, but you can't make it drink." Forget every worn-out phrase you've ever heard.

7. Stick with an upbeat tone.

Avoid negative expressions when you can send the same message with positive words. "I won't be able to get delivery for you on that new option until June" becomes "I'll get delivery for you on that new option in June." "I can't do that" becomes "Let me tell you what I *can* do."

8. Make your nonverbal communication reinforce your words.

Your vocal quality and your body language combine to account for as much as 93% of the messages people receive from you. Is your 93% consistent with your 7% (the actual words you choose)? In other words, let your voice and body language strengthen, not contradict, the message you send with your words.

9. Speak less; listen more.

The buyers you call on should monopolize the conversation. The more buyers talk, the better they feel about you and the more you will learn about what it takes to get the sale. Speak no more than 30% of the time. (74)

10. Learn and grow.

Every time you're unsuccessful in a communication situation, learn from it. When you make mistakes, don't get defensive and deny your error and don't go to the other extreme of punishing yourself for your communication blunders. Instead, every time you fail to communicate, say to yourself, "I just learned one more way not to speak to someone in that situation."

— — —

11 Ten Tips for Avoiding Common Communication Errors

Put it before them briefly so they will read it, clearly so they will appreciate it, picturesquely so they will remember it and, above all, accurately so they will be guided by its light. —Joseph Pulitzer

English is a tough language, whether you're speaking or writing. When you face a buyer, you need a good vocabulary and you need to know how to use those words accurately. This list addresses some of the most common speaking and writing errors that plague sales professionals. If you often make these blunders, we recommend several actions. First, find a communication role model in your life to study and emulate. Second, read more. Third, consult these communication guides—*The Elements of Style* by Strunk and White and *The Little English Handbook* by Corbett. Fourth, attend the next communication seminar you learn about.

1. Run all your documents through a spell-checker before you print them out.

Don't let common misspellings like "ocassion," "supercedes," or "dependant" make it onto paper.

2. **Look up these commonly confused words in a dictionary to make sure you're using each properly.**

All the words below are spelled correctly, so a spell-checker won't catch you if you type the wrong one—but your buyer might.

- a lot / allot
- adverse / averse
- advice / advise
- affect / effect
- all ready / already
- alternate / alternative
- assent / ascent
- capital / capitol
- cite / sight / site
- complementary / complimentary
- council / counsel
- definite / definitive
- disinterested / uninterested
- fewer / less
- flaunted / flouted
- forego / forgo
- imply / infer
- its / it's
- lay / lie
- principal / principle
- proceed / precede
- reluctant / reticent
- stationary / stationery
- than / then
- their / there / they're
- your / you're

3. **Learn to pronounce words correctly.**

Look up the correct pronunciations of the following commonly misspoken words:

- forte
- harass
- institution
- leisure
- library

- memento
- nuclear
- prerogative
- realtor

4. Follow "either of," "neither of," "each of," or "every" with singular forms.

"Either of these products is a good choice" is correct. "Either of these products are good choices" is not. "All of" can be plural: "All of those products are good choices." If you want to use "they/them" to avoid having to specify gender, be sure to use plural forms elsewhere: "all employees" instead of "each employee."

5. Use "you and I" where you might say "we," and "you and me" where you might say "us."

You wouldn't write, "between we," so don't write, "between you and I." You wouldn't say, "Us are here," so don't say, "You and me are here."

6. Learn how to use "whom" correctly.

Here's one way to remember the difference between who and whom: whom with an *m* is parallel to pronouns with *m*: me, him, them. "I met him; whom did you meet?" "They're going now; who else is coming?" Usually people won't mind if you say "who" when technically you should say "whom," but making the mistake the other way around can brand you as both pretentious and ignorant.

7. Be aware of any idioms or regional pronunciations you learned growing up.

People in New York wait "on line," but the rest of the country waits "in line." People in the South say "you all" to mean "all or both of you," but people from other parts of the country don't understand that nuance. If you say "irregardless" or "I could care less," don't you mean "regardless" and "I couldn't care less"?

8. Be careful with apostrophes.

An apostrophe is useful for showing possession, but where to put the apostrophe can be tricky:

- belonging to Tess: Tess's
- belonging to the Jones family: the Joneses'

- belonging to Sid and Nancy together: Sid and Nancy's house
- belonging to Sid and Nancy separately: Sid's and Nancy's proposals

An apostrophe can also indicate where a character has dropped out of a word: shouldn't, 'twas, the '90s. Be careful: some word-processing programs automatically flip that apostrophe the wrong way when you type it at the front of a word.

9. Don't use quotation marks for emphasis.

Typing too many quotation marks looks "weird," doesn't it? Use italics instead.

10. Don't splice sentences with a comma.

This is incorrect: "We analyzed the data thoroughly, we could not reach a conclusion." Replace the comma with a semicolon, or turn the line into two sentences. Sticking "however" in the middle doesn't solve the problem.

▬ ▬ ▬

12 Ten Ways to Keep Your Selling Skills Sharp

The will to succeed is important, but what's more important is the will to prepare. — Bobby Knight

A saw never sharpened will eventually become dull and useless. In the same way, selling skills that lose their edge lose their impact. Unless you work at improving your skills and techniques, you will be overtaken by competitors who do. The following tips will ensure that no matter how sharp your competitors are you will be sharper.

1. Start a personal library.

This book is a good beginning to building your library. Check best-seller lists, get recommendations from friends, note the titles of books and authors your colleagues are discussing.

2. Subscribe to at least one well-respected general business magazine and the most respected journal in your industry.

Business Week, Fortune, and *Forbes* feature cutting-edge stories that help you keep abreast of the changing business world. Read the trade journal in your specific industry to learn about developments affecting your company.

3. Set aside three hours a week for reading.

Keeping a library and taking out subscriptions without reading the material is like having a personal art gallery without ever looking at the pictures. Commit to the same regular reading schedule every week.

4. Play audiotapes in your car.

More and more books are coming out on audiotape. When you're on the highway, pop a tape in the player, concentrate on the road, and arrive at your destination a little smarter.

5. Carry learning materials in your briefcase.

Think of all the time you waste in doctors' waiting rooms, airport lounges, and outside buyer offices—time you could use to sharpen your skills. Pull out your newspaper, magazine, book, or tape player.

6. If you sell technical equipment or services, schedule regular updates from appropriate suppliers.

If your vendors don't offer training programs, find some who will.

7. Form a "Mastermind Group."

Serious sales professionals join a Mastermind Group of other serious sales professionals—a safe place to ask delicate questions, put your toughest sales problems on the line, and get honest answers. Check with local sales associations for help in locating or organizing one.

8. Keep an open mind.

Your decline begins the first day you believe you know it all. Then you stop learning and start losing. Your competitors begin to close the gap and your customers start to feel you're not the resource you once were. Remember, anything you don't know represents an opportunity to grow.

9. Hire a personal coach.

Let this professional help you improve the image you project.

10. Attend at least one personal development seminar every year.

Call your local college, university, or chamber of commerce. Check into any one of the several national seminar providers who may conduct programs in your area. Attend conferences sponsored by professional associations. After each seminar ask yourself what you learned that will improve your next call on a buyer or customer. (4)

✓ Master TIPPS (Time, Information, People, Place, Stress)

Successful salespeople realize that sales result from setting goals and crafting plans to achieve them. They make the most of time spent on the telephone, in the car, in airports, and in lobbies. They know that stress is part of their profession and have developed strategies to cope with it. They rarely wake up in the morning wondering what to do that day. They rarely go to bed at night lamenting how little they did. They don't wish for luck because they know how to follow the "tipps" in this chapter to make their own luck.

■ ■ ■

13   Thirteen Tips for Time Management

> *Yesterday is a cancelled check; tomorrow is a promissory note; today is the only cash you have — so spend it wisely.*   — Kay Lyons

Certain conditions can put you at an advantage or a disadvantage relative to your competitors. For instance, the helpfulness of your support staff, the number of buyers in your market, and the quality of your products can all make every presentation either a tough sell or an easy sell. However, one factor levels the playing field. Neither you nor your competitors have more than 60 minutes to an hour, 24 hours to a day, or 7 days to a week. Time is the great equalizer.

1.   **Change your mind-set—start viewing time as a precious, finite resource.**

Time spent is time irreplaceable. You cannot expand, manufacture, or "save" time. For example, you'll never get a second chance to make better use of the 10 seconds it will take you to read this item in this list.

2. Get the most out of each moment of your selling day.

Periodically ask yourself this question: Am I making the best use of my time now?

3. Establish goals.

It's amazing how effectively and efficiently you manage your time once you decide what you want that time to produce. Develop goals that are professional (e.g., sales quotas, buyer contacts) and personal (e.g., exercise, family relationships). (25)

4. Adopt a comprehensive calendar and contact management system.

There are several on the market. Some are low tech; others are high tech. The important issue is not whether the system is electronic, but whether you get the most out of it and maintain the discipline to use it. A contact management system is your "Triptik" for achieving your goals.

5. Arrange your day so that the most difficult and valuable challenges coincide with your peak energy levels.

The availability and needs of your buyers and customers often direct your calendar. Whenever you're in charge of your time, schedule the toughest challenges for those parts of the day when you have your greatest physical and psychic energy. (8)

6. Spend less time on routine, non-value-added tasks.

Your three most valuable professional pursuits are (1) planning your sales calls, (2) making your sales calls, and (3) meeting the needs of your ongoing customers. All other activities are secondary. *Prioritize* your "to-do" list to keep these three pursuits foremost. *Delegate* clerical tasks to others. *Automate* by learning every possible advantage that your most frequently used software program can give you. *Eliminate* nonessential tasks. (14)

7. Handle each piece of paper only once.

Respond to it, file it, route it, or destroy it. Don't put it into an ever-expanding in box or "get to" pile.

8. Handle electronic messages only once.

E-mail and voice mail can quickly clutter your life. Once you've heard or read the message, take one of four actions: answer it, delete it, route it, or print it. If you print it, see tip #7.

9. Clean up the clutter in your car, your desk, your office, and your computer files.

Clutter saps your discipline, your time, and your energy. Use these simple criteria to define clutter: if you haven't looked at it in a year, if it is changing color or fading, if colleagues make fun of it, or if you don't know why you saved it in the first place, it's clutter.

10. Ask the most efficient salespeople you know to share the one time management technique that has been most useful for them.

No one is born efficient. People develop smart habits and strategies over time. Find out what those are. Next time you're at the water cooler, the pub, or the golf course with a colleague, exchange time management tips.

11. Build personal and family time into your calendar.

The goal of time management is *not* to turn you into an efficiency-driven selling machine. The goal is to make your working hours as productive as possible so that you can enjoy all the benefits that sales success will bring. Twenty years from now you'll not want to look back at your life and regret the time you did not spend with family. (9, 22)

12. Maintain your health.

Time devoted to your spiritual and physical well-being is time well spent. You cannot exert energy if there is no energy reserve from which to draw. (7, 9)

13. Stop enabling people who may be robbing you of your valuable time.

Exit gracefully from conversations that waste your time. Distance yourself from colleagues whose personal inefficiency harms your productivity. (19, 20)

14 Nine Ways to Maximize "Pay Time" and Minimize "No Pay Time"

Time is really the only capital that any human being has, and the only thing he can't afford to lose. —Thomas Edison

The more of your day that you fill with activities that make money, the more successful you will be. Think about what you do each day. How much of your effort generates income ("pay time") and how much of it only supports the generation of income ("no pay time")? Here's how to keep these two in perspective.

1. Watch what you do.

Pay-time activities include finding buyers, getting appointments, making sales calls, making referral calls, and servicing your customers. Pay time typically occurs between 8 A.M. and 5 P.M. Most no-pay-time activities are best scheduled for before 8 A.M. or after 5 P.M. These activities include writing proposals, organizing your contact management database, writing letters or e-mail to buyers and clients, doing research on more buyers on the Internet, checking out the competition's Web pages, designing a specialized mailing to a specific database, planning workflow, and so on. Keep a journal of the percentage of your day you spend in each type of activity. Unless pay time is consistently 90% or more of your effort, reorganize your day.

2. Stay on goal time, not clock time.

Your purpose is to accomplish goals, whether that takes one hour or eight hours. Start your day by saying, "This is what I will accomplish today." (For example, set up five appointments with new buyers.) When you've accomplished that goal, stop working for the day. Go home to your spouse and children, play golf, or do whatever else you choose to do as a reward for success.

3. Keep a "cookbook" and manage it hard.

Plan the precise ingredients that must go into your day. Map out the specific behavior you need to reach your daily goals and plot your progress throughout the day. Most contact management systems allow for tracking and tallying daily performance.

4. Focus on the moment.

Stay 100% mentally focused on what you're doing. Don't keep one foot in today's cookbook and the other foot in some opportunity for another day. The resulting "mental pollution" will cloud your focus.

5. Maintain a healthy self-esteem.

Your emotional well-being is a key to remaining in pay time. You need to know how to handle the rejection embedded in the no's you collect throughout the day, every day. Keep your mind off yourself and on your revenue-generating goals. (22, 23, 43)

6. Activate a support group.

You can face the business of selling alone, or you can share your lessons with others in the safe environment of a support group of your peers. Learn what others are doing to manage their days and keep no pay time to a minimum.

7. Keep a journal.

It's not enough merely to track your daily behavior in your cookbook or contact management system. You also need to keep a personal journal to record your lessons learned, your shortcuts, your attitude assessment, and your interpersonal behavior. Learn how these factors contribute to your pay time/no pay time split. Get ideas for changes.

8. Establish a prospecting system.

Create a process that forces you to systematically perform the grunt work that's a part of sales prospecting. Make sure it covers generating referrals and introductions as well as working leads generated through advertising, add-on sales, direct mail, broadcast fax, association selling, or directory cold calling. Use the system to maximize your pay time.

9. Establish a selling system.

If you don't have a plan of your own, you'll become part of someone else's. If you don't have a system of selling, you'll be prisoner to the buyer's system—one designed to keep you permanently in no pay time as you cough up your expertise for free. The purpose of this book is to give you a system that keeps you in pay time and in charge of your sales calls.

▬ ▬ ▬

15   Eleven Qualities of a Successful Sales Plan

You read a book from beginning to end. You run a business the opposite way. You start with the end, and then you do everything you must do to reach it. —Harold Geneen

Are you working backwards? Or are you systematically striving toward desired ends? You need a sales plan—one that establishes goals, priorities, timetables, and necessary resources. A sales plan that will achieve your ends has these characteristics.

1.   Sets measurable, specific, vivid, and motivating goals.

Where do you intend to be in one year? What measures will you use to gauge your achievements: Number of buyers contacted? Percentage of sales to certain types of customers? Sales volume? Profit? Ranking among your peers?

2.   Identifies the enabling objectives necessary to achieve ultimate goals.

If your goal is to be named salesperson of the year in your company, what objectives must you reach on the way to that outcome? How many new buyers must you contact? What post-sell strategies will you employ with existing customers? What new work habits must you develop and what old habits must you drop? What values will you need to embrace? What internal relationships will you cultivate? Hurdlers don't cross the finish line without first jumping over intermediate hurdles. What are yours?

3.   Outlines a logical order among the intermediate steps.

What is the logical sequence for achieving your ultimate goal? What must happen first, second, third, and so on?

4.   Establishes a reasonable yet challenging time line.

When will you achieve your ultimate goal? *When* will you jump the intermediate hurdles?

5.   Pinpoints the barriers between you and your objectives.

Why haven't you been achieving your objectives? What are the constraining forces either in you or in the environment? To what degree have they been talent, skill, or attitudinal shortfalls? To what degree are they resource deficiencies? To what degree has your choice of buyers been to blame? To what degree have others legislated limitations that have constrained you? What else has stood in the way?

6. Specifies strategies, procedures, and tactics.

A goal without a corresponding action is a wish. Goals with actions are blueprints for success. What actions will overcome the barriers that have kept you from achieving your objectives?

7. Summarizes the resources needed.

What money, material, supplies, equipment, facilities, information, education, training, support, counsel, or staffing do you require?

8. Establishes accountability.

If this is your personal plan, then you are solely accountable. What will you do to hold your feet to the fire? If the plan involves others, who will be responsible for achieving what specific objectives by what specific date?

9. Is in writing.

Plans not written are dreams. Plans written become vows. Don't just dream about success, vow to succeed.

10. Is shared and negotiated with those responsible for implementing it.

The more people who see your plan, the more pressure you'll feel to make it happen. The more people who see your plan, the more others will want to help you achieve it. The more you involve others in helping you create the plan, the more excited they will be to be a part of it.

11. Signifies commitment.

Start your plan only once you become totally confident in it and fully committed to it. Make sure all others affected by the plan are equally confident and committed. Sign on before you sign off.

━━ ━━ ━━

16 Thirteen Strategies for Serving Large Territories

Henceforth I whimper no more, postpone no more,
*   need nothing,*
Done with indoor complaints, libraries, querulous
*   criticisms,*
Strong and content I travel the open road.
                                    — Walt Whitman

Selling door-to-door can be a tough way to make a buck. It's even tougher when the doors are hundreds of miles apart. If you manage accounts in territories covered by lengthy car trips or plane flights, this list will help you maintain your health, your sanity, and your expense account.

1. Plan your route to maximize return on investment.

Apply a logic to your itinerary that saves time, hassle, and energy. Look for ways to call on the most important buyers in the shortest period of time at the least expense.

2. Learn and use a software routing program if your market is extremely large or complicated.

Software programs can help you plan your itinerary efficiently. Ask your colleagues which ones they use.

3. Stick to the travel plan.

Be disciplined. Unless there are unforeseen emergencies, stick to your itinerary.

4. Place a reminder call to buyers or customers on the itinerary 24 hours before scheduled appointments.

The only thing worse than losing a sale is spending hours getting to an appointment only to discover the buyer forgot about it.

5. When your route involves frequent flying, work with a travel agent who knows you as well as your mother does.

Make sure your travel agent knows your preferences regarding:

• Small commuter planes

- Window, center, or aisle seating
- Seating in the front, middle, or back of the plane
- Airlines of first choice and last choice
- Cities with multiple airports (e.g., Midway or O'Hare in Chicago; LAX or John Wayne in Los Angeles/Orange County; LaGuardia or JFK in New York)
- Minimum acceptable connection time between planes
- Car rental agencies of first choice and last choice
- Hotel chains of first choice and last choice
- Desirable amenities or special hotel services (e.g., nonsmoking rooms)

6. If your route requires extensive driving, get a full-size car loaded with options.

You will spend a great deal of time in your car. Make sure it as safe, comfortable, and luxurious as possible. Invest in a hands-free cell phone.

7. When you travel overseas, schedule downtime to recover from jet lag.

Some people require 24 hours to recover. Others simply need six to eight hours of rest. Most people experience greater jet lag heading east than heading west. Don't schedule the trip so that you run from baggage claim to a taxi to the appointment.

8. Travel in casual clothes.

Unless you're trying to sell something to the captain of your flight or the manager of the gas station, dress comfortably.

9. Carry enjoyable diversions with you.

Read novels on planes. Keep tapes or CDs of your favorite music or books in your car. Load fun games on your laptop. Find ways to relax during travel.

10. If you travel with a laptop or handheld computer, keep it in sight.

Many a traveling sales professional has been victimized by a computer thief. Be especially careful when you send computer bags through metal detectors at airports.

11. Pack light and pack smart.

Check bags on flights only if you must, to avoid the delays and unpleasant surprises that often await you at the luggage carousel. Save your back by packing light and using bags on wheels. Take clothing that you know you look good in and you know you will wear. Maintain a complete duplicate set of travel toiletries at home ready to throw in your bag so that you'll never have to worry about leaving your deodorant at home.

12. Eat light and eat smart.

Cut down on fat and calories and increase your consumption of water, juices, fruits, and vegetables. Eat plenty of protein at lunch for afternoon energy. Drink alcohol only at the end of the day and only in moderation. For overseas meals, don't eat food when in doubt, unless failure to do so would offend your host.

13. If you frequent the same hotels in the same cities, get to know the desk clerk, the bell captain, the wait staff, and the management.

These people are your extended family on the road. They anticipate your needs and make your life just a little easier. View the extra tips you give them as an investment in your physical and psychological well-being and in your ability to sell.

▬ ▬ ▬

17 Ten Guidelines for Phoning across Time Zones

> Let your fingers do the walking.
> — Advertisement for Yellow Pages

Some salespeople work in space measured by square feet. Others work in territories measured by square miles. And still others define their territory as global. As your territory increases, you'll want to be adept at managing the phone challenges created by time zones.

1. Know the time in the city you're calling.

If your market is the U.S., know in which time zone each city you call is located. Memorize the time difference in each continental zone plus Alaska, Hawaii, and Puerto Rico. If your market is global, do the same thing for each city you call. Get a detailed map that pinpoints the time zone location of each of your customers.

2. When placing calls halfway around the world, note the date differential.

Depending on the global destination of your call, you may be calling one day (24 hours) ahead or behind your current calling date. Be sure you and the other party are aware of both the time and date differences between the two of you.

3. Place the call so that it arrives within an 8:30–5:00 span at the destination.

Yes, most companies have voice mail or answering machines. But unless the call is an emergency, business etiquette dictates that you contact buyers and customers during their workday, not yours.

4. Specify times in the other party's time zone when you arrange for a return call or meeting.

You show your sensitivity and good manners when you leave messages that specify times relative to the other person's time zone, not yours.

5. When leaving a message on voice mail, indicate the zone from which you're calling as well as the time you left the message.

Say something like, "This is Ms. Katherine Smith returning your call. It is now 3 P.M. your time, 2 P.M. my time."

6. Make telephone appointments whenever you can.

International telephone tag is costly. Ask an assistant or colleague of the party you want to speak with when that person is most likely to be available for a return call. Choose a time within the window you're given, and ask for that party to be available then. When the other party will be calling you back, give at least two alternative times when you will be sure to be in your office.

7. Alert your telephone receptionist or support staff when to track you down.

Staffers who receive your calls should be able to connect those calls to you at almost any moment in the day. They should also have daily updated knowledge of which long-distance callers are most important.

8. **When arranging a conference call across time zones, recognize time differentials.**

When parties in the call cross time zones, make sure that each person expects the call at the right time. When parties are on different sides of the international date line, be sure to verify calendar days.

9. **When leaving a message on a long-distance call, include the area code with your number.**

If you're calling Kreskin or another clairvoyant, feel free to skip the area code. Leave the U.S. calling code for international callers.

10. **Keep your long-distance callers aware of changes in your area code.**

As cell phones and fax machines tax the capacity of local phone lines, more of us are having our area codes reassigned. You might choose to communicate a change in area code to your customers in person, via e-mail, over a fax line, or through the post office. Whichever mode you choose affords you an opportunity to make a positive contact with them. Take full advantage of that opportunity. For example, you might want to announce a new product line along with your new telephone number.

▬ ▬ ▬

18 Thirteen Ways to Make Valuable Contributions to a Meeting

No grand idea was ever born in a conference, but a lot of foolish ideas have died there.

— F. Scott Fitzgerald

Unless you work by yourself, you attend meetings from time to time. They may be called by your sales manager or sales team. Meetings hold great promise as a decision-making tool. Unfortunately, that promise is too rarely achieved. Here's what you can do to help the meetings you attend be more productive and make yourself a more valuable team member in the process.

1. **Read the agenda.**

Do any advance research necessary to hit the ground running and ready to contribute to the meeting's goals.

2. Arrive on time.

If you'll be late or absent, notify the leader. Take along work with you to use the time it takes for the meeting to get under way. Put it away as soon as the meeting begins.

3. Position yourself to contribute.

Grab a seat that affords you the greatest eye contact with the largest number of people.

4. Question anything you don't understand.

If you're not clear about the goals of the meeting, ask what they are as the meeting opens. If anyone uses a term you don't understand or mentions a project new to you, ask respectfully for an explanation.

5. Contribute actively.

Participate, speak up, and be candid. Give the group the full benefit of your knowledge. Don't withhold comments only to share them privately with individuals following the meeting.

6. Be concise.

Don't monopolize discussions or elaborate excessively. When you speak, get to the point. Contribute with as few carefully crafted words as possible.

7. Stick to the agenda.

Don't go off onto tangents. Don't get ahead of the plan. Don't change the focus to meet your needs.

8. Build on the present discussion.

Whenever possible, connect your comments to those of the person who spoke just before you. Don't allow important thoughts to die without a response.

9. Fix the future, not the past.

Help steer the team away from placing blame and getting mired in the past. Keep your contributions focused on improving the future and encourage others to do the same.

10. Challenge shoddy thinking.

Question specious assumptions. Attack bad ideas without attacking the people who have them. Say something like, "I have a problem with treating the issue in that way." Don't say something like, "I don't agree with your idea." Depersonalize disagreement.

11. Stay cool under fire.

Remain calm when your ideas and your positions come under attack. If people take potshots at you, tell them how inappropriate you found their remarks without firing back at them.

12. Contribute in between meetings.

Perform post-meeting follow-up as promised—within 24 hours when possible.

13. Avoid the seven deadly sins of meeting participation.

Avoid these no-no's at your meetings. Not only will they block team progress, they will give you a black eye with the team leader and most group members.

- Using a meeting as a forum from which to launch personal or hidden agendas.
- Intentionally withholding information the team needs.
- Leaking confidential meeting information.
- Using a meeting as a substitute for communication that should be one-on-one.
- Criticizing team members or team meetings to outsiders, rather than to team members.
- Displaying any form of destructive, vindictive, or abusive behavior.
- Failing to support group decisions reached through democratic processes.

▄▄ ▄▄ ▄▄

19 Thirteen Guidelines for Working with Tough Coworkers

The best way to get rid of an enemy is to turn him into a friend. —Abraham Lincoln

Working on a sales team can be heaven or hell. At its best a sales team is a mutually supportive, close-knit crew who look out for, and bring out the best in, each other. At its worst a sales team is a divisive collection of individuals who get in each other's way. Use the advice in this list for those times when one or more of the members of your team is getting in your way.

General Advice

1. Analyze the situation.

What is the problem? Most challenging coworkers fall into one or more of the categories in the next section of this list. Which are you encountering?

2. Practice empathy.

Put yourself into your coworker's shoes to discover reasons— legitimate or otherwise—for the troubling behavior. Are there extraordinary pressures on your coworker right now? Is his or her job less secure than it was in the past? Are there problems at home? None of these explanations can excuse the behavior you're experiencing, but they will help you identify the pain or fear that's at the root of the behavior. This identification enables you to respond less emotionally, and therefore more powerfully, to what's going on. (49)

3. Talk with trusted colleagues.

Do your friends experience similar trouble with this person? If so, continue with the advice on this list. If not, *you* may be the problem. Try to figure out why others don't share your frustration. Ask your friends how they see you contributing to the difficulty no matter whom they see as the major antagonist. Take care not to gossip negatively about coworkers behind their backs.

4. Be careful.

You have limited influence over your coworkers. Unless you're on a self-directed team, they probably don't feel accountable to you. They can grow defensive quickly when you point out faults to them.

Advice for Dealing with Nine Tough Coworkers

5. The *Deadweight* doesn't carry a fair share of the load, shirks difficult assignments, and rarely delivers on promises to help or cooperate with you.

- Examine your personal prejudices. Is there any chance that your reaction is clouded by racism, sexism, regional bias, lifestyle, religious intolerance, or other forms of bigotry?
- When the Deadweight *does* help you, be generous with your thanks. Praise the behavior you want.
- Consider confrontation. Play the role of reporter. Describe the behavior you see and why it's a problem. Don't attribute intent; talk instead about the consequences of the behavior for the coworker, the company, customers, buyers, you, and the team. Ask for help in averting the consequences.

6. **The *Rumor Monger* gossips about others, loves to pass on bad news, and is a one-person grapevine.**

   - Avoid the Rumor Monger as much as your job permits.
   - At every opportunity correct distortions and untruths you encounter in the grapevine. ("Actually, that's not the case. I was there—let me tell you what was said.")
   - When confronting the Rumor Monger, expect denial. Have such well-documented evidence that he or she can't duck responsibility.

7. **The *Leech* sucks precious moments of your workday by gabbing about any of a dozen topics unrelated to sales, takes an interminable time getting to the point when talking business, or may be an advice seeker whose need for help exceeds your time or capability.**

   - Don't become so hardened to Leeches that you quickly dismiss people who have a genuine need for a listening ear.
   - When the Leech says, "Do you have a few minutes?" say, "Yes, at around 3:30; what are we going to talk about?" If it's truly important, he or she will return at 3:30. If not, you've saved yourself precious time.
   - When all else fails, keep your office door closed or pile papers on your side chairs and on the floor. You might also position your desk so passersby cannot easily get your visual attention. If you work in a cubicle, turn only your head to speak when the Leech shows up.

8. **The *Back Stabber* takes credit for your accomplishments, whispers sour nothings in the boss's ear about you, and says**

one thing to your face and does the opposite behind your back.

- Take action. Of all the troublesome coworkers on this list, this is one you can't afford to tolerate.
- Rethink your interpretation of the Back Stabber's behavior. Is there any chance you're misconstruing this person's motives because of your insecurity, bias, or not having all the facts?
- Before confronting the Back Stabber, gather your evidence carefully. Stay calm. Present facts, not innuendo, hearsay, or supposition. Don't attribute motive or intent. Describe the behavior that must end. Ask what you can do to ensure that it ends. Without threats, describe the consequences of more of the unacceptable behavior.

9. The *Empire Builder* cares far more about his or her career than about the good of the company, fights for maximum organizational resources at any cost to others, and looks for every opportunity to hog the limelight.

- Be honest with yourself. A high-performing salesperson is often mistaken for an Empire Builder by lower achievers. We hope you're not one of these.
- Give your boss rational, statistically supported, and well-documented arguments for the resources you require that the Empire Builder is competing for.
- Confront the Empire Builder, if necessary. Be direct, specific, and demonstrate your unwillingness to be intimidated. If this doesn't work, it may be wise to bring in a third party—perhaps a common boss—as a mediator.

10. The *Jabber* pokes at your sensitive spots under the guise of a good-natured ribbing, embarrasses you in front of others, and plays practical jokes.

- The first step is to protect yourself by realizing that the problem is not any weakness of yours. The Jabber is a small person who needs to pull you down to size.
- Be prepared the next time the Jabber embarrasses you or others. Respond on the spot to gain the advantage of surprise. Repeat what the Jabber said. Don't attribute motives. Describe the destructive results you see of the Jabber's behavior. State that it must stop.

- Turn down apologies from chronic Jabbers. Say, "That apology may be real for you, but it's not real for me. The only thing real for me would be never to experience that again."

11. The *Know-It-All* has an inflated ego, offers unwanted information and advice, and is the first to say "I told you so" when you suffer the least setback.

   - If you believe you work with several Know-It-Alls, it may be that you're overly sensitive when your coworkers make justifiable offers to help you increase your effectiveness.
   - Tell the Know-It-All that advice has more impact when it has been requested.
   - Remember that when the Know-It-All insists on telling you how to do your job, you can simply say "Thank you" and then ignore the advice.

12. The *Griper* resists change, expects the worst, and complains about support staff, coworkers, management, buyers, and customers.

   - Avoid associating with Gripers if possible.
   - Don't get caught up in the Griper's negativity. Assert your own realistic optimism. Counteract the Griper's complaints with facts.
   - Focus the Griper on the benefits of any change that you need him or her to support.

13. The *Short Fuse* flies off the handle at the slightest provocation, is highly judgmental of others, and behaves unprofessionally with others, to the point of shouting, name calling, finger pointing, foot stomping, and even profanity.

   - Let the Short Fuse blow off steam. If the situation permits, listen to cut through the anger.
   - Once the Short Fuse winds down, respond slowly and calmly, yet assertively, to bring the Short Fuse down to your level of emotionality.
   - Find an opportunity to give the Short Fuse specific feedback on the negative impact of blowing up. "When you react that way, other people, including me, don't want to be around you."

20 Seventeen Guidelines for Working with Tough Bosses

A boss is someone who's early when you're late and late when you're early.   —Author unknown

You've probably worked for managers you hoped would be there forever. You've probably also worked for managers you hoped would disappear before you returned to work in the morning. Just in case your sales manager is in the latter category, consider the advice on this list.

General Advice

1.   Analyze the situation.

What is the problem? Most bosses who inspire complaints fall into one or more of the categories in the next section of this list. Which is yours?

2.   Use empathy.

Put yourself in your manager's shoes to discover reasons—legitimate or otherwise—for the behavior that drives you crazy. Are there extraordinary pressures on your boss right now? Is he or she on the outs with upper management? Is his or her position less secure than it once was in the organization? It's freeing to recognize that if you lived in your boss's skin you might behave the same way. This understanding enables you to respond more powerfully and less emotionally. (49)

3.   Talk with colleagues.

Find out if your coworkers are experiencing similar problems. If they're not, admit that your performance, rather than the boss's behavior, may be the problem. If they share in your misery, you might organize an informal support group to work within the system to bring about change. This might include group delivery of a request to the boss for changed behavior.

4.   Don't retaliate.

When someone in authority abuses that power, it is tempting to act like a vengeful victim. Rather than looking for a way to get back at the person, identify positive steps to take such as the ones in the section below.

5. Get a life!

If the specific suggestions below don't work, take steps necessary to spend less time with your boss. Do what you can to shelter your customers from the trauma and frustration you experience. Don't let it affect your self-confidence and your ability to sell. Whatever you do, don't take your manager's problems home with you.

Advice for Dealing with Twelve Tough Bosses

6. The *Puzzle* rarely states clear expectations, fails to give complete instructions, and provides little or no performance feedback.

   - Don't wait for expectations; state what you think they are and get a confirmation or denial.
   - When you get an assignment, tell the Puzzle exactly how you're going to handle it and what outcomes you're shooting for; get an OK before you proceed.
   - Hand your boss a blank performance review with a suggested date for a meeting to discuss it.

7. The *Bully* issues orders rather than requests, manages through intimidation, and rarely asks for your ideas or suggestions.

   - Look for the first opportunity to point out, with evidence, how the behavior is harming the bottom line.
   - Make it in your boss's best interest to change; show how the behavior is causing pain for the boss or how ending the behavior will relieve pain.
   - Send the colleague your boss trusts most to have a heart-to-heart discussion with the boss.

8. The *Turbo* has unreasonably high expectations, expects you to drop whatever you're doing to meet his needs, and drives himself unmercifully while expecting the same of you.

   - Show your boss how the intense pressure in your job is harming your ability to serve the company well.
   - Better yet, show how reducing the pressure will enable you to improve your contribution to the bottom line.

- When your boss hits you with an unexpected last-minute assignment, give an impact statement of what that will do to the priorities you're now working on and suggest a better way to get everything done.

9. The *Showboat* enjoys the limelight, takes credit for your successes, and disassociates herself from risky ventures until they start to pay off.

   - The smartest strategy may be to continue to help your boss look good, while letting the right people know how you've contributed to successful projects.
   - Look on your own for ways to make your work better known throughout the organization.
   - If you choose to confront, start off by saying, "I'm concerned that the value of my work is not always matched by the amount of credit it receives." Then ask for the specific credit you feel is justified without usurping the boss's own need for glory.

10. The *Ostrich* avoids confrontation, doesn't want to hear bad news, and ignores signs of poor performance.

    - Resolve your disagreements with others before they reach your boss.
    - Emphasize the positive before you direct discussions to problems that need to be addressed.
    - Offer alternative solutions for every problem you identify.

11. The *Dumper* gives you the dirty work, stays busy with easy tasks and fun jobs, and is one of those rare bosses who delegates too much.

    - Work at becoming more efficient to handle all the work thrown your way.
    - Delegate more yourself; don't allow your desk to become a bottleneck.
    - Be prepared to negotiate early, on the spot, when your boss unloads on you. Point out a better way to get things done—one that he or she is likely to approve.

12. The *Withholder* manages close to the vest, rarely gives you sufficient information to do your job, and may delegate responsibility but without the necessary authority.

- When you get a delegation, anticipate the information you'll need and ask for it on the spot.
- Show your boss how much more effective he or she can be by letting go of certain current responsibilities.
- Show your boss how poorly things are going because you don't have the authority to represent him or her properly in assignments you have.

13. The *Pet Owner* gives favorites the best assignments, the best performance reviews, and the best raises.

- Consider that you may be doing a poor job of playing the rudimentary office politics it takes to get in your boss's good graces.
- Consider that your boss may feel that you're not doing the quality job you think you are. Ask your boss and others whose opinion you value.
- Ask yourself, "What can I do to cause my boss to put me in the favorable light others are in?"

14. The *Chicken* fears going to bat for you and your colleagues, can't get what you need from upper management, and is reluctant to make decisions.

- Encourage your boss. Do your best to build up his or her self-confidence without being an obnoxious sycophant.
- Strongly assert your realistic optimism in situations where your boss may be afraid.
- Offer to represent your boss in situations he or she may not want to confront.

15. The *Hypocrite* feels immune from sacrifices you are asked to make, says one thing to your face and another behind your back, and doesn't feel the need to follow the rules.

- If you choose to confront hypocritical behavior, don't ascribe intent, accuse, or complain of unfairness.
- Focus on the gap between what your boss believes and how you believe others view the behavior.
- Recommend how your boss might deal with the negative perceptions that others—not necessarily you—have.

16. The *Deaf Ear* rarely has time or the desire to listen to your

problems, finishes your sentences for you or wanders off mentally as you speak, and is not easily approachable.

- Ask yourself what you might be doing to discourage your boss from listening to you. Is your message focused and to the point or do you ramble and beat around the bush? Does your boss not value your work and therefore not your words?
- Send messages to your boss at the time, in the place, and in the format that experience has told you get the best response.
- Focus on your boss's self-interests in the messages you send. Ask your boss to put everything aside to hear the critical information you have.

17. The *Perfectionist* wants it done his or her way, feels results are never good enough, and criticizes liberally, while praising sparingly or not at all.

- Make sure you're as dedicated to total quality and continuous improvement as you should be. Rather than you working for a perfectionist, it may be that your boss supervises a tolerator of mediocrity.
- Repeat back your boss's most unreasonable demands so he or she can hear how ridiculous they are.
- Let your boss know how important praise is to the staff, including you. Ask what you can do to begin earning it.

▬ ▬ ▬

21 Seventeen Questions to Help You Sell with Integrity

> *The problem with being a liar is you need a terrific memory.*
> — Mark Twain

We all know salespeople whose greatest skill is fabricating the truth and remembering what they said to whom. But deceit will always catch up with the deceitful. Your goal is to connect the needs of the buyer with the solutions you can deliver — not to make a sale at any cost. The questions in this list will help you keep on the straight and narrow. You'll sell both with integrity and financial success. Can you answer with a resounding yes to each of these questions for the sales you make?

1. Did I get the appointment to make the sales presentation without resorting to lying or deception? (119)

2. During the sales presentation was I careful to listen to the needs of the buyer and offer only responsive solutions?

3. During the sales presentation was I careful not to lie, stretch the truth, or exaggerate the benefits that my service or product provides?

4. During the sales presentation was I certain not to withhold any information the buyer needed in order to make the best decision?

5. During the sales presentation did I answer all questions directly and forthrightly?

6. During the sales presentation was everything I may have said about the competition and the competition's products or services truthful?

7. During the sales presentation was I thinking "How can I help this buyer?" even more than I was thinking "How large a contract can I get?"

8. Can I describe my conduct throughout this sale with pride to my parents, spouse, or children?

9. Can I look myself in a mirror and say, "You did your best to satisfy the buyer's needs fully within the limits of the buyer's budget"?

10. If a panel of objective experts in sales saw and heard everything I did in my presentation, would they conclude that my approach was honest and ethical?

11. Did I follow up the sale with an effort to make sure the customer received the value that I sold?

12. The last time I learned after a sale that the customer was confused or mistaken, did I call immediately to clarify and explain?

13. The last time a customer called with a complaint, did I ensure that the customer was made whole with speed, pleasantness, and generosity?

14. Do I get referrals to new buyers from the customers I sell?

15. Do I get thank-you notes from the customers I sell?

16. Would I be willing to send my résumé to a random sample of my customers if I was looking for a new job?

17. Am I proud of the work I do?

━━ ━━ ━━

22 Thirteen Tips for Maintaining Personal Balance

> *Perpetual devotion to what a man calls his business is only to be sustained by perpetual neglect of many other things.*
>
> — Robert Louis Stevenson

How good is it to be the best salesperson in the world but the worst parent or spouse? How fulfilling is a fat bonus check when you don't have the time to spend it? Would you be happy to receive the salesperson of the year award flat on your back? Financial success without personal happiness is a hollow victory. Professional fame without good health is an empty conquest. Which of the tips in this list will you use to ensure life-work balance?

1. **Align your values with your behavior.**

What are your values? How important are family, spirituality, and health? How important are service, integrity, and responsibility? How about wealth, possessions, and fame? Whatever your values, are you acting in concert with them? Once you live your life, spend your time, and follow priorities that are consistent with your most cherished values, you'll begin to build life-work balance.

2. **Ask your friends or loved ones if they think your work is consuming too much of your life.**

If they answer yes, ask for specific examples of how you do this. Listen carefully and nondefensively to what they tell you. Denial will be your biggest enemy here. In order to avoid it, request positive suggestions of what you can begin doing right away to keep work in perspective. For example, you might start leaving work a half hour earlier or make a lunch date with your significant other in the middle of your workweek. (9)

3. If you strive for a bigger paycheck every year, know why.

Money is not a goal in itself. What will more money do for you? Is it a way to keep score? Is it validation of your worth as a person? Are you out to prove something to someone? Are you intent on keeping up with the Joneses? Do you need too much "stuff" in your life? Or are you building a financial base that will both support your family and enable you to help others in need? Be honest!

4. If you've been depressed or distraught for more than a month, seek professional help.

Talk to your clergy, physician, or psychologist. Don't trust do-it-yourself remedies to recover from severe mental anguish.

5. If your marriage is suffering because of work, seek professional help.

Your church, synagogue, or community center may sponsor a marriage encounter. Most couples return from these events with a renewed commitment to working together to achieve a balanced relationship between their personal and professional lives.

6. Work smarter, not harder.

Time in the office isn't necessarily goal-directed activity. When there is more work to be done than you have time for, find better ways to do it. Don't just set aside more time to do it in the same old—and perhaps inefficient—way. Get training in time management. Learn better use of your computer software, contact management system, and other time-saving aids. (13, 14, 108)

7. Copy role models who are happier than you, not those who merely earn more commissions than you do.

You undoubtedly have friends and coworkers who make more money than you do, but who haven't found much contentment in life. You also know people who are happier and more contented than you are regardless of the money they make. Connect with this latter group. Spend more time with them. Learn their secrets. Model yourself after them.

8. Develop a support system.

Maintain closeness with a circle of loyal friends, helpful coworkers, and loving family members. Test reality by having them continually review your life-work balance. Be there for them when they need you, and let them be there for you when you need them.

9. When you experience burnout, negotiate for a leave of absence.

Extended time away from the daily routine is an exhilarating elixir. It will give you a chance to recharge your mental and physical batteries, develop perspective on life, and find answers to questions such as those posed in #1 and #3 of this list.

10. Take extended vacations.

To protect yourself from burnout, take all the vacation days coming to you and schedule them into concentrated periods. For instance, if you're going to take four weeks of vacation, two shots of two weeks of solid respite are more refreshing than using up the four weeks with 10 two-day escapes. One reason for this is that intense professionals usually need two to three days to get work out of their hearts and minds before they can begin to truly enjoy and benefit from a vacation.

11. Contribute time to the helpless, sick, homeless, or hungry.

Stop donating money and start donating time. Many burned-out and depressed salespeople find that donating time to charitable causes has more therapeutic value than months of counseling.

12. Listen to your spouse and kids.

We did not say "talk" to them. Devote an entire day to renewing the bonds with the most important people in your life. Ask questions about their most cherished activities. Find out what you've been missing in their lives.

13. Focus on one priority at a time.

When you're working, concentrate on work; when you're making money, make the most you can; when you're doing a job, give it your all. When you play, play hard; when you're on vacation, have fun; when you're with family, show them your love. Maintain the cleanest possible breaks between your work and the rest of your life.

▬ ▬ ▬

23   Thirteen Empowering Responses to Adversity

When one door is shut, another opens.
  —Miguel de Cervantes

Your best customer defects to the competition. You lose your job. The bank calls to say that your car is to be repossessed. Your marriage is on the rocks. You get bad news from your doctor. Your best friend is leaving town. Your dad just passed away. If even one of these things has happened to you lately, you're a candidate for this list. Scour it for ideas that will get you back on track.

1.   Keep it in perspective.

Something awful just happened to you, but your world isn't falling apart. If you don't believe this, think back to past adversities and notice that your world is still intact. (22)

2.   Grieve properly.

There is nothing wrong with feeling bad. In fact, denying your emotions may slow your return to normalcy. Expect to proceed through the grieving stages of disbelief, denial, anger, bargaining, self-pity, depression, and acceptance. Do not linger at any one stage. If you are unable to progress to acceptance, get help.

3.   Maintain confidence in your resilience.

Don't underestimate your power to bounce back. Use this dreadful event as an opportunity to prove what you're made of. Recognize that your greatest limitations are self-imposed. You can overcome almost any disadvantage of the past by vowing to do so. (107)

4.   Take care of yourself.

Continue to do the things you've always done to remain healthy and energetic. Increase your exercise regime. Build a reservoir of strength to draw from when you need it. (7, 9)

5.   Distract yourself.

Every time you catch yourself complaining, worrying, or feeling hopeless, snap out of it. Quickly immerse yourself in an activity that will fill your mind with uplifting thoughts.

6. Find the opportunity.

Every adversity represents a change in the status quo. Every change in the status quo creates a new opportunity somewhere in your life. Channel the energy that some people put into anger or despair into searching for that opportunity.

7. Take a chance.

When things were going along smoothly, there was little incentive to shake things up. There was little reason to take risks. Adversity often gives you the courage to gamble for a chance at something better. For example, getting fired from a cushy sales job may encourage you to take a crack at that consulting dream you've always had but were too fearful to pursue.

8. Accept help.

You probably have family members, friends, and colleagues who can offer emotional support in your despair. Don't go off by yourself to lick your wounds. There's safety in numbers.

9. Take advantage of your mistakes.

Learn. Never say, "Boy, did I blow that!" when you can say, "I just learned one more way not to . . ."

10. Don't hold grudges.

Don't waste time placing blame or asking, "Why did this happen to me?" Realize that holding a grudge drags you down in the eyes of others, makes you unhappy, and limits your potential.

11. Write about it.

Write the complete story of what happened to you. Note every detail. Compose the dialog. Include a description of your feelings. The next day read the story. Add a happy ending. Record the actions you'll take to make it so.

12. Pray.

Take advantage of the unshakable belief you have in something greater than yourself. Ask God for the strength to survive and even thrive in the face of this catastrophe. If you're not religious, find another spiritual core that will help you heal.

13. Set a high recovery goal.

Decide right now that you will emerge from the adversity stronger, happier, and more useful to your family and your customers than before it occurred.

▬ ▬ ▬

24 Fourteen Antidotes for Stress

If you can't stand the heat, get out of the kitchen.
—Harry S Truman

Stress isn't necessarily bad. It is present in everyone's life to some degree. In his book *Margin*, Richard A. Swenson claims that the issue is not stress anyway, but rather *margin*. He offers the formula

$$POWER - LOAD = MARGIN$$

Power is the energy, stamina, and strength we have to live our lives. Load is made up of the physical, emotional, and psychological demands made on our lives. Margin, therefore, is the reserve we have to deal with the challenges thrown at us by a difficult world. It is the reserve energy you have left to make sales call after sales call. It is the resilience you have to rebound from a confrontational buyer. It is the capacity you have to persist in the face of overwhelming odds. If you suffer from excessive stress (too little margin), what is the root of the problem? Do you have too little power or have you taken on too much of a load? This list focuses on strategies to increase your power and reduce your load.

Ideas to Increase Your Power

1. Heed the advice of the power-building lists in this book.

The majority of the lists in this book are aimed at increasing your power. A handful of them are particularly helpful.

- 6: Fifteen Affirmations to Get Through a Tough Day
- 7: Eleven Actions That Increase Your Energy
- 9: Twenty Areas of Life Where Your Actions Need to Match Core Values

- 12: Ten Ways to Keep Your Selling Skills Sharp
- 13: Thirteen Tips for Time Management
- 22: Thirteen Tips for Maintaining Personal Balance
- 23: Thirteen Empowering Responses to Adversity
- 107: Nine Ways to Become More Resilient in Times of Change
- 108: Fifteen Ideas for Better Use of Information Technology

2. Remain active.

Get off the sofa and get into some rock-climbing gear. Put down your Game Boy and get onto the tennis court. Put out the fireplace and put on your cross-country skis. Leave the barbecue and head for the swimming pool.

3. Adopt a hobby.

Find a retreat from the wars of work that both exercises and relaxes your mind. Collect coins, fall in love with antiquing, play a musical instrument, build model ships, learn a craft, take a class on painting, start sewing clothes, get absorbed in golf, study ancient cultures.

4. Take frequent short breaks.

Treat yourself between sales calls to a few minutes of relaxation or pleasure.

5. Take restful vacations.

Take them in lumps of as many days as possible. If you limit yourself to two days at a time, and it takes you two days to begin relaxing away from work, you get little value from your time off.

6. Find your 30 minutes.

Reserve 30 minutes to an hour each day for yourself. The very beginning or the very end of the day works best. Do what *you* want to do during that time. Keep it sacred. (13)

Ideas to Reduce Your Load

7. Heed the advice of the load-reducing lists in this book.

Several lists in this book contain load-reducing advice. Look at these first:

- 8: Ten Hints to Beat Procrastination
- 19: Thirteen Guidelines for Working with Tough Coworkers
- 20: Seventeen Guidelines for Working with Tough Bosses
- 102: Nine Strategies for Preventing Buyer's Remorse
- 103: Eleven Responses That Heal the Customer Who Feels Betrayed
- 118: Ten Expectations to Have When Your Company Is Merged

8. Simplify your life.

Understand the difference between needs and wants. Cut back on the expense and complexity of your lifestyle. Reduce the amount of "stuff" and the number of gadgets in your life. Buy fewer items that plug in or require batteries.

9. Leave work stress behind.

When you come home at night, leave your shoes at the front door to symbolically separate from the stress producers in your work. Change out of your sales professional "uniform" immediately. Write a story of the rigors of your day into a journal at the end of the day.

10. Confront toxic people.

You probably work with someone or serve a customer who challenges you. This person may demand too much, drain your time, antagonize you, complain constantly, abuse you emotionally, or behave in a dozen other nerve-rattling ways. It may be time for you to tell that person: "Get right or get out!" Depending on the person, the exact words you use to convey the message will differ. The end you seek is always the same: to get this person to end the objectionable behavior or exit your life. (19, 20, 92)

11. Delegate.

Very few professionals make the best use of their assistants. If you have one, discuss how you can delegate more effectively. Start off the meeting with this question: "What ideas do you have for how you can help me be more efficient and effective?" Delegation works at home, too. If you have children, are they carrying their fair share of the chores? For major home improvement tasks, do more hiring of professionals in place of do-it-yourself projects. (112, 116)

12. Automate.

Take advantage of every opportunity afforded you by modern technology to do your work in less time. For instance, take a class on how to take full advantage of the time-saving features of your computer and its software. Most people have mastered much less than 25% of their computer's capability. (108, 110, 111)

13. Negotiate.

Talk to your boss about your workload. Can you make a case for having some of it redistributed to others in order to achieve better team results? Talk to yourself about your career. Can you make a case for lowering your career goals a notch or two in order to reduce the pressure? (91)

14. Eliminate.

Every sales professional is doing at least one thing that if eliminated wouldn't harm his or her productivity in the least. This might be an unnecessary habit or ritual that uses time without providing any return. Ask colleagues if they notice anything in your behavior that fits this category. Offer to return the favor.

▬ ▬ ▬

25 Sixteen Goals That Successful Salespeople Achieve

> *Every calling is great when greatly pursued.*
> — Oliver Wendell Holmes Jr.

The remaining chapters in this book lay out the actions that will set you apart from amateurs. This list is a gateway to those chapters. It identifies the most important goals that successful sales professionals meet. If you haven't achieved all these goals, you've got the right book in your hands. Consider two strategies at this juncture. One is to read the rest of *Close the Deal* chapter by chapter to learn how to achieve these and other crucial selling goals. Another is to turn first to the cross-referenced lists you need right now.

1. Know the market better than the competition.

Be on top of what buyers need and what they'll need in the future. (26, 28–30)

2. Get past the receptionist more often.

Passing gatekeepers takes more than old ploys; they have a few old ploys of their own. (38)

3. Convince more buyers to meet with you face-to-face.

Once you get past the gatekeeper, the challenge is to get the decision maker to give you an appointment. (39)

4. Stop wasting time and money on people who won't buy.

Sending literature to "tire kickers" is a waste of printing and postage. Have you noticed how few of those expensive packets you mail out convert into sales? And start presenting only to serious buyers. (59, 77)

5. Hold buyers' attention throughout your presentation.

Keep them from looking at their watches and saying, "You've got two more minutes." (52, 83, 86, 87, 109)

6. Hear from the committees you present to.

Don't settle for "We'll get back to you." (59, 86)

7. Create instant rapport with every buyer.

It's all a matter of analyzing and adapting to each buyer's personality style. (60–69)

8. Get buyers to say, "Wow, am I ever glad *you* showed up!"

Relieve their innermost pain. (70–80)

9. Feel good about asking for the order.

The secret is not to ask. (77–81, 92)

10. Keep price from ever being an issue again.

How would you like to actually take advantage of having a high price? (77, 78)

11. Profit from the no's you get.

They'll do more for you in the long run than the yeses. (92, 93)

12. Get buyers to be honest with you.

They have been conditioned to lie. (59, 77, 78)

13. Prevent buyers from giving your ideas to the competition.

Keep your solutions from showing up in their proposals. (59)

14. Get credit from your customers for all the times you jump through the hoop for them.

You need all the credit you can get. (104)

15. Get the other members of your sales team to work with you.

You can encourage better teamwork. (112)

16. Protect your best customers from the competition and get more business from them.

Don't just sit around waiting for them to defect. (94–105, 115)

✓ Know Your Market

3

The ideal goal of every manufacturer is to operate a plant at maximum capacity with minimum inventory. Under this scenario product would go immediately from the last stage of production onto a truck to be routed to a customer. One necessary condition for achieving this goal is to predict market conditions with laser accuracy. In the same way, sales professionals practice "just-in-time selling." They understand what's needed by what buyers almost before the buyers realize it. They know the market.

---

26 Ten Methods to Track Market Trends

> I don't set trends. I just find out what they are and exploit them.   — Dick Clark

A sure way to miss your mark as a salesperson is to assume that your customers will want tomorrow what they want today. One day there will no longer be a market for that hot product or service you're selling today. Will you be the first to recognize that change? One day a new market may emerge to gobble up that outdated inventory or treasure that old-fashioned service you're ready to give up on. Will you be the first to recognize that trend? The suggestions in this list will keep you on the leading edge of your markets by building your "Market Quotient."

1. **Spend at least three hours a week reading magazines and journals that report general market trends.**

Consider these sources:

- *Wall Street Journal*
- *American Demographics*

- *US News and World Report*
- *Time*
- *Newsweek*
- *Business Week*

2. If you sell to a specific industry, read its trade magazines.

Discover emerging trends even before your customers experience them.

3. Subscribe to Internet services that feed market information to your computer.

The generic name for these services is "point cast." They are usually free and are the quickest way for you to receive breaking news affecting your customers and their industry. They enable you to determine the categories of information you want and to specify your data needs within those categories.

4. Subscribe to newsletters in your field.

Most newsletters pay staff to track trends. Let them earn their money.

5. Set up a monthly "Trend Watch" lunch with colleagues.

Gather once a month with peers to check perceptions, validate assumptions, develop insights, share market information, and test your sense of market reality.

6. Attend meetings of your trade association.

Attend these meetings as if you were a dry sponge. Soak up as much information from as many sources as you can. Attend sessions, participate in roundtables, network over meals.

7. Subscribe to services that provide industry- or market-specific polling data.

If you are selling to a large industry or market, there's a company somewhere collecting data from that industry or market and selling it to people like you.

8. Talk with salespeople outside your industry.

Tracking trends is nothing more than acquiring competitive intelligence. Salespeople who deal with the public on a daily basis, even if they're not in your market, are sources of valuable insight. Invite some of them to your "Trend Watch" lunches (#5 in this list).

9. Talk with your customers.

Ask customers how they see their tomorrows. The hope, uncertainty, and anxiety they express foretell the future. Their concerns and their anticipations may point the way to prospective opportunities for you.

10. Open your eyes, ears, and mind.

On the way home from the hospital a frightened new mother confided to her mom that she had no idea how to take care of her infant. The mother's advice was simple: "Study your child. *She* will show you what to do." That is the best advice to a trend watcher. Study your market. *It* will show you what to do.

— — —

27 Ten Techniques for Conducting a Competitor Analysis

Treating a competitor's brand as if it didn't exist doesn't mean your customers will do the same.
— Margie Smith

Sports teams have to learn as much about their opponents as they can. What are the other team's strengths and weaknesses? Where are we most vulnerable to them and where are they most vulnerable to us? What are our best opportunities to defeat them? In the same way, successful salespeople make a conscious effort to acquire strategic information about competitors.

1. Ask four basic questions.

Here are the key questions for conducting a competitor analysis:

- What are their strengths in the marketplace?
- What are their weaknesses in the marketplace?
- What major threats do they pose to our survival?
- What major opportunities exist to outsell them?

Depending on the competitor, the industry, and the competitor's relationship to you, other more specific questions will emerge from the four basic questions. For example: "What kind of training have their salespeople received?"

2. If the company is publicly traded, buy stock in it.

As a stockholder you will receive reports discussing strategy, missions, financial performance, and long-range goals. If the company is part of a larger, publicly traded holding company, you should buy stock in the holding company. You may have mixed feelings about making money on your investment, but what a nice way to hedge your bet.

3. Ask for permission to visit the company to perform benchmarking.

This may sound like a crazy idea, and many competitors may turn you down, but some will not. A few will even buy your lunch! Ask to see whatever "best practices" within your competitor's operation you can learn the most from. Gain the intelligence that will make you more competitive, and copy those great ideas that will work for you.

4. Develop a file of competitors' ads and promotional brochures.

Study prices, promotional features, and ad copy. Does a particular competitor appear to focus on operational excellence (low price, efficiency, reliability), product leadership (invention, product development, cutting-edge technology), or customer intimacy (total, customized, and personalized solutions)? (97)

5. Visit their Web sites on the Internet.

What promotional services does a site offer? What does the site say about the company? Check out your competitors' Internet presence once a week.

6. Hire a media clipping service.

These services will scan publications and clip stories on companies you designate. They cover the hundreds of papers and magazines you don't have time to read.

7. Buy competitive products and study them in detail.

Car companies, appliance manufacturers, and computer manufacturers buy one another's products. They want to see how well they are made, how they differ from their own products, and what they can legally copy.

8. **Listen carefully to what your customers say about your competitors.**

Your customers can provide loads of strategic data about your competition. Ask them for the differences they experience between your products and services and those of your competitors. Use this information to develop better products and services as well as more effective sales strategies. (30, 100, 104, 105)

9. **Ask your employees, coworkers, and family members for their opinions about your market generally and your competitors specifically.**

Your family, coworkers, and employees have a vested interest in your success. Ask them to tune into your competitors' ads, products, and promotions. Measure their impressions.

10. **Shun strategies you would not want your competitors to use on you.**

The strategies in this list are ethical. They don't harm your competitor. Learning the competition does not mean you have to lie, cheat, or steal. (21, 119)

━━ ━━ ━━

28 Fourteen Sources of Market and Customer Information

Before you build a better mousetrap, find out how many mice are out there.—Mortimer Zuckerman

Market research always has been and always will be the key to long-term company survival. You need to understand who the buyers are, where they are, how much money they have to spend, *and* how many of them are out there. This list directs you to sources that provide that information.

Local Market Analysis

1. **Chamber of commerce.**

Study the membership list. What start-up companies have recently joined? What companies are no longer members? What new opportunities appear to exist for you? If your chamber of commerce has a Web site, check it out. Is the chamber itself a potential customer?

2. Convention bureau.

What kinds of organizations find your region attractive as a meeting site? What products and services do their members look for during their stays in your city? If your bureau has a Web site, check it out. Is the bureau itself a potential customer?

3. City, county, and state offices of economic development.

Get on their mailing lists to receive their publications and reports. What new initiatives are under way that your product or service can assist? What companies are moving into your region? What national or international companies have established local subsidiaries? If these offices have Web sites, visit them.

4. Local newspapers.

Read them daily. Who is proposing to do what? Who is doing what? Check the classifieds to see who is hiring and therefore growing.

5. Local business paper.

Your city may have a paper dedicated solely to business news. These are founts of information on the commerce of your region. For example, local business papers will tell you what companies are doing well or planning major expansions and who's recently been promoted to what position.

6. The business development center of your local college or university.

Many colleges and universities have established offices to promote emerging entrepreneurs. Contact these offices to find out who is doing what. You might even be one of the emerging entrepreneurs they can help.

7. The local Yellow Pages.

How do the major companies that serve consumers directly position themselves with consumers? Does this positioning give you new ideas on how you might serve those companies or even compete with them?

8. Annual reports.

Surf the Internet or your local library for the most recent annual reports of the top dozen or so nearby companies that you'd like to do business with. Learn where they're headed and dream up some ways you might help them get there.

National Market Analysis

9. *The Wall Street Journal.*

This entire publication will help you. Pay particular attention to the "What's News" section on the front page of the first section and the entire first page of the second section.

10. *Business Week.*

Reading this magazine cover to cover for six months is tantamount to taking a marketing course in an MBA program.

11. Reports from the federal government.

You pay your taxes. Why not tap into the voluminous databases available to the taxpaying public? Start your search at the GSA (Government Services Administration) Web site or contact the local liaison office of your congress member.

12. The national Yellow Pages.

These are available on CD-ROM. Ask your local Yellow Pages representative for information on how to purchase them.

13. Industry-wide publications.

Read the trade publications published for your market. Join organizations that publish useful newsletters and organize valuable trade conferences where market trends are revealed. Seek information not only for your primary market (e.g., breakfast cereals), but also for related markets (e.g., breakfast foods).

14. A company database of all "hot information" your colleagues have heard.

Coworkers hear things about industry and market trends as they call on customers, talk to suppliers, or schmooze with colleagues on the golf course. Set up a centralized database where all such information can be posted.

29 Ten Dimensions That Define Your Market

Every crowd has a silver lining. — *P. T. Barnum*

Yes, it is possible to sell ice in Alaska and coals in Newcastle, but there may be better markets for ice and coal. Some buyers are perfectly suited to, and highly interested in, what you offer; others won't be easily sold. What is the ideal profile of the buyers you intend to go after? Which will find your product or service most useful and attractive? What are your best markets and which will waste your time? Study the dimensions in this list to create the combination of factors that best defines your target markets. Be creative. Involve others in brainstorming to identify your best opportunities.

If You Sell to Commercial Clients, Study . . .

1. Standard industrial classification.

Go to your library or search the Internet for a listing of the standard industrial codes published by the federal government. Just a few examples of the broad categories containing these codes are

- 1500: General Building Contractors
- 2000: Food and Kindred Products
- 2300: Apparel and Other Textile Products
- 3300: Primary Metal Industries
- 3600: Electronic and Other Electric Equipment
- 4700: Transportation Services
- 5300: General Merchandise Stores
- 8200: Educational Services

2. Tax status and ownership.

Which of these best defines your market?

- Profit or not-for-profit?
- Publicly owned or privately held?
- Public sector or private sector?

3. Company life/growth cycle.

Does customer maturity affect your success?

- New or mature company?
- In an emerging or level business?
- Growing, stagnant, or declining revenues?

4. **Size, concentration, and reach.**

How does size affect needs for your wares?

- Small, medium, or large employee base, capital outlays, and revenues?
- A few locations or spread out over a wide area?
- Local, regional, national, or global?

5. **Proportion of profit customers generate.**

Do you want a few customers that each generate a large portion of your earnings, or will you be better off with large numbers of customers each providing a smaller piece of your gain? This analysis can also be applied to individual consumers.

If You Sell to Individual Consumers, Study . . .

6. **Demographics.**

What easily measurable dimensions define your target audience?

- Age
- Location
- Occupation
- Gender
- Ethnicity
- Religious affiliation
- Health
- Marital status
- Dependents

7. **Psychographics.**

How does the psychosocial makeup of consumers affect their interest in your product or service?

- Attitudes
- Opinions
- Values
- Beliefs
- Lifestyle

8. Socioeconomic class.

Who can best afford to say yes to you?

- Income
- Level of debt
- Credit rating
- Savings
- Stock and bond ownership
- Home ownership
- Total assets

No Matter Where You Sell, Study . . .

9. Relationship to you.

How close do buyers already need to be to you before you can sell to them?

- Friendly, neutral, or hostile?
- Ignorant of your existence or already aware of you?
- In agreement with your basic philosophies or antagonistic to them?

10. Loyalty.

Conventional wisdom says that you need to spend five times more on finding a new customer than on selling more to an old one. Does this relationship hold in your business? What percentage of your marketing effort should you exert on prospecting for new gold and how much on refining the gold you already have? (104)

■■■ ■■■ ■■■

30 Eleven Guidelines for Creating a Customer Advisory Group

> *Profit comes from repeat customers: those that boast about the product or service.*
>
> —W. Edwards Deming

No matter how much the world of business may change, one factor will never change: *Your most valuable sources of information are your customers.* They will tell you what you're doing right, what you're doing wrong, and what you need to change immediately to remain competitive. Customer advisory groups may be the best consultants you'll retain. Follow these guidelines to get the most out of them.

1. Position the group as a win-win opportunity for members.

If customers believe they're only doing you a favor, getting them to join will be a difficult sell. Make sure potential members understand that membership provides an opportunity to improve their business as they help you redesign yours.

2. Choose members for the right reasons.

Select advisory group members who are perceptive, vocal, and motivated to participate. "Figurehead" members selected for their fame or position, but who won't attend group meetings or give follow-up a high priority, will be of little value.

3. Use the group in a strictly advisory capacity, not as another opportunity to sell.

Demonstrate to members that you need their advice to serve them better. Confirm this message through your actions.

4. If you sell different product lines to different customers, organize the groups along common interests.

For example, you may choose to organize groups along these lines:

- Large retail customers
- Small retail customers
- Large wholesale customers
- Small wholesale customers
- Domestic market
- International market
- New customers
- Long-time customers (29)

5. Make the members feel special.

Membership should be an honor and a privilege. You want members to feel good about serving you. Treat them to the best in transportation, parking, refreshments, meals, and meeting space. Have the CEO give them their charge and put in an appearance now and then at meetings. Write up their recommendations in prestigious company publications. Thank them publicly.

6. Reward them for participating.

Provide rewards they would value. Consider members-only discounts on your products, dinner passes, tickets to the theater or to sporting events, coveted club memberships, or other attractive gifts. (32)

7. If you are a major supplier within an industry, have customers elect their own representatives.

Major producers often set up advisory councils composed of members selected by members of the industry itself. For instance, some auto dealer associations have this relationship with auto manufacturers.

8. Unless there is a crisis, schedule no more than two meetings per year.

Gathering more often will be seen as a chore and an unreasonable imposition.

9. Take advantage of information technology to conduct virtual meetings.

Consider these options for meetings that don't require travel or face-to-face discussions:

- Electronic chat rooms on the Internet
- Videoconferencing
- Questionnaires e-mailed or faxed to members and e-mailed or faxed back to you (108, 111)

10. Appoint an effective group leader.

Someone who knows how to run effective meetings and who understands your business thoroughly should lead the customer advisory group. You need to trust that the group's recommendations will be creative yet well thought through and that their ideas will be appropriate to your mission.

11. Act on their recommendations.

If you follow the advice given on this list, the ideas that you get from your customer advisory group will enable you to advance the fortunes of your business. Implement the ideas that will work. Tell them why you might choose not to implement others. If you ignore their suggestions or drag your feet in applying them, you may never again have customers who are willing to serve on the advisory group.

▬ ▬ ▬

31 Thirteen Smart Price-Setting Strategies

What we obtain too cheap, we esteem too lightly.
—Thomas Paine

This may be the most vexing question facing marketers and salespeople: What price will maximize the income I receive from my sales? Experts who research this question typically answer it with three words: It all depends. That's because there is no magical formula that fits every pricing situation with total certainty. Even so, there are several schemes that savvy sellers consider when they set their price.

1. Give it away free with no strings attached.

Many companies share ideas and even provide free services through their Web sites on the bet that they'll attract enough paying business to cover the costs of the free services.

2. Give it away free for a limited time.

Long distance and cellular access providers have used this tactic to induce customers to shift from competitors and to sign up as first-time subscribers. This approach and the one preceding make sense when your production costs are low, perceived value is high, profit margins are high, and you're entering an exploding market.

3. Sell it at cost or below cost.

The loss-leader strategy can be used when you have a popular item that will encourage subsequent purchases of other items that consumers, attracted by your low price, learn about. Supermarkets lure food shoppers into their stores with buy-one, get-one-free specials.

4. Offer free or deeply discounted peripherals.

When you maintain the basic price of your key product or service, you help to reinforce the message that it is of high quality and value. At the same time, deeply discounting attractive accessories encourages consumers to buy the key product. TV marketers often pitch that ordering a product by a certain date will get you a free video showing you how to use it along with a month's supply of the consumables the product uses.

5. Price the items in a package separately.

A motivational speaker who normally charged companies $5,000 for an all-day program got less price resistance when she began quoting clients on a per-participant basis. Her new charge of $95 per employee up to 50 (guaranteed minimum), plus $50 for each additional participant, was more popular and made more money for her in the long run.

6. Bundle the price.

The opposite approach to #5 is to establish a single price for a combination of product and service features. You may also sell the individual items of the bundle separately and offer a discount for the total bundled package. Bundling works well when the product or service has many options or add-on features. Computer hardware manufacturers bundle the price.

7. Meet your competitor's lowest price.

This is a common pricing strategy, particularly among retailers who engage in heavy advertising campaigns.

8. Price at cost plus markup.

Once you determine costs, add on a standard margin that will sell enough of the product to provide a targeted profit. This is the most traditional form of pricing.

9. Price at "cost-plus."

The "plus" is a fair profit margin negotiated with the customer or changed according to market conditions. Some auto manufacturers will work only with selected vendors who are willing to follow this pricing strategy. Expect customers to ask to see invoices for your costs.

10. Offer discounts.

For commercial sales the most common discounts are given for quantity purchases or prompt payment of invoices. Discounts to individual consumers take many additional forms. One is the "calendar" discount used to encourage business during slow business periods: for instance, a local gas station may offer a five-cent-per-gallon discount on Tuesdays. Coupons are another popular form of consumer discounting.

11. Use market pricing.

This widespread tactic among airlines and hotels is also known as "demand pricing." Two fliers on the same airline depart and return on the same day. One has to take two planes to get to a destination 1,000 miles away; the other takes only one plane to go 700 miles yet pays a higher fare than the first flier. Why this seeming incongruity? One is flying into a market that the airline has decided fliers will pay more to reach by air.

12. Establish prestige pricing.

When your product or service enjoys a reputation of quality and status, you may be able to reinforce and even enhance that reputation by attaching a markup higher than competitors do. Consider the premium you pay for designer labels on clothing.

13. Use new product price skimming.

Some businesses charge an inordinately high price when a product or service is first introduced. If the product is well accepted, they will "skim the cream" until competitors mobilize to enter the market and force them to lower their price. The first Internet access providers extracted a high monthly charge until alternative services became available.

━━ ━━ ━━

32 Thirteen Qualities of Attractive Premiums

A small gift is better than a great promise.
— German proverb

Premiums are the gifts salespeople offer as incentives to get people to buy. You also give them out to existing customers as expressions of gratitude. A cleverly conceived premium is not a bribe to change a decision, but a marketing tool to draw the buyer to a point of interest and to show sincere appreciation to a customer. Used by the smallest of companies to the largest of firms, attractive premiums can open the door and keep 'em coming back! From key rings to fine wines to vacation trips, premiums make an impact. Here's what you should give away to get the most back:

1. Usability.

For premiums, value equals use. Favor function over form. For example, a multipurpose golf tool works better than a bag of tees. A first-aid kit at a trade show works better than a 60-second electronic foot massage.

2. Reusability.

Single-use premiums expire without lasting impact. Functional and reusable premiums are smarter. Custom holiday ornaments, umbrellas, and coffee mugs are examples of reusable gifts.

3. Prominence.

You want your premium on your buyer's desktop, not in a drawer. The higher the visibility, the more likely and lasting the impact. Select premiums that people want to show off. A clock will sit on a desk in plain view; a letter opener will be hidden. Key rings are usually found in pockets, not out of them.

4. Originality.

Think creatively. An artist's rendering of the city or an attractive photograph may be around an office for years. The calendar your competitors send out won't even get up onto the wall.

5. Uniqueness.

A handcrafted wooden pen with the initials of your customers engraved on the barrel may be prized more than a designer pen that's three times more expensive and three hundred times more common.

6. Timelessness.

Calendars are doomed at year's end. So is anything with a date unless it's a collector's piece such as a Rockwell portrait or other designer-styled gift. Think long-term.

7. Close fit to your business.

Match your premium to your market and your company. This is why dentists give toothbrushes and floss. A bicycle sales or repair shop can give away reflective strips imprinted with its name. An environmental firm can give a personalized water-testing kit.

8. Appeal to current interests.

Techno toys are hot. Computer mouse pads, a custom computer game, and audio or video discs are examples. Gadgets that blink, make sounds, or require a human touch to activate are quite memorable.

9. Visibility to other people.

Sometimes your premiums are more than a way to influence one buyer; they're part of an overall marketing campaign. In this case, choose gifts that many people will eventually see. T-shirts, hats, visors, and other monogrammed clothing make good billboards, as do window decals and windshield protectors. Custom collector lapel pins worn on hats or jackets can be quite popular. Stuffed animals sporting a logo are often a winner.

10. Lightweight for items you'll mail.

Weight and packaging costs can run up your investment in a premium without adding value for your customer.

11. High value to the customer, low cost to you.

Often you can buy bulk copies of a best-selling book, audio-tape, or CD direct from its publisher at a good discount. If you order in the hundreds or thousands of copies, the publisher may even imprint your logo on the product at a low cost. Your customers will value a nice premium like this at its retail cost of $15 to $30, but the actual cost per unit to you may be only half of that.

12. A slogan worth quoting.

At a computer trade show, one company put such a clever message on a button that everyone "had to have one." Its advertising message was everywhere. Build a slogan around a theme or current marketing campaign to put on the lips of customers (e.g., Nike's "Just Do It"). Keep the message inoffensive; avoid sexual innuendo. If you're marketing internationally, be sure to check for language that translates properly.

13. Chocolates are always a winner.

An exception to many of the "rules" in this list is chocolates. Delightful bites are a hit at trade shows, at holiday time, or really anytime. Many chocolatiers do logo imprinting and will even design a custom mold for your firm. Do this one right and customers will remark throughout the year how much they liked your sweet gift.

---

33 Six Methods to Create a Sales Forecast

My interest is in the future because I am going to spend the rest of my life there.

— Charles Kettering

Given the market you're in and the condition of the economy, what's a reasonable sales target for you and your company? While there is no single foolproof method for computing those targets, there are proven techniques that have withstood the test of time. Most sales professionals use one or a combination of all six. Regardless of the forecasting method you use, make sure your resulting sales target is both motivating and achievable.

1. Trend analysis.

Add a percentage increase to this year's sales to forecast next year's. *Example*: projecting a 7% increase on current sales of $660,000 results in a sales goal of $706,200.

2. Sales force survey.

Lead a discussion among sales personnel of the major trends affecting the market and the impact those trends will have on sales volume. Following the discussion, have each person submit a dollar estimate. Drop out the highest and lowest and compute the average of the remaining estimates to get your forecast.

3. Chain ratio.

Use this formula: (number in total market) × (% market share you expect) × (unit price) = sales forecast. *Example*: (250,000 homeowners in your market with furnaces) × (14% expected market share) × ($120/yearly maintenance contract) = $4.2 million in total maintenance contract work.

4. Test marketing.

Direct a sales campaign to a small randomized sample of the market and extrapolate the results to the entire market.

5. Trend analysis reflecting expert opinion.

Choose estimates from trade associations or industry experts. Adjust the estimates (% increase or decline) according to the knowledge you have about your competition. *Example*: If experts estimate your total market will decline by 11% in the coming year, you might reduce your sales target by only 7% because you know an advantage you will have in the coming year over most competitors.

6. Statistical computer analysis.

Use correlation and regression techniques based on algorithms and computer models. **Caution:** The fact that a computer provides a forecast does not necessarily make it any more reliable than the preceding five methods. Remember the law of statistical analysis: Garbage In–Garbage Out.

━━ ━━ ━━

34 Twenty-Five Strategic Questions to Improve the Impact of Sales and Marketing Campaigns

Whoever sows sparingly will reap sparingly, and whoever sows generously will also reap generously.
—2 Corinthians 9:6

Some of the toughest decisions executives make are concerned with marketing. Marketing decisions are inherently fraught with ambiguity and uncertainty. What is the best copy for an ad? Where should the ad appear? How many times should it run? Should we run different ads for different buyers? Depending on your selling responsibilities, these questions may or may not appear directly relevant to you. But if you believe they have no application to your daily duties, think again. The answers to these questions affect everyone in the company—*especially* those in sales. You may not be responsible for answering them, but you can't represent your company well without knowing what the answers are.

Corporate Identity Decisions

1. Who are we . . . what is our corporate mission?

2. When buyers think of us, what do we want them to think?

3. When buyers think of us, what *do* they think?

4. If we can't be all things to all people, what can we be to what kinds of people?

5. Who else in our industry might answer question #4 the same way we did?

6. How are we different from the competition identified in question #5?

Buyer Identification Decisions

7. Do we have different customers for different product lines?

8. How large (in numbers) is our potential market?

9. Where are buyers located?

10. What are their values?

11. How much do they typically expect to spend for our product?

12. What reasons do our current customers give for having made a purchase decision?

Strategic Marketing Goals

13. Do we want to maintain or increase market share? If increase, by what percentage?

14. Do we want to maintain or increase customer share? If increase, by what percentage?

15. Are we planning to roll out a new product? If so, where do we want to position it in the market?

16. If we have different product lines, have we established specific marketing goals for those respective lines?

17. Do we need to create a public relations campaign? If so, with what goals?

Marketing Budget Decisions

18. How much will we allocate to our total marketing budget?

19. If the budget is limited, where should we put our money?

20. Which goals identified in #12–17 are most crucial for our short-term survival/long-term success and should therefore receive the highest consideration?

Advertising Media Decisions

21. Given our goals and our budget, what is the best way to reach the buyers defined by #6–11?

22. What advertising media will be most cost-effective for our strategic goals?

23. Given our corporate identity (#1–6) and our buyers (#7–12), what should we emphasize in our ad copy?

24. What does our internal advertising capability position us to do well, and what will we outsource?

25. How will we measure the impact of our marketing campaign?

▬ ▬ ▬

35 Fifty Business Terms to Master

> *And all your future lies beneath your hat.*
> —John Olham

One of the surest ways to lose credibility on a sales call is to look dumbfounded when a buyer says, "To meet our Hoshin planning goals for TQM we're reengineering our POP processes. Do you have a UPC product that will help us?" The vocabulary of business executives is replete with acronyms, jargon, and bureaucratese. This list will help you to build that vocabulary.

1. **Brand Equity:** Portion of a product's value attributed solely to its brand name.

2. **Break Even Quantity:** The number of units that must be sold in order to cover the costs of producing those units.

3. **Buy Forward:** Purchasing an entire year's inventory at a discounted price.

4. **Buyer's Remorse:** Regret a buyer feels after a purchase. (102)

5. **Cash Cow:** A product or operation that generates considerable profits.

6. **CQI (Constant Quality Improvement):** A management philosophy based on continually improving products, processes, and outcomes. See TQM.

7. **Co-op Advertising:** Advertising paid for by the retailer and the manufacturer together.

8. **Cumulative Discount:** Quantity discount for purchases over a period of time.

9. **Dog:** A product that has cost disadvantages and too few buyers for market growth.

10. **Drop Shipper:** Merchant wholesaler that buys directly from manufacturers or suppliers and arranges for shipment to end users. Sometimes referred to as a Desk Jobber.

11. **EDI (Electronic Data Interchange):** Computer-to-computer linkages between manufacturers, retailers, distributors, financial institutions, and others.

12. **FOB (Free on Board):** Designates the point at which responsibility for merchandise shifts from seller to buyer.

13. **Fixed Costs:** Costs required to run the business or a project regardless of the output created.

14. **Full Disclosure:** Legal concept requiring divulgence of information so purchaser may make safe and informed decision.

15. **Hoshin Planning:** A method for strategic planning that uses specific tools to forge individual ideas into a consensus decision. (In Japanese "hoshin" means "shiny needle," like the needle of a compass giving direction and focus.)

16. **Inelastic Demand:** Changes in price have little effect on demand for the product. (When demand is "elastic," price changes have a powerful impact on consumer buying.)

17. **Inventory Turnover:** The number of times a company or operation sells and replaces its merchandise in one year. Also known as "turn."

18. **JIT (Just in Time):** An approach to managing inventories and projects so that what you need for the next step in the manufacturing process is there when you need it: not sooner, and definitely not later.

19. **Letter of Credit:** Common method for international payment; usually provided by the buyer's bank.

20. **Leverage:** Using borrowed funds to invest such that the return on the investment is higher than the cost of borrowing the funds.

21. **Loss Leader:** An item sold at cost or below cost to attract customers to other items.

22. **Marketing Mix:** Combined decisions regarding product, promotion, place, and price (the "four P's") that determine the key dimensions of a marketing campaign.

23. **Markup:** An amount added to the cost of a product or service in order to set its selling price.

24. **MSA (Metropolitan Statistical Area):** A distinct metropolitan area with a population of at least 50,000.

25. **Mission Statement:** A written document detailing the purposes of the organization, its reasons for existence. See Vision Statement.

26. **NPV (Net Present Value):** Investment minus the value today of future expected cash flows from the investment.

27. **Net Sales:** Total sales minus returns.

28. **OEM (Original Equipment Manufacturer):** A business that purchases goods and incorporates them into products it manufactures.

29. **Overhead:** The costs of running a business that go on regard-

less of activities that contribute directly to productivity (e.g., utilities, rent, and insurance).

30. **Positioning:** Establishing an image with consumers for a product or service that distinguishes it from the competition.

31. **Product Life Cycle:** A marketing model that assumes that all products and services pass through four predictable stages: introduction, growth, maturity, and decline.

32. **PM (Push Money):** Money passed directly to a retailer's sales staff for selling a manufacturer's products.

33. **POP (Point of Purchase):** The physical location where the customer pays for product.

34. **Price Ceiling:** The maximum amount customers will pay. (31)

35. **Price Floor:** The lowest price that will still yield a profit. (31)

36. **Price Lining:** Selling products at a range of prices, each indicating a different level of quality or features. (31)

37. **RFP (Request for Proposal):** Invitation from a buyer for bids from potential suppliers. (85)

38. **Reengineering:** Process of redesigning organizations or departments so that they focus on processes (what they do to serve customers) rather than operations (jobs, titles, hierarchy, and function).

39. **ROI (Return on Investment):** Net profits expected from a given investment expressed as a percentage of the investment.

40. **SPC (Statistical Process Analysis):** Using statistical analysis to ensure that manufacturing of products and delivery of services don't deviate from optimum levels of quality.

41. **SBU (Strategic Business Unit):** Separate business system within one organization run as if it were an independent company.

42. **Stock Turnover:** The number of times during a given period a company's stock is sold.

43. **TQM (Total Quality Management):** A management philosophy stressing constant improvement in all business processes. See CQI.

44. UCC (Uniform Commercial Code): Legal guide to commercial practices in the U.S. (119)

45. UPC (Universal Product Code): Computerized coding system on products read by electronic scanners.

46. URL (Universal Resource Locator): An Internet address. (110)

47. Virtual Corporation: Conducting business with a minimum of full-time employees through a combination of outsourcing and computer networking.

48. Vision Statement: A document describing the aspirations and desired future state of an organization. It often includes a statement of corporate values and beliefs.

49. Warranty: Assurance by seller that goods or services will perform as represented.

50. Zoning: A method for scheduling calls that divides a large territory into manageable zones. (16)

✓ Find Buyers

4

Many salespeople report that what they enjoy most about selling is closing the sale and getting their commission check. What most salespeople enjoy least about their occupation is generating leads and making cold calls. The irony of selling is that the joy of the sale depends on the grief of prospecting. The tips and strategies in this chapter show you how to reduce the grief and increase the joy.

■ ■ ■

36 Forty Sources for Leads

> *Beaten paths are for beaten men.*
>
> *— Eric Johnston*

The three most important factors in real estate value are location, location, location. The three most important factors in selling are leads, leads, leads. You require a constant supply of new buyers to call on. The best way to find new buyers is to look for them in new places. Here are 40 places you will find them. We bet you can think of 40 more.

Through Personal Networking

1. Current customers
2. Former customers
3. Customers of current and former customers
4. Next-door neighbors
5. Customers' next-door neighbors
6. Local chamber of commerce

7. Local office of economic development

8. Your family

9. High school or college reunion attendees

10. People you meet on vacation at the beach, in the mountains, or at the amusement park

11. People in chat rooms and other locations on the Internet

12. Your attorney

13. Your banker

14. Your accountant

15. Your physician

16. Your clothier

17. Colleagues at seminars, conferences, and conventions

18. Current and former colleagues

19. Patrons in bookstores, particularly in front of the business shelf

20. The person sitting next to you on an airplane, especially in first class

21. Acquaintances in airports, restaurants, hotel bars, ski lodges, golf courses, malls, museums, doctors offices, and anywhere else

22. Buyers that turned you down in the past

23. The names you're afraid to call because you believe they won't listen to you

24. Contacts at social, professional, or fraternal clubs

Through Typical Marketing Strategies

25. Responses to radio or TV ads

26. Responses to printed ads

27. Responses to telemarketing

28. Mailing lists developed at trade shows

Through Marketing Services and Publications

29. Mailing lists from qualified list brokers

30. Trade association lists

31. Hoover's (in book form, on CD-ROM, or at Internet site)

32. Moody's Industrial Directory

33. Standard & Poor's Register of Corporations, Directors, and Executives

34. Dun's Direct Access (Dun and Bradstreet) accessed through your computer

35. National Trade and Professional Associations (Columbia Books)

36. Middle Market Directory (Dun and Bradstreet)

37. Encyclopedia of Associations (Gale)

38. The International Corporate 1000 (Graham and Trotman)

39. TrackAmerica: Information on 10 million U.S. businesses and 90 million consumers accessed through your computer

40. Business Lists on Disc (American Business Information): over 9 million businesses on CD-ROM

▬ ▬ ▬

37 Thirteen Tips for Increasing Your Net Worth Through Networking

I never met a man I didn't like.   —Will Rogers

The success of Amway, Excel, Mary Kay, and other direct marketing companies is no secret. The fortunes of these enterprises grow through the networking prowess of those who sell their products. No matter what you sell, the more effective your sales network, the more likely you are to succeed. Professional salespeople understand this basic principle and use ideas like those in this list to broaden and increase the quality of their personal networks.

1. **Have your 30-second commercial ready.**

Be prepared to give a very brief explanation of your business purpose when you first speak to someone at a meeting. Focus on the value you add to your clients more than on the features and benefits of your products (e.g., "Our hotel provides corporate groups with a conference environment where they can play as hard as they work").

2. **It's OK to feel hungry when expanding or tapping into your network, but don't look and act famished.**

Aggressiveness will cause people to resent your taking advantage of their friendship to make a sale or to gather other names. (3)

3. **Give something.**

Provide value to your colleagues in exchange for their help. Practice the rule of giving out at least one lead for every one you receive.

4. **Listen for opportunities.**

Your ears may be the most important marketing tool you have. When you meet people for the first time, listen to the names they drop and the opportunities they reveal. (74)

5. **Tap into alumni networks from schools and continuing education programs.**

Starting with your high school graduating class and moving up through the present, think of every school that gave you a diploma or certificate and every continuing education program you ever attended. Make sure your name remains on their mailing lists. Obtain those lists so you can network with former classmates.

6. **Create a memorable business card.**

Without being showy or gaudy you can turn heads with your business card. Here are several business card enhancements we've seen used singly or in combination. Whichever you choose, get feedback on the tastefulness of your design before you execute it.

- Hire a graphic artist to create a four-color design that enhances your information.
- Hire a graphic artist to create a personal logo to go on your card and stationery.
- Use both sides of the card for your message.

- Include information of value to your buyer. For instance, a speech consultant prints the "Seven Deadly Sins of Speech Making" on the reverse of his card.
- Fit more valuable information on it with an oversized card that folds down to business card size.
- Print the card on plastic or another medium rather than paper.

7. Give out your business card only when there is good reason to.

For potential buyers, this means only after you have set up an appointment with someone or he or she has agreed to accept your phone call to set up an appointment. For colleagues, this means once the two of you identify mutual interests and believe you can help each other. Does this sound too conservative to you? If so, think of how you felt about the last salesperson you met who stuck a business card into every hand within reach and then taped one to every pay phone in the building. Were you eager to work with that person?

8. Maintain a presence at trade associations.

Take every advantage of membership events by getting and giving business cards and networking.

9. Collect business cards with a vengeance.

Try to get into the *Guinness Book of Records* for the most business cards ever collected. As soon as possible after receiving a card, write notes on the back indicating the value that person can be to your sales goals. If the person is a buyer, make preliminary notes about that buyer's needs and level of satisfaction with current suppliers.

10. Encode business card data into a contact management database.

Consider a computerized business card management system. This can become your electronic Rolodex.

11. Obtain and encode personal information into the database.

Use this information to send congratulatory notes on personal events and commemorations such as:

- Birthdays
- Anniversaries

- Graduations
- Confirmations
- Bar Mitzvahs
- Christenings
- Births
- Marriages

Create "tickler" files with the personal information you encode. The software should signal you one week before an anniversary, graduation, or birthday so you can send a card or make a phone call.

12. **If you do a great deal of business overseas or with foreign-born customers, program your tickler file to recognize customs and celebrations.**

It's better not to make any gesture than to make an inappropriate one. Learn about the customs and traditions that international associates would be pleased for you to acknowledge and get some coaching on how to do it. For instance, when working with Islamic colleagues, buyers, or customers, you'll want to know the meaning, the customs, and the dates of Ramadan. (113)

13. **Scan the local paper and trade journal for stories about people in your network.**

Send congratulatory, handwritten notes each time you read something flattering about people you know.

■ ■ ■

38 Nine Strategies for Getting Past the Receptionist on the Phone

> *It still holds true that man is most uniquely human when he turns obstacles into opportunities.*
>
> *—Eric Hoffer*

The telephone is undoubtedly the most cost-effective way to contact a buyer. However, buyers often create filters and gatekeepers to screen calls. The tips in this list will increase your chances to get past the filters, both human and psychological, and make the appointment. Use the ideas that suit your style and are likely to work with the receptionists you encounter.

1. Ask for the buyer as if you were calling your best friend.

"Good morning; is Jennifer in?" Don't say, "My name is [. . .]." Don't give a company name. Don't say, "I'm calling for [. . .]." If the receptionist has revealed his or her name, say, "Hello, Pat; is Jennifer in?"

2. Turn the receptionist into an ally.

You (with a more traditional opening): "Good morning; my name is [. . .]. I'm calling to talk with Jennifer Smith. With whom am I speaking?"
Receptionist: "This is her secretary, Pat Morris."
You: "Ms. Morris, if you were me and you needed to speak to Ms. Smith, what would you do?"

3. Avoid a direct response to a receptionist's screen.

Receptionists have three questions in their repertoire to fend off salespeople: Who's calling? What company are you with? What's it about? That's the bad news. Here's the good news. Many receptionists don't get paid enough to handle responses that don't fit with those questions. Consider these responses to the typical screens:

- "I'd be happy to tell you, but it's important I speak to her directly."
- "I'm not exactly sure."
- "Do you think this will take long? I'm calling long distance."
- "Is it raining there?"

4. Throw the receptionist off balance.

Move the receptionist off his or her scripted brush-off through unexpected responses and questions. Don't sound like a salesperson—put the receptionist off guard through "pattern-interrupt" phrases. For example:

Receptionist: "Thank you for calling ABC Company."
You: "Hi, is Jennifer in?"
Receptionist: "What company are you with?"
You: "I have to have a company?"
Receptionist: "What's this about?"
You: "I'm not sure. That's why I'm calling her."
Receptionist: "What are you selling?"

You (confused): "I don't understand."

Receptionist (again): "WHAT are you selling?"

You (still confused): "Is it possible that Jennifer may be trying to sell *me* something?"

5. **When nothing else works, pull out a few more stops.**

- "How have you been trained to deal with people on the phone you don't know personally? Why do you think you were trained that way?"
- "What do you need to know about me personally before you put this call through?"
- "What are you hoping to accomplish by keeping me from talking to your boss?"
- "Are you willing to risk the company losing money by not putting this call through?"
- "Since you won't put me through, would you be kind enough to give me your name? That way when someone calls in about the inquiry, I'll be able to tell them who it was I spoke with from your company."

6. **Overcome your internal programming.**

Recognize why you will be uncomfortable interrupting the receptionist's automatic questions.

- We are each programmed by our experience for certain routine encounters—programming we need to break.
- At some level the receptionist represents your parent telling you to be obedient.
- You received messages early on in your childhood that said, "Be nice to strangers on the phone."
- You'll tend to play the receptionist's part for her, thinking about how she's going to trap you. As soon as you start thinking the receptionist's part for her, it's two against nobody, and there's nobody left to do the selling.

7. **Never leave your name or number with the receptionist.**

If the buyer is not in or is busy, find out if it makes sense to keep trying. "If you were me, would you call back?" (Assuming the answer is yes.) "I'm sure she doesn't want to play telephone tag. When would be the best time?"

8. **When routed to voice mail, consider leaving no message at all.**

But listen intently to the buyer's voice for auditory clues to how best to communicate later with the buyer.

9. **When routed to voice mail, leave a memorable message.**

Consider these options:

- "These are the three reasons you should return my call."
- "Pressing delete will erase this message; it won't delete your problem."
- "Pressing delete could be a very costly mistake. Are you willing to risk it?"
- Leave your name and phone number at the start, then cut off your message abruptly at an intriguing point as if the phone line were disconnected.

▬ ▬ ▬

39 Sixteen Strategies for Getting More Appointments with Buyers over the Phone

A wise man will make more opportunities than he finds. — Francis Bacon

Success! You've gotten past the receptionist. Now what? How do you convince the buyer who takes your call to give you a face-to-face appointment? Here are two different scenarios for the call. The second probes more deeply than the first, which leaves a bit more to accomplish at the appointment. Pick and choose strategies from within each scenario to find an approach that feels right for you. The final section of this list provides some guiding principles for getting the appointment regardless of strategy.

Caution: The strategies in this list may become less appropriate as the sophistication and organizational level of the buyer increases. In all cases, practice being gentle and sounding sincere when you use these ideas.

A Less Probing Scenario

1. **Establish a mini-contract.**

"Pat, this is [. . .] [pronounced clearly and slowly]; does my name sound familiar? [Proceed regardless of the response.] Let me tell you why I'm calling. I work with [name of one of your customers known to the buyer]. Now, I'm sure the last person you wanted to talk to today was someone in my business. I thought it might make sense for you and me to spend one or two minutes on the phone asking each other some questions to determine if it makes sense for you to invest more time on this phone call. Is that fair?"

2. Probe for pain.

Have 7 to 10 questions ready to help the buyer feel the pain he or she experiences. "People generally decide to invite us in because they have problems with [two of the strongest pains you relieve]. Do either of these strike any chords? [Wait for a response.] Oh, tell me a little bit about that. How long has it been this way? Have you tried to do anything in the past to fix it? Did it work?" Abandon your script once the buyer has "cracked" a little and opened the door for you to "pick" at his or her pain. (76)

3. Set an appointment.

Once you hear legitimate pain, ask, "Pat, may I make a suggestion? Based on the problems you've shared with me, it sounds like it would make sense for you to get out your calendar and invite me in to talk further. Is that fair?"

4. Measure the buyer's commitment to the appointment.

"Pat, I am noting our appointment on my calendar; should I do it in pen or pencil? Pencil means I have to confirm, pen means you will definitely be there."

5. Establish the contract for the first meeting.

"Pat, what things would you like to accomplish by the end of our meeting? [Wait for a response.] OK, good, I've written them down. Now, to make our time more effective, would you do some homework? [Wait for "Sure."] Think some more about the areas you'd like to see improvement in. I'll ask you to share these when we meet, OK? See you on the [day of the meeting]. Good-bye." (59)

A More Probing Scenario

6. Establish a mini-contract.

"Pat, this is [. . .] [pronounced clearly and slowly]. My name doesn't ring a bell, does it? [response] I didn't think so. Let me tell you why I called and you can decide if you want to talk to me or not. I'm a salesperson, we sell [your product], and, guess what, this is a sales call. I'm probably the last person you wanted to talk with right now. I've got a 30-second commercial I'd like to deliver to you, and then you can decide if it makes sense to spend another two or three minutes on the phone, is that fair? [Wait for a yes.] My 30-second commercial is actually a question. I'm assuming there are a whole lot of things you're going to have to feel comfortable about before you would seriously consider taking 45 minutes of your time to invite me in there to sit with you face-to-face. Is that a fair statement, Pat? [Wait for an answer.] What are some of the things you'd have to feel comfortable with to even *consider* doing that? [Interrupt as soon as Pat starts to answer.] Pat, I've got a problem—my 30 seconds are up. [pause] I don't suppose you'd like to continue the conversation?"

7. Probe for pain.

"All right, go ahead, so what are some of the things you'd have to feel comfortable about? [Work off Pat's responses.] Who do you use now? [Pat responds.] Oh, nice company. [pause] Were you involved in the decision to bring them in? [Pat responds.] How long have they been with you? [Pat responds.] You must like what they do for you. [Pat responds.] Let me ask you this. Nobody's perfect. If they could be doing one thing better, just one, what would it be? [Pat responds.] That's interesting. Why'd you pick that one? From what I hear around the industry, the firm does a great job in that area. [Pat responds.]" (76)

8. Dig even deeper for pain.

Expose enough pain to get the appointment.

- "It's probably not the case with you, but . . ."
- "Based on priority, what do you look for in a supplier: service, technical expertise, reliability, personal attention, or price?"
- "I doubt it would matter if you could speed up the . . ."
- "Sometimes when I talk with people for the first time, they may be thinking their business is different, or they don't think they can unhook from their present supplier without a lot of aggravation, or they don't feel someone new could help them. [pause] Are any of these the case here?"

• When nothing elicits pain, ask this: "I get the feeling you might have decided to give up trying to find a workable solution. Is that a fair statement?" (75)

9. Set an appointment.

When the buyer agrees to make an appointment with you, a little bit of "hard-to-get" will help to get the buyer to stick with the commitment.

You: "Get out your calendar."
Pat: "I have it."
You: "What day are you looking at?"
Pat: "Next Tuesday at 10 A.M."
You: "Got a problem. That won't work for me. Would you be kind enough to pick another time?"
Pat: "How about Thursday?"
You: "That's fine. What time?"
Pat: "2:30."
You: "OK, 2:30 works for me, too."

10. Increase the buyer's commitment to the appointment.

Another tactic to increase the likelihood that the buyer will honor the appointment is to give the impression that you are rearranging your schedule to meet at the selected time. When you have to shuffle your schedule to accommodate buyers, they feel more committed to being there for you.

11. Establish the contract for the first meeting.

Get the buyer's commitment for specific outcomes of the meeting. "Pat, just so we understand one another and there are no surprises or disappointments, I'd like to establish a couple of goals for our meeting on [date and time]. What do you hope we can accomplish by the end of the meeting? [Wait for a response.] Great; I've written those down. Between now and then will you do some homework to ensure a productive meeting? [Wait for "Sure."] Will you write down the three most nagging problems on which you'd like to see improvement? [Tailor this last question to fit your business.] See you on [day of the meeting]. So long." (59)

Guiding Principles

12. Have fun.

If you aren't loose, you can't be creative. When you're not creative, you lose opportunities. Don't be anxious—be relaxed and playful. Most traditional salespeople telegraph their cold-call "blues" through the telephone wire, and the buyer picks up on that. Talk as if you are having a conversation with your best friend. Act as if you are financially independent and don't need the business. If that was in fact true, wouldn't you make totally stress-free cold calls for appointments, and wouldn't you end up seeing more people?

13. Overcome the common appointment stalls.

Consider these options for the "send me literature" stall:

- "How large is your office? I probably have enough literature to fill half of it, and most wouldn't address your specific problems. I don't know if what I have would be of interest to you, but it may make sense for us to get together and find out. What do you think?"
- "It's probably not the case, but a lot of times when people ask to see literature it's their way of politely trying to get rid of me. Is that what's happening here?"
- "When people ask for literature, they want to know if I can help them, if their time with me would be worthwhile, or it's a way to politely close the door. Which one describes you?"

Consider these options for the "write me a letter" stall:

- "I'd be happy to do that. May I ask you a question? [response] Why am I doing that?"
- "Sure. And you never see anyone unless they send a letter first?"

Consider these options for the "we're interested, but not right now" stall:

- "So you want to fix the problem, but not until next year? [response] There must be a reason."
- "Experience tells me that when someone says they have a problem, but they don't want to fix it, there's usually a problem I don't know about."

- "It's OK to say no and I'll go away, no hard feelings."

14. Prepare for other stalls.

Note your phone-tested responses to the 10 most common objections you hear. Keep that list in front of you on paper or a computer screen when making calls. Under pressure from a skeptical buyer, you may not remember what to say and how to say it. The prompts will help, and the buyer has no idea they are in front of you.

15. Never hang up first.

Don't wimp out. Don't hang up until the line goes dead. And even then, call right back and ask, "Did we get disconnected?"

16. Don't book appointments with buyers who have no pain.

There are no "social calls" in sales—only in taking care of customers who've already bought.

━━ ━━ ━━

40 Nine Creative Ways to Get the Appointment

You're given a bag of cement and a bucket of water. You can either build a stepping stone or a stumbling block. The choice is, and always has been, yours. —Author unknown

Regardless of unrelenting technological and cultural changes affecting the sales profession, one thing never changes: You can't make the sale if you can't get the appointment. In fact, many professionals believe the toughest part of the job is getting into the buyer's office. The items in this list might make the difference between tripping over a stumbling block and standing on a stepping stone.

1. Shoot for the top.

Get the name of the company president. It's easier to work your way down the hierarchy than up. You never know—the president may end up personally escorting you to the purchasing agent's office.

2. Ask for an appointment in a telegram.

When is the last time you received a telegram? Follow up with a phone call.

3. Pay for the appointment with philanthropic "currency."

Do you want to stand out from your competition? Offer to pay for the appointment. Since direct compensation to the buyer could be viewed as a bribe or kickback and would violate most organizations' code of ethics, consider these payments:

- A contribution to the buyer's charity of choice
- A contribution to the charity the organization sponsors
- A contribution to the local children's hospital or to St. Jude's
- A contribution to the local homeless shelter

Present your proposal as follows to avoid any sense of impropriety: "I've pledged to give $50 to the Salvation Army for each appointment I have this month. Would you like to help me increase that gift?"

4. Pay for the appointment by actually buying the buyer's time.

If you're calling on an attorney, accountant, physician, dentist, or any other professional who sells time, pay for an appointment. Tell the professional that since you bought the time you expect the same professional courtesy he or she offers any other paying customer: listening with an open mind.

5. Send a gift.

Find out what the buyer values. It might be a pack of excellent cigars or a short set of premium golf balls. A gift certificate to a haute cuisine restaurant is always appreciated, as is a selection of premium imported coffees. Use your creativity: a dog lover might well appreciate an assortment of gourmet dog treats. Attach a note saying you'll call next week about the reason for the gift. (32)

6. Ask customers to make an initial contact on your behalf.

You probably ask current customers for referrals. Go one step further. Why not ask them to make the initial contact for you? The receptivity to your messages will increase. Send a token of appreciation for making the call.

7. Attach a note requesting an appointment to a news clipping about the company or about the buyer.

Scan trade papers and your local paper for stories about the buyer or the company. Attach a personal note to the clipping commenting on the story and requesting an appointment.

8.   **Request an appointment via e-mail.**

Obtain the buyer's e-mail address and send a short, pithy, and intriguing note requesting an appointment. (111)

9.   **Mail the buyer a fictional news story dated in the future describing the phenomenal financial success he or she realized by buying your product or service. Follow up with a phone call.**

Use your word processor and clip art to create a short (50-word) "newspaper article" describing how your product helped the client achieve phenomenal growth and success.

━━ ━━ ━━

41   Seven Steps for Remembering a Person's Name

The true art of memory is the art of attention.

—Samuel Johnson

Perhaps the most valuable "nuggets" of information a sales prospector digs up are the names of all the people to deal with in the buying organization. Learn people's names, spell them correctly, pronounce them properly, and *remember* them. Increase your ability to remember names and you'll increase your success.

1.   **As you are introduced, concentrate on the person.**

You don't have to be brilliant or have a photographic memory to remember names. You simply have to work at it. Block out all distractions. Fight any temptation to mentally wander from the face you see and the name you hear.

2.   **Scan the person's face for an unusual or distinctive feature.**

Listen with your ears and your eyes. Imagine you are looking at a topographical "map." Hone in on any distinctive features of that map. Scan the eyes, cheekbones, hairline, facial structure, mouth, birthmarks, or moles. Pick the most likely facial feature your eyes will gravitate to the next time you meet the person. Choose only permanent features—not something like a hair style that may be different the next time you meet. (74)

3.   **Decide if you will put a priority on first or last names.**

Naturally you'll want eventually to remember the full names of your buyers, but if you're meeting six people all at once that may be too much to expect. Decide whether the degree of formality of this particular meeting suggests you refer to the first or last names of those attending.

4. Repeat the person's name.

"Hello, Kathy Morris." Say the full name clearly. It is vital to listen to the name and clearly repeat it. Don't bother adding something like, "It's nice to meet you." That will only distract you from the name you want to remember. If you're not sure of the pronunciation from the introduction you heard, say, "I'm sorry—could you repeat your name?" When you're sure you understand it, say, "Kathy Morris, hello."

5. Link the distinctive facial feature with the name as you repeat it.

As you repeat "Kathy Morris" think about the most distinguishing facial feature you noticed. For example, her protruding chin might strike you. If you're focusing on "Kathy," you might see a huge cat leaping off her chin. To remember "Morris" you might see Morse code dots in the place of a mole or other mark on her chin. Take a second to fix the image of your choice to the facial feature. The next time you see Kathy Morris your eyes will be drawn to the cat or to the Morse code. Or, when you really get good with this memory system, you'll see a cat with Morse code tattooed on its side and remember her full name.

6. Glance back at the person a few times to reinforce the link between the name and the mental picture.

During the meeting replay the visual link you made between the cat or the code and Kathy's chin.

7. At the end of the day write down the names of all the people you met and the mental picture you associate with them.

As you write down a name, say it out loud to yourself. Articulate the name slowly and purposefully. Enter this list into a high-tech (computer) or low-tech (file card) database.

42   Fifteen Ways to Warm Up to Cold Calling

> During my 18 years I came to bat almost 9,000
> times. I struck out almost 1,700 times and walked
> maybe 1,800 times. You figure a ballplayer will
> average about 500 at-bats a season. That means I
> played seven years in the major leagues without
> even hitting the ball.   —Mickey Mantle

It's exciting to pick up the telephone to call buyers who are waiting to hear from you. We bet you could make these calls all day, every day, and with your eyes closed. You don't need advice to help you with this seller's dream. You *do* need this list for the kind of prospecting most salespeople would rather not do—cold calling. Some salespeople see an impending cold call as a threat to their self-esteem; others see it as an opportunity to make money. Look for at least one idea in this list to help you overcome your reluctance to make cold calls, and turn threats into opportunities.

1. **Recognize that you'll need to make some finite number of dead-end calls before the next positive response.**

You have no idea what that number is. It might be one—this next call. Or it might be 100, and this next call will reduce the number to 99. Either way, make the call!

2. **Build rewards into your day for achieving milestones.**

Once you achieve each milestone (e.g., 25 calls), do something like read your favorite section in the newspaper, go out for some ice cream, or call a good friend to plan your weekend.

3. **When the last call was a real bummer, use a prescribed routine to get beyond it.**

Maybe it's a cup of coffee, reading a page in a favorite book, going outside for fresh air, or a few moments of prayer. Get back to the phone within 15 minutes.

4. **View the next call as your first call of the day.**

Even though it may be 3 P.M., assume you've made no calls yet today. Imagine this one coming up is your first. Be as fresh and energetic as you were at 8 A.M.

5. View the next call as the one that will decide whether you can pay your bills.

Be sure to call this person who is waiting to put money in your pocket.

6. View the next call as an opportunity to help someone solve a problem.

You have a great job. You help people relieve their pain. Get busy so you can find someone who needs you. (1)

7. Practice positive mental imaging.

Try this sequence:

- Close your eyes.
- Take a deep breath.
- Picture in your mind the smile that must have been on the face of the last buyer who accepted your proposal.
- Exhale slowly with this picture in your mind.
- Put that same smile on your face.

8. Recall your favorite positive affirmations.

Woody Allen said, "Eighty percent of success is simply showing up." General George S. Patton said, "I don't measure a man by how high he climbs, but by what he does after he falls down." (6)

9. Picture your competitor sitting at a phone about to dial the same number.

Don't wait another second. Your competitor has this buyer in mind, too, and may dial the number faster than you will.

10. Think about the cold calls that resulted in meetings and in sales.

Yes, you've had rejections, but you've also had successes. Think about all the cold calls that confirmed your belief in yourself and your product.

11. Next to your telephone, post the running total of the sales volume that's resulted from cold calls.

Calculate the sales you've generated throughout your career that can be traced to an initial phone call. Keep that number next to your telephone. Bump it up every time you have another success.

12. Next to your telephone, post your current year's sales to date and current year's sales goal.

Successful salespeople have vivid, specific goals. Stop focusing on your reluctance to call and start focusing on the likelihood this next call will get you closer to your goal. When it does, update your sales figure.

13. Hone your appointment-getting skills.

Become so good with the tactics described in Lists 38 and 39 that you know reaching a buyer on the phone means getting an appointment.

14. Stop waiting for cold calling to be enjoyable.

Don't kid yourself. This is one of the most miserable parts of your job. And your competitor hates it even more than you do because—thanks to this book—your conversion rate is higher. (23, 24, 43)

15. Recognize that you make money only when you make a sale or keep a current customer happy.

If you can't get yourself to call a buyer, *at least call a customer.*

▄▄ ▄▄ ▄▄

43 Fourteen Methods for Rejecting Rejection

God doesn't require us to succeed; He only requires that you try. — Mother Teresa

No one in any profession is successful 100% of the time. Babe Ruth struck out twice as often as he hit home runs. Michael Jordan missed over half the shots he took. Worldwide best-sellers *Gone With the Wind, 7 Habits of Highly Effective People,* and *Chicken Soup for the Soul* were at first thrown in the reject pile by acquisition editors. (Our first book, accepted by only one of five publishers, is now read in thirteen languages.) Keep rejection in perspective as you move toward your goal.

1. Expect your share of rejections.

Babe Ruth swung for the fences almost every time he came to the plate. He didn't sulk the many times he missed the ball. He knew that strikeouts came with home run hitting territory. They come with your territory, too. (23, 25)

2. Focus on the long term.

Tomorrow, you'll barely remember those rude words barked at you today. Next week, you'll have to struggle to recall them. By next month, they will have evaporated in your memory. In the context of your total life, that last rejection was no big deal. Life goes on. (22)

3. Develop perspective on your pain.

Remember three things:

- Like all other adversities you've experienced, this too shall pass.
- At this instant there are many people, perhaps some very close to you, who are suffering from far greater tragedy and heartache than you.
- Selling is a profession, not a life.

4. Understand why people are mean.

Those people who are ugly, rude, and nasty to you are usually that way because they are frustrated, pained, or afraid. Recognizing that their meanness is rooted in their own dispositions or inadequacies helps to protect you from an emotional beating. (49, 53, 103)

5. Separate your "I" from your "R."

Your "I" is your *identity*—your feelings of value as a person. Your "R" is the *roles* you play—in this case, the role of cold caller. On a scale of 1 to 10, you are always a 10 in your self-worth, your identity. That's because you have unconditional positive regard for yourself, and well you should. How you rate yourself as a cold caller, on the other hand, can fluctuate between a 1 and a 10. This rating has nothing to do with who you are.

6. View rejection as a statement about an interaction between two particular people at a particular time.

What just happened is not a statement about you, but about the failure of two people to connect. The buyer said no to you, not *about* you. Even though your proposal was unsuitable, you were not.

7. View rejection as an invaluable lesson.

Snubs teach you something about prospecting, qualifying leads, or building rapport. Don't think, "Boy, did I just blow that call!" or "I failed again!" Instead think, "I just learned one more way not to make a sales call."

8. Take stock of your achievements.

Reflect on your past accomplishments. Give yourself the credit you deserve for getting to where you are now. Notice how the significance of recent setbacks pales in comparison to what you have attained in your education, your career, and your life. (22)

9. Take a mental or physical break.

When the downside of selling gets to you, get away from it all.

- Go to the zoo.
- Fly a kite.
- Watch a sunset.
- Rent a Marx Brothers movie.
- Take a child to an amusement park.

10. Study the percentages — get a reality check.

You are in a profession where the numbers are fairly predictable. You know about how many people you have to call to get an appointment and about how many appointments will result in a sale. Don't start focusing on rejections until they accumulate in numbers that run significantly above expectations.

11. Talk about your feelings with family and friends.

You live and work with people who have a vested interest in your happiness and success. Talk about your feelings. Give them a chance to help you gain perspective.

12. Acknowledge the facts of business cycles.

All business has its ups and downs. The smaller the business, the more wild those ups and downs can be.

13. When you're in a "down," work harder to get yourself into position for the next inevitable "up."

When you're in a sales slump, give yourself permission to hear twice as many rejections as usual. At the same time, make

twice as many calls to get your sales up to where they were before.

**14. When the rejections you get make you feel depressed, seek
professional help.**

Normal feelings of rejection pass within a few days. If yours last
for weeks or longer, get a referral for competent help *now*.

▬ ▬ ▬

44 Ten Ways to Get the Most Out of a Booth at a Trade Show

> Make no little plans; they have no magic to stir
> men's blood. . . . Make big plans, aim high in hope
> and work. —Daniel H. Burnham

One of the greatest sales challenges is to get buyers to give you an
appointment. Wouldn't it be nice if buyers came to *you*? Well, they
do when you exhibit at a trade show. Perhaps the best thing about
trade show selling is its cost: the expense of a sales call performed
at a trade show booth can be half the expense of making a direct
sales call. Even more dramatic is the comparative cost of closing a
sale. On average it takes only one follow-up call to close a booth-
generated lead. What's your experience on a direct sales call? The
national average is about five. So trade show booths can be
hotbeds of inquiries, leads, referrals, and sales—but only if you
know what you're doing.

1. Choose the right show.

Contact the IAEM (International Association of Exposition
Managers) or your trade association for information on the types,
sizes, locations, and attendance of the shows available. Choose a
show whose characteristics best fit your distribution channels,
marketing strategy, and selling style. Make a final decision on the
best show for you by attending the show yourself and doing on-
the-scene evaluation. Get answers to questions like these:

- Is it well run and well attended?
- Do the kind of people who come to this show buy my prod-
  uct?
- How does our exhibit compare to the ones set up here?

- How do exhibitors at the show feel about the quality of the leads they receive?
- Are our competitors here? What kind of booth traffic are they getting?
- How does traffic flow in the room, and what, therefore, will be the best location for us at the next show—assuming the show will be in the same location?

2. Advertise your appearance.

If you opened a store in a shopping mall, you'd expect to do advertising and promotion to get people in the door. The same is true at a trade show.

- Send personal letters, postcards, or e-mail to prospective buyers announcing your appearance at the show.
- Tell current customers about your booth with stickers on everything that goes out to them starting three months before the show.
- Consider including teasers in your mailings—for example, a coupon redeemable at the booth or part of a premium that will be made whole at the booth. For example, you can mail out the jacket of a hardback book you'll give to those who present the jacket at your booth.
- Advertise in the show guide or in the trade magazine of the association sponsoring the show.
- Think about PR placements on local radio or TV stations.
- Check into the possibilities for promotion in conjunction with the host hotel or convention center—for example, on closed-circuit TV.
- Put a special show message on your Web site.
- Reinforce your presence at the show with a hospitality suite.
- Take advantage of other advertising opportunities show organizers offer. (45)

3. Get a good location.

Register early. Ask for the best booth position possible. Do whatever you can to get into the busiest traffic pattern. Find out how assignments are made. Typically the best spots are issued to companies that ask for prime space, sponsor a portion of the conference (e.g., a meal), register earliest, pay a premium, or have exhibited longest at the show. Few exhibitors will think to ask to be placed next to a popular competitor or another exhibitor likely to attract large crowds—but these are great locations.

4. Set realistic goals.

What value do you hope to generate at your booth? Is it realistic to expect such outcomes?

- How large a mailing list do you hope to create from visitors?
- How many leads or referrals will you generate?
- How many sales calls will you make?
- How many sales will you close?

5. Design your booth.

Many of the people who attend the show will walk by your booth without stopping. When they do stop, the average trade show goers will dwell about 30 seconds before moving on. How will you give your exhibit extraordinary eye appeal and stopping power?

- Build your exhibit around your product. The whole purpose of exhibiting is to sell the product.
- Don't cause sensory overload for visitors. Keep your booth tasteful and uncluttered.
- Show as much of your product line as possible. People expect to see more than catalog pictures.
- If possible, demonstrate your product. Show how what you say about your product is true. Let visitors see your product in actual use, and maybe even operate it themselves.
- Give away samples of your product or, if that's not feasible, distribute samples of products made by your product.
- Consider hiring a professional artist, merchandiser, or booth planner to design your exhibit.

6. Ship smart.

Most major trade shows retain a "drayage" firm to ship your exhibit for you and get it back to you in one piece. When your exhibit is complex and heavy, it's a good idea to turn shipping over to these professionals. Since it is often difficult to pinpoint arrival dates for long-distance shipments, drayage contractors offer storage at the destination until show time. Ship early. Most problems associated with booth setup can be traced to a late shipping date.

7. Educate and motivate booth personnel.

Make sure exhibitors have this knowledge:

- Why this particular show was chosen and its role in the firm's marketing strategy.
- The specific selling goals for the show.
- Why they were selected to make this a successful show—they are like stars in a Broadway play.
- That they are not at the show to educate the public but to get sales from qualified buyers.
- The kinds of people likely to arrive and the names of specific VIP customers to fawn over.
- Features and benefits of products on display, but more important, the solutions those products have provided to current customers.
- How to demonstrate products and answer the most common questions.
- Costs of products and details of special offers.
- Knowledge about competitors—particularly those at the show.

8. Greet visitors in the right way.

Make sure exhibitors follow these do's and don'ts of booth behavior.

- Don't sit down, look bored, read, or play with your laptop.
- Don't assume the "executioner stance" (arms folded over chest).
- Don't impersonate the "carnival barker" (ready to grab people and pull them into the booth).
- Don't nag visitors with a version of the old retail store opening, "May I help you?"
- Don't eat or smoke. If you have a drink, keep it out of sight.
- Don't carry on private conversations with fellow salespeople or those in the next booth.
- Do have the booth covered at all times.
- Do dress in a manner consistent with your company's image.
- Do put chairs outside your booth for visitors who may want to sit down with you to talk.
- Do engage visitors with traffic-stopping questions such as, "Did you stop here earlier?" and "Have you ever exhibited at

this show?" and "What does that decal signify on your badge?"

- Do ask questions to stimulate conversation and to learn if visitors have any reason to be interested in your product. ("Does your current software program enable you to . . . ?")
- Do limit your talking so that visitors can tell you what they want in a hurry.
- Do stop telling your story to visitors who are not potential buyers so you can move on to the next person.

9. Follow up.

Make the most of your trade show investment by following up right away with the people you meet. That follow-up may be a telephone call, mail, e-mail, or all three. Respond in the manner, and with the material, appropriate to your product. Move each visiting buyer closer to becoming a customer.

10. Evaluate.

Monitor the effectiveness of your booth daily. If results are not what were expected, you may be able to take corrective action on the spot. After the show, assess how well you attained each of your pre-show goals. Make decisions for future show participation. Will you exhibit again? At this show? What changes in show strategy are indicated?

▄▄ ▄▄ ▄▄

45 Twenty-One Ways You and Your Company Can Make a Splash at a Trade Show

Be not forgetful to entertain strangers, for thereby some have entertained angels unawares.

—Hebrews 13:2

A trade show is an opportunity to see people, shake hands, pass out business cards, and talk about your product to hundreds of buyers at one time and in one place. You might even have a chance to solve problems and close sales. But we want you to think bigger than this. Why not stick out above your competitors? Consider these ways—some costly and not so costly—to have a memorable trade show presence. Once you see these ideas, you'll think of another 21 on your own.

1. Two weeks before the show, send a welcome letter to all registrants; include coupons for a free gift to be picked up at your booth or an invitation to your hospitality suite. (46)

2. Have hot food at your hospitality suite throughout the day; advertise it heavily. (46)

3. Sponsor a meal at the show where your CEO can welcome guests from a lectern onstage.

4. Sponsor a special program for spouses.

5. Sponsor a professionally supervised children's hospitality suite with videotapes, games, refreshments, and evening baby-sitting.

6. Sponsor the keynote speaker introduced by your CEO.

7. Charter a bus providing free guided tours of the host city.

8. Sponsor complimentary transfers from the airport to the hotel.

9. If attendees receive a "welcome" bag or basket when signing in, pay for something special to go in the basket.

10. Provide an attractive shoulder bag bearing your logo to each participant. (32)

11. Pay for the entertainment at any extravaganzas.

12. Pay for the cost of table centerpieces at dinner.

13. Pay for a special dinner dessert named after your company and perhaps in a presentation reflecting what you do (e.g., milk chocolate molded in the shape of your product).

14. Underwrite the costs of trophies for a golf tournament.

15. Pay a professional photographer to take free portraits of family members attending the show.

16. Sponsor refreshment breaks.

17. Provide free popcorn in the afternoon in bags imprinted with your company's name and logo.

18. Provide company merchandise for gifts, premiums, and raffle prizes. (32)

19. Sponsor a drawing for a cruise or Caribbean vacation.

20. Rent an oversized booth with a stunning decor and valued giveaways.

21. Set up a computer with Internet access at your booth. Provide free e-mail service. (110)

■■■ ■■■ ■■■

46 Ten Tips for Working a Trade Show

It's show time! — Entertainment catch phrase

Trade shows are to salespeople what Christmas is to retailers. All year long you look forward to a brief period when you have the potential to sell a great deal of merchandise. But you will realize the potential of trade shows only if you focus your efforts and energy. The tips in this list will help you develop that focus.

1. Obtain a list of attendees at least two weeks before the show.

What current and former customers will attend? What buyers will be there? What appointments do you plan to get? Whom will you target for bonding and rapport building? What buyers will you target to close at the show?

2. Plan your attack.

Leverage the time and energy available to you to achieve optimum results. Draw up a plan with specific goals like these:

- Reestablish relationships with former customers.
- Refresh relationships with current customers.
- Make sales calls on a specific number of new buyers.
- Learn about new market trends.
- "Listen" to the current market.
- "Shop" the competition.

3. Use a team approach.

If you attend the show with colleagues, assign individuals to certain parts of the show plan. Take advantage of the talents and interests of team members as well as their personal contacts. Meet in the middle and at the end of the day to debrief. Check in with each other early in the morning to agree on the day's tactics. (112, 116)

4. Arrive a day early and stay a day later.

Arriving early ensures that you are rested and organized on the first day of the show. It will also give you chance to make opportune calls on other participants who might arrive early. Staying a day later gives you a chance to unwind, collect your thoughts, and begin to devise your post-show strategy.

5. Reserve a room at the same hotel as the show.

Saving money by staying at a less expensive hotel is penny-wise and pound-foolish. Staying elsewhere squanders the opportunity to prospect in elevators, the lobby, the restaurant, and the workout room.

6. Bring more marketing materials than you think you'll need.

It is much better to bring brochures and business cards back to your office than to run out of them at the show.

7. Run plenty of "30-second commercials."

Prepare a standard half-minute description of what you do. Focus your presentation on how you add value to customers rather than on the features or benefits of your product. ("I provide manufacturing companies with a patented, trouble-free commercial filter that cuts their production downtime dramatically.") Run this commercial for everyone you meet. (37)

8. Buy breakfast, lunch, or dinner for buyers and customers.

Never eat alone at a trade show. Arrange as many of these meals as you can prior to the show. Leave a few slots open later in the schedule for new people you meet at the show.

9. Eat, drink, and rest wisely.

Trade shows can be exhausting. Eat healthy, drink alcohol only in moderation, and get good sleep. Get to bed early enough to take advantage of the camaraderie that often builds among early risers. One of them just might be a major buyer. (7)

10. Debrief.

At the end of the show, compare results with your plan. What worked and what didn't? What will you do differently next time? What's your plan for post-show action?

▬ ▬ ▬

47 Seventeen Ingredients of a Successful Direct Mail Marketing Campaign

Doing business without advertising is like winking in the dark. You know what you are doing, but nobody else does. —Author unknown

In 1667 William Lucas mailed a printed price list of seeds and plants to his customers. The British gardener is thus credited with being the first direct mail marketer. Years later Ben Franklin offered over 600 books through his catalog book-selling business. To this day direct mail marketing remains for many products the most powerful communication tool. The success of your campaign depends on three factors: (1) the accuracy and appropriateness of your mailing list; (2) the attractiveness of the offer you communicate in the mailing; and (3) the quality of the package you mail—the envelope, the letter, the brochure or catalog, any inserts, and the response device. According to the so-called 40-40-20 rule, attributed to direct mail marketing expert Ed Mayer, the mailing list and the offer are each twice as important as the package itself. (34)

1. Determine your expected profit.

What does history lead you to expect as a response rate to your mailing? 2%? 5%? 8%? Given the net profit from each order and the total cost of the mailing, is this mailing worth doing? If it isn't likely to turn a profit, can it be justified with other criteria, such as its positive impact on future mailings or letting customers know you're still alive? (31, 33)

2. Test, test, and test again.

Experiment with price, letter length, brochure copy, font size, color, mailing lists, and more. Change one variable at a time to learn what works best.

3. Conduct research.

Survey the customers on your mailing list. Get an accurate picture of your average customer and track trends. Make the questions brief, clear, and easy to answer whether asked through the mail or over the telephone. For mailed surveys consider offering a gift to increase the response rate. (26, 28)

4. Keep records.

One of the most common reasons for failure in direct marketing is the inability, or unwillingness, to maintain good records of inquiries, response rate, sales, returns, cost of guarantees, and other factors. A good database of seasonal, monthly, and regional performance enables you to target your mailings to your most cost-effective time periods and locations.

Regarding Your Mailing List

5. Build your own mailing lists.

Tap these sources:

- Referrals and recommendations from others inside and outside your organization
- Previous inquiries and requests for information
- Past sales records
- Routine office correspondence
- Government sources
- Directories
- Daily news from the business section of your newspaper
- Trade or business publications
- Lists in trade magazines

6. Rent or buy mailing lists.

These are available from list brokers, mailing list services, trade publications, and trade associations. Before using one of these services, investigate the quality of the names on the lists it provides. Buy a small portion of the list to evaluate; ask current service customers how well they like the lists; find out how frequently the lists are culled and updated.

Regarding Your Offer

7. Make it look different.

Better yet, *make* it different. It's hard enough to get people's attention in the mail. If your offering looks like the same old stuff, no mailing list and no package are going to pay off for you.

8. Make it better.

Send out nothing but top-notch materials. Use your mailing to announce revolutionary new products.

9. Don't offer a "bargain."

Buyers are highly sophisticated today. They know that a reduced price means either a product that's not selling or the imminent unveiling of a new model that will make obsolete the one you're offering. Rather than promote a low price, promote high value. Many people are willing to pay for quality.

Regarding Your Package

10. Use "AIDA."

A: Grab the reader's undivided *attention.*
 I: Generate *interest* by showing the buyer the gain from using your product.
D: Create *desire* with a compelling offer.
A: Tell readers what *action* you want them to take.

11. Design the outer envelope.

It can contain teaser copy ("Guess who's coming to dinner?"), attractive graphics, or simply your organization's return address. Try to make it look like a piece of individualized first class mail. Consider a color that might distinguish it in a pile of mail.

12. Design the cover letter.

Keep the letter and the paragraphs within it short. A headline can serve where no salutation is feasible. Use illustrations when possible—they increase readership. Use the closing paragraph to ask for the sale and to indicate how you look forward to being of service. Take advantage of the most highly read portion of any letter: the postscript. (48)

13. Design the brochure.

A professional graphic designer with brochure experience should lay out your brochure. It should contain a bold and intriguing headline that makes the reader want to devour the rest of the copy. The text itself should be benefits-oriented with a special emphasis on the pain your product or service relieves. Answer these questions about your brochure.

- Does it feel exciting and dramatic?
- Does it feel personal and special?
- Is it clear what product or service is being advertised?
- Is there enough information to interest the reader?
- Is there one focal point or "big idea" that has the stopping power to grab the reader's eye?
- Does it pose questions whose answers will cause buyers to identify with the problems solved by your offer?

14. Use humor somewhere in the package.

There's no better way to get the attention of your readers than to make them laugh. Imagine a utility company mailing featuring a cartoon with the following script: "Electric power plants of the future will have two employees—a man and a dog. The man will be there to feed the dog. The dog will be there to keep the man from touching the controls." This piece will be read!

15. Give readers something of value in the package.

Here are some possibilities for package premiums.

- Twenty humorous quotations
- Calendar or personal planner
- Exotic tea bag
- Refrigerator magnet
- Short self-scoring test
- Attractive wall poster
- Booklet of business stories or humor
- Chance to win a prize
- Puzzle or brain teaser (32)

16. Design the response piece.

An effective response piece makes it easy for the buyer to reply. It typically restates the offer made in the letter, outlines the payment options, and states any guarantees. Consider personalizing the response by having callers (to an 800 or 888 number, of course) ask for someone by name.

17. Get your mailing out on time.

When your package needs to be in the mail by a particular date, allow twice as much time as you estimate you'll need. Few direct mail marketers ever made the mistake of sending out a mailing too early.

▬ ▬ ▬
48   Sixteen Tips for Getting Your Letters Read

> *The finest eloquence is that which gets things done.*   — David Lloyd George

Think for a moment about all the unsolicited, prospecting letters you receive. How many do you throw away before you even open them? How many do you throw away after a quick glance inside? Would you like your letters to get a better reception? Try a few of these ideas. (11)

1.   Use plain envelopes without windows.

They should say "open me," not scream "junk mail."

2.   Don't fill the envelope with inserts.

This is not an opportunity to send every brochure in your office to buyers. Limit yourself to one brochure and perhaps a postage-paid reply card with a real stamp on it.

3.   Address the envelope and letter to a specific person, not "Occupant."

Addresses printed on the envelope rather than on a label look more personal.

4.   Use a first class stamp on the envelope.

Metered mail says "throw me away."

5.   Use white or conservatively colored paper.

Many people are turned off by bright colors.

6. Use a readable font.

Go for at least a 12-point size, perhaps in a sans serif font.

7. Through variation in fonts, underlining, bold, and italics, draw attention to important phrases and words.

Don't overdo it, though. Don't get too fancy with colors, although you might want to use color to highlight one or two key words in the letter.

8. Experiment with unusual letter layouts and formats.

Meet with a graphic designer to redesign your letterhead or lay out your letter in an eye-pleasing format.

9. Grab your reader's attention at the beginning of the letter.

Try one of these attention getters.

- Tell a story.
- Quote a startling statistic.
- Quote a satisfied customer.
- Make a surprising statement.
- Describe the reader's problems.
- Refer to a current news story.

10. Keep the text simple

- Select words that are descriptive, vivid, short, and forceful.
- Avoid lengthy, convoluted sentences.
- Use correct grammar and punctuation.
- Keep paragraphs short—three to five sentences.

11. Write with a "you attitude."

Use second person pronouns (you, your) as opposed to first person (I, me, mine, our, we). Identify with the reader's pain.

12. Write with an informal, flowing, style.

Use conversational language. Read your letter out loud to make sure it's reader friendly.

13. Don't end the first page with a period.

In a two-page letter arrange for the last sentence of the first page to continue onto the second page.

14. Call for action.

In the last paragraph ask the reader to do something.

15. Sign your name in blue ink.

Sign in a color different from the type font to make it clear the letter and signature weren't mass printed. Under your signature include the most prestigious title to which you are legally and ethically entitled.

16. Add a postscript that poses an intriguing question.

Research has shown the postscript to be the most often read portion of a letter.

✓ Analyze Buyers

5

Parents with more than one child soon discover the differences in their offspring. Even identical twins can show dramatic variance in abilities, talents, personalities, emotional makeup, thought processes, and communication style. These children grow up to be adults. Those adults become your buyers. And no two of them are alike. Like parents, you have to deal with a broad spectrum of personalities, each of which challenges your interpersonal skills in a new way. Although the following lists won't turn you into a psychologist, they will increase your ability to adapt your selling style to the buyers you meet.

49 Ten Psychological Principles You Need to Know

> *When dealing with people, remember you are not dealing with creatures of logic, but with creatures of emotion, creatures bristling with prejudice and motivated by pride and vanity.* —Dale Carnegie

Astute salespeople understand the wisdom of Carnegie's observation and apply that wisdom each time they make a sales call. In many respects they are unlicensed psychologists who just happen to be selling a product or service instead of seeing patients. Although no list can provide an in-depth analysis of the intricacies and subtlety of human behavior, the following 10 principles provide a solid foundation. Study them to understand your buyers better.

1. We all walk around with mental scripts written by our parents and other authority figures.

Our parents and early authority figures are always with us. DNA and chromosomes do not determine values, beliefs, prejudice, and fear; we learn these once the umbilical cord is cut. On the stage of life, many of us are still reading off scripts written long ago.

2. **We do what we do because of the significant, emotional events that shaped our early years.**

An adult who was a child of the Depression is different from an adult who was a child of the Vietnam era. Both are different from adults who grew up watching MTV. Knowing the events that affected people in their youth provides insight into what they believe as adults.

3. **We are all psychological "icebergs"; some have higher "water lines" than others.**

Most of an iceberg is not visible to the naked eye, but is below the water line. Similarly, many of our fears, prejudices, and beliefs are unseen by others and are also unknown to the self. Behaviors are observable; motives and fears are not. Those people with a "high water line" conceal their emotions. Others display their emotions more freely.

4. **We are all pain avoiders and pleasure seekers.**

This principle does not mean that we are unbridled hedonists. Rather, it emphasizes the two major motivating forces of all human beings. People differ according to the relative power of pleasure and pain; it's vital to know which of these plays a bigger role for each person you hope to influence. You wouldn't want to sell pain avoidance to a pleasure seeker, or vice versa. Finally, you need to know exactly how each person defines his or her pain and pleasure.

5. **We can all be described as having degrees of OK-ness and not-OK-ness.**

A basic tenet of human behavior is that most people, regardless of how well they function in society, are victims of low self-esteem, insecurity, and other forms of "emotional baggage." Indeed, a recent study of the Harvard School of Medicine reported that 18% of the U.S. population not under any form of psychiatric care should be.

6. **Despite our unique personalities, the specific environment in which we find ourselves often shapes our behavior.**

Honest folks have been known to steal. Calm people sometimes blow up. Aggressive personalities will retreat under the right circumstance. The people around us and other pressures in a situation have powerful effects on our behavior. Where we are influences what we do.

7. We need more TLC.

Research confirms that when babies are deprived of physical touching and cuddling they grow up with more emotional problems than babies who receive physical stroking. As children mature, emotional stroking becomes as important as physical stroking. Survey after survey confirms that the #1 complaint employees have about their jobs is that they do not feel appreciated. They don't hear enough praise, recognition, and commendation from their bosses for the work they do.

8. We hear what we want to hear and see what we want to see.

No two people will interpret the same event in exactly the same way. This does not mean that one is right and the other wrong. It simply means our perceptual filters differ because of our contrasted personalities, needs, and experience.

9. When our egos are threatened, we become defensive and sometimes attack.

We all need to feel safe and secure. When that security is threatened or our sense of self is imperiled, we become highly protective. We may go beyond a defensive posture to attack the person challenging our well-being. (103)

10. Drugs, stimulants, diet, and sleep deprivation can affect our personalities.

Drastic mood swings can be traced to changes in body chemistry, which are partially influenced by eating, drinking, and sleeping habits. Many people rely on caffeine in the morning, nicotine throughout the day, and alcohol in the evening, all of which alter their moods from their natural states. A large number of Americans get too little sleep and lose their ability to deal effectively with the emotional pressures of life. (7)

▬ ▬ ▬

50   Four Ways to Categorize Personality Types

> *What a man is is the basis of what he dreams and thinks, accepts and rejects, feels and perceives.*
>
> —John Mason Brown

You need a foundation for effective bonding and rapport with your buyers. The more you know about people, the easier it is for you to adapt your style to them. Although each person on the globe is uniquely different from every other person, psychologists have provided useful categories for simplifying these differences. This list summarizes the four categories comprising the DISC system. Once you understand these four distinct types, you'll be able to place your buyers in one of the categories and respond according to the advice in Lists 62–65 in the next chapter.

1.   **Dominants (D): "Let's get it done now—*this way.*"**

Dominants have a high need to control and be independent. In negotiations they tend to keep information to themselves, identify the other person's weakness, and exploit that weakness for personal gain. They focus on the bottom line, which for them means winning. Dominants want to draw their own conclusions instead of being led to the conclusion. Dominants tend to talk more than they listen.

2.   **Influencers (I): "I'm glad you're here. Let's talk about what we can do for each other."**

Influencers, like Dominants, are assertive and have a need for autonomy. However, they are "softer" and have a greater need for recognition and acceptance. They love to talk and will provide a great deal of information about their needs. They don't try to win at your expense because of their need to be liked. In negotiations they rely heavily on gut feelings and impulsive decisions, which sometimes sours their long-term satisfaction with a deal. They, more than the other three types in this list, are susceptible to buyer's remorse.

3.   **Steady Relaters (S): "The most important thing is that we both come out of this feeling good about each other and the deal."**

Steady Relaters want to maintain working relationships and avoid conflict at all costs. They control their negative emotions so as not to offend. Like Influencers, they have a need to be liked and to build relationships. However, they are far less assertive and impulsive. Because change makes them uncomfortable, they are especially skeptical about new ideas, products, and procedures. They do make decisions, but those decisions tend to be agonizingly slow.

4. **Compliants (C): "Let's take this more slowly; I want to be absolutely sure we cover every base."**

Compliants are risk-averse and motivated by security. Because of their strong need for perfection and their underlying insecurity, they continually seek reassurance that they are doing the right thing. They focus on details, making sure that everything works the way it should and that there will be no surprises. They make decisions slowly and systematically, weighing all criteria. Because of their insecurity and need for reassurance, they will seek more information during the sales call than either Dominants or Influencers.

▬ ▬ ▬

51 Ten Signs of Interpersonal Style

Some people light up a room by walking into it; others light it up by walking out.

—Author unknown

You are a detective, searching for clues to reveal the best approach to take with a buyer. Should I stress facts or emotion, statistics or anecdotes, numbers or words? Should I be direct or indirect, assertive or compliant? Should I be strictly business or friendly? The answer to each of these questions is the same: Comfortably adapt to the manner of the person in front of you. Make your style congruent with that of your buyer. These outward signs will help you define that style.

1. **Office or work space.**

   - Is it well organized and neat or a mess?
   - What kind of wall decorations do you see? What's their message?
   - How many family photographs are around?
   - Is the area bright and open or dark and closed?

- What personal artifacts do you see?
- How is the furniture arranged?
- Are you offered a seat across the desk or next to the person? (61)

2. Clothing.

- How neat and clean is it?
- Is it trendy, classic, or out of date?
- Is it coordinated or clashing?
- Is it flashy, tasteful, or subdued?
- Is it well fitted or sloppy?
- Is it well cared for or unkempt? (61)

3. Facial expressions.

- Does this person smile, frown, or do a bit of both?
- Are you getting good eye contact?
- Do you see a "yes" face (eyebrows raised) or a "no" face (eyebrows lowered)? (61)

4. Initial contact.

- Were you seen on time or kept waiting?
- Were you made to feel comfortable by a warm greeting?
- Did you receive a friendly or a detached handshake?
- Did the conversation start out sociable or get down to business right away?

5. Rapport.

- Does the person seem interested in you or only in business?
- Does the person make small talk or stick to the purpose of the meeting?
- Does the person display a sense of humor?
- Is the person a gracious host?

6. Vocal indicators.

- Is the person's speech slow and deliberate or quick and spontaneous?
- Do you hear varied vocal inflections or a boring monotone?
- Are the voice tones warm and soothing or harsh and brusque?
- Do you hear a haughty or a humble tone?
- Does the person reveal true emotion with the voice? (60)

7. **Conversation pace.**

   - Is the interaction slow or fast?
   - Is it pressured or relaxed?
   - Is it smooth or disjointed?
   - Is it forced or flowing? (60)

8. **Language.**

   - Is the person's speech negative and whining or positive and inspiring?
   - Is word choice measured and precise or spontaneous?
   - Is the language colorful and expressive or dull and lifeless?
   - Is the language pompous or down to earth?

9. **Gestures.**

   - Does the person seem spirited or stoic?
   - Are gestures calm and controlled or nervous and fidgety?
   - Are they natural and comforting or forced and irritating?
   - Are they controlling? (61)

10. **Focus of comments and questions.**

   - Do the person's words focus on facts and hard data or feelings and speculation?
   - Are they penetrating or superficial?
   - Are they unequivocal or tentative?
   - Are they businesslike or informal?

▬ ▬ ▬

52 Twelve Ways to Tailor Your Sales Presentation to How Buyers Screen the World

> *Each mind has its own method.*
>
> — Ralph Waldo Emerson

Buyers have distinctive perceptual screens, which define how they view the world and how they process information. Give two buyers the same facts and their contrasting screens will cause each to react differently. The four perceptual screens of most interest to sales professionals are (1) need for detail, (2) sameness-difference, (3) directedness, and (4) primary motivation.

The Need for Detail Screen

1. Learn whether you have a big-picture or detail-oriented buyer.

Big-picture people absorb information in large chunks and want the total view; detail-oriented people absorb minutiae and want the fine points. Ask a simple question: "Ms. Buyer, we have an awful lot to cover today. Would you like me to begin with a broad overview or get to the details immediately?" The responses could range from "Just give me a broad brush" to "I need to know exactly how your system replaces each of the services I'm now receiving."

2. Give a brief overview to the big-picture buyer.

Hit the highlights. Get quickly to the bottom-line benefit of using your product or service. Offer a brochure or binder with details that the buyer can refer to at a later time. Remain sensitive to a possible desire by the buyer to hear the details after getting the big picture.

3. Meet the needs of the detail-oriented buyer for specific information.

Make sure you know the ins and outs of your product or service. Present the technical fine points. Describe everything that is pertinent to your product and then some for those buyers who thrive on particulars.

The Sameness-Difference Screen

4. Learn whether you have a "sameness" or "difference" buyer.

"Sameness" people relate your product to what they've already experienced; they look for connections between what you say and what they know. "Difference" people compare how your proposal is unlike what they already have; they are also quick to point out what is wrong with your presentation, publication, or product. Ask a question about a comparison between two items. For example, "How would you compare your new computer with the one it replaced?" Does the buyer focus first on the contrasts or first on the similarities?

5. Dwell on similarities with "sameness" buyers.

Emphasize how similar your product or service is to what they already know or use before you describe the differences.

6. Focus on contrasts with "difference" buyers.

Demonstrate the distinctiveness of your product. Touch on the similarities only if the buyer did in answering your comparison question.

The Directedness Screen

7. Learn whether you have an inner-directed or an other-directed buyer.

People who are inner-directed look inside themselves for answers and decisions. Outer-directed people want to bounce ideas off others before committing themselves. Ask the question, "How will you know [your product or service] is right for you?" Does the answer show this buyer to make independent decisions or seek consensus?

8. Speak in the language of inner-directed buyers.

Encourage them with statements like these: "I'm sure you know what's right for the company" or "You can decide for yourself what's right for you."

9. Speak in the language of other-directed buyers.

Tell third-party stories and share testimonials from satisfied customers. Offer lots of data to buttress your argument. Make all the references you can to magazine, newspaper, or trade publication articles.

The Primary Motivation Screen

10. Learn whether you have a "pain avoiding" or a "pleasure seeking" buyer.

Pain avoiders want mostly to elude the agony of conflict, criticism, or anger. They also fear loss of job, acceptance, prestige, or profits. They don't want to be hassled. By contrast, pleasure seekers go after growth, excellence, beauty, recognition, promotion, stature, and income. Ask the question, "What do you want from [name what you sell]?" When you get a response, follow with the question, "Why is that important?" The answer will tell you whether this buyer is hoping to move away from pain or move toward pleasure with the help of your product or service. (70, 75)

11. Appeal to pain avoiders.

Ask questions to learn the specific pain the buyer wants to relieve. Use words like "fix," "solve," "repair," and "alleviate." Show how your product or service relieves the buyer's distress. (76)

12. Appeal to pleasure seekers.

Ask questions to learn the positive things the buyer hopes your product or service will provide. Use words like "grow," "achieve," "realize," and "accomplish." Show how you can help the buyer fulfill his or her dreams.

53 Seven Fears All Buyers Have

> The optimist proclaims that we live in the best of all possible worlds; and the pessimist fears that this is true.　　　　—James Branch Cabell

Fear could be the most powerful motivator affecting your buyers. In order to maintain an image of power and control, buyers may not reveal the underlying anxieties affecting their decisions. Some of these anxieties are obvious; others are subtle. You'll increase your sales once you help your buyers discover their fears, show that you are sensitive to those fears, and lead buyers to the conclusion that your product will replace fear with peace of mind.

1.　Fear of buyer's remorse.

Buyers are afraid that even though buying from you today looks like the thing to do, they'll regret that decision tomorrow, next week, or next month. This fear increases in direct proportion to the price and the number of choices they must pick from. (103)

2.　Fear that the wrong choice will diminish respect and esteem from others.

Peer pressure does not lose impact once we leave our teens. We continue to vie for the approval and recognition of our peers. This fear increases if the buyer has strong social needs, serves a domineering boss, works in a team environment, or is employed by a company demanding continuous improvement and excellence.

3. **Fear of losing self-esteem.**

We all want to feel good about ourselves. Making the wrong decision and suffering the consequences of that error can cause self-
respect to plummet. (62)

4. **Fear that the wrong decision could ruin a career.**

For some buyers the wrong decision might mean a pink slip. A corporate culture where one mistake is your last mistake creates
paralysis by analysis. Of course, the right decision of significance
could bring kudos and eternal gratitude from upper management
and even shareholders.

5. **Fear that the wrong decision could mean disaster or the end of
the company.**

Some decisions carry life-and-death consequences for the person
or the company. A buyer who realizes the company is on the edge
of survival may lack the courage to make a decision of major pro-
portions. A buyer who has to be very careful with limited
resources is in the same position.

6. **Fear of the unknown.**

Regardless of assurances and guarantees from you, buyers may be
more content to stick with a painful status quo than to opt for an
uncertain future. They may not like what they currently have, but
they *know* what they currently have. The future is too big a question mark to take any risks. This fear is especially pronounced for
buyers whose job may not be assured and for those who lack self-
confidence.

7. **Fear of relinquishing control to you.**

Like all people, buyers want to feel in control and have the upper
hand. They want to call the shots, establish the agenda, and have
autonomy. They are comforted by the power of being able to delay
purchase decisions as long as they want. Once you interfere with
that control, you reduce their power and elevate their fears. The
advice in the following chapters allows buyers to feel in control of
the buying process.

---

54 Eleven Negative Assumptions Most Buyers Have about You and the Sales Process

> *A foreigner scarcely counts as a human being for someone of another race.* — Pliny

You want to get into a buyer's office to sell your product. A buyer wants to make sure your product is the right product and you're the person to buy it from. As you create the relationship you hope will end in a sale, each of you has assumptions about the other. Once you understand some of the low opinions buyers have of you and the process about to begin, you'll be in a better position to build rapport and make the sale. (102)

1. Buyers believe their time is more valuable than your time.

They'll feel put out having to fit you into their busy schedule, and show little regard for yours.

2. Buyers believe that it's OK not to answer your unsolicited phone call or to delay returning it.

After all, they don't know you from Adam or Eve, may be loyal to another supplier, and may not care to invest energy and time in cultivating a new business relationship.

3. Buyers believe that canceling an appointment with you may cause an inconvenience, but is not wrong.

Again, they are very busy. You can always reschedule. They feel that you're the one who stands to make money on the deal, so you should tolerate any inconvenience rescheduling might create.

4. Buyers believe it's OK to mislead you.

They might schedule an appointment to get you off their back with no intention of honoring it. They might lie about current suppliers. They might mislead you about whether and how much money has been allocated to solving their problems. They may claim wrongly to have the power to make a decision.

5. Buyers believe most salespeople are trained to manipulate and use psychological "games."

Have you listened to dozens of psychological tapes, attended days of training in the manipulation of others, and mastered a complete repertoire of negotiation tricks? Buyers believe you have. They see you entering their offices with an arsenal of selling deceptions that they must defend against.

6. Buyers expect to feel pressured.

They expect you to back them into a corner and try push them into a hasty decision.

7. Buyers feel that strong resistance is their only defense.

Given their expectations of impending pressure and manipulation, buyers feel justified in being inflexible, stubborn, and resolute. If they start to like you and the product, their internal alarm may cause them to "come to their senses" and conclude that their positive response must be irrational and foolhardy. This often happens just when you begin to think you've made the sale.

8. Buyers feel that giving in too early is losing the game.

In a game each side makes "moves." Buyers often judge that buying at the first sales call is giving in too early and is therefore the "wrong move." Thus, they feel no remorse in calling you back a second or third time before giving in.

9. Buyers believe that even though you may look like a nice person your job forces you to compromise your ethics and integrity.

In surveys measuring the most trusted occupations in America, salespeople never score in the upper ranks. Parents rarely brag about their son or daughter the salesperson.

10. Buyers believe it's OK to get free consulting from you.

They see nothing wrong with using your expertise to help them make a good decision with your competitors. After all, you called them, they didn't call you, and you're on their territory, not vice versa. Be ready with strategies to keep from giving away your knowledge without payment for what it's worth. (55, 59)

11. Buyers believe that stalling and delaying are right and necessary.

They believe that the more they control in the negotiation the greater their psychological security. Their ultimate control is deciding whether or not to place the order. The longer they delay that decision, the greater their security.

━━ ━━ ━━

55 Seven Ways You Don't Want to Enable Buyers to Abuse You

Remember, no one can make you feel inferior without your consent. — Eleanor Roosevelt

Psychologists tell us that without knowing it we encourage many of the most frustrating and irritating acts others commit toward us. That's what *enabling* means — reinforcing the very behavior we want a person to end. Some of your buyers may be leading you along, refusing to return your calls, or treating you disrespectfully *with your help*. When you stop doing the things on this list, you'll start gaining more respect and getting more sales.

1. Don't give buyers free consulting.

Should buyers get all the information they need to make an informed decision? Always. Should they use you as an unpaid consultant? Never. *Do* help buyers discover that you can help them solve their problems. *Don't* show them how until they become customers.

2. Don't prepare detailed, costly proposals without assurance that the proposals will receive serious consideration.

Buyers should receive a written proposal if they need one. Unfortunately, some buyers request proposals *after* they have selected suppliers just to meet their business or political requirements of getting multiple bids. Don't play the game. Get a guarantee that your proposal will be viewed in fair and open competition.

3. Don't allow you and your proposal to travel up and down the buyer's organizational hierarchy.

It's possible that decision makers at several levels will need to have input in the buying decision. That doesn't mean you should be expected to make several presentations over an extended period of time to different groups. One of the up-front contracts to make with your buyer concerns the conditions under which you are willing to make a presentation. Get agreement that each presentation you make will be followed by a mutually agreed upon action by the buyer. Stick to your position. (59)

4. Don't tolerate open-ended indecisiveness.

If buyers believe that you'll hang around indefinitely, and they are in no hurry to make a decision, you will end up hanging around indefinitely. Extract an up-front agreement from buyers on how long you're willing to hang around. If you haven't done this and a selling cycle is beginning to drag, impose your limit at that point to see whether you have a truly interested buyer. (59)

5. Don't let your products or services be demeaned.

Some buyers will minimize what you do and what you sell. If you allow that to pass without challenge, you're reinforcing the notion that you're just another salesperson with a product no better than anyone else's. If you don't show respect for your profession, your product, and your company, who will?

6. Don't let your company or coworkers be demeaned.

Be open and candid in accepting responsibility for past failures to satisfy customers. At the same time, stand up for the integrity, competence, and commitment of your team. Buyers who demean your people to your face are saying even more to others behind your back. Be sure they have the facts about any situations they claim knowledge of and defend the honor of the good people who work in your company. Your loyalty will not be lost on buyers.

7. Don't enable buyers to put you in ethical or legal dilemmas.

Should you bend over backwards to get a sale? Certainly. Should you marshal all the resources at your disposal to make the buyer happy? You bet. But don't ever let that mean that you compromise your integrity or sell your soul. (21, 92, 119)

▬ ▬ ▬
56 Ten Steps for Discovering the Buyer's Budget

I have enough money to last me the rest of my life, unless I decide to buy something.

—Jackie Mason

One of the toughest selling tasks is to discover the amount of money your buyer has available for a purchase. Yet without probing the budget, you may fail to qualify the buyer—that is, determine if the buyer can afford your product—and waste both your time and the buyer's time. These strategies tell you if the money's there without making you come off as intrusive or manipulative.

1. Before you probe the budget, review the pain.

The best transition into a budget discussion is to reinforce the reason that the budget exists: removing the buyer's pain. Summarize the pain, then confirm that the buyer is willing to pay for its removal. "Pat, let's see if I have this right. You said that these are the greatest problems you're having with your current hardware: . . ." (75)

2. Ask the money question.

In a matter-of-fact, cordial tone open the discussion with this non-threatening question: "Pat, do you have a budget set aside for the solution to your problem?"

3. If the answer is no . . .

Respond with a softening statement to validate the buyer, followed by a question to initiate the budget discussion. "That's not unusual. How do you plan on moving forward?"

4. If the answer is yes . . .

Ask, "Could you share that figure with me in round numbers?" The key elements of this strategy are the words "share" and "round numbers." Asking the buyer to "share" creates a psychological bond. Asking for an approximation relieves pressure while still getting a dollar amount fairly close to what's going to be available.

5. If the buyer offers a budget figure you believe is too low . . .

Say, "That could be a problem." This response also opens the budget discussion for further probing. Consider these additional questions when the proposed budget is too low:

- "What will we do if the investment needed is higher than you've planned for?"
- "In case we can't go first class, are there some problems we can leave unsolved if we have to? Which ones?"

- "Are you really committed to solving these problems?" (89)

6. **If the answer is "yes, but I can't share that with you"** . . .

Validate the unwillingness and apply "bracketing." Bracketing identifies the low and high budget range. Set the lower end of each range at the price you want to get. (You'll see why at the next step.) "That makes sense, and I understand. Pat, as you probably imagine, we have many products that might solve your problem. Some of our solutions range in price from $10,000 to $18,000 and others $18,000 to $35,000. I understand this is confidential information, but off the record which range do you have in mind?"

7. **After the buyer selects one of the ranges** . . .

Move toward the lower end of that range. The buyer expects you to pick the larger number; surprise him or her by picking the lower one. That's why you set the range in your brackets as high as you did. "I *thought* you might pick the $18,000 to $35,000 range. I see you closer to the $18,000 than the $35,000. Is that fair?"

8. **If the buyer insists that you reveal your price** . . .

Reveal it. If a specific price has been established and is documented in brochures or catalogues, simply announce the price. However, if the price is negotiable depending on the extent and nature of the buyer's specific problem, quote a price high enough to seem reasonable (perhaps 20% over where you hope to settle).

9. **If you're selling a big-ticket item and the buyer is unwilling or unable to commit a budget for the item** . . .

Try selling smaller pieces. Could you sell an initial fact-finding study? Is there a one-day consulting project you could deliver? Is there a 30-day trial you could sell? Maybe the buyer can't spend the entire sum without a committee but is able to spend a smaller amount. Unbundle the product or service and sell what you can.

10. **Do your homework on the buyer's historical spending habits.**

If you are selling a big-ticket item, find out whether the buyer purchased other big-ticket items in the past, even if those items are unrelated to what you are selling. Learn what this buyer is typically willing to spend to solve problems.

▬▬ ▬▬ ▬▬

57 Twenty-Seven Facts to Learn about Your Buyer

> *A man's most open actions have a secret side to them.* —Joseph Conrad

There is much to learn once you establish rapport with your buyer—crucial information that will help to confirm the buyer's pain and will tell you how to best translate that pain into a decision. The questions on this list are for the individual in the company you're dealing with on a day-to-day basis. Certain of them are equally relevant for other key decision makers you'll meet in closing the sale. Get answers to these questions both by asking them and also by listening to others speak, observing their actions, and doing research on the company through every available source.

Personal Questions

1. Where does he/she live?
2. What kind of car does he/she drive?
3. Married?
4. Children?
5. Grandchildren?
6. What stands out in his/her upbringing and family life?
7. Where was he/she educated?
8. What degrees does he/she hold?
9. Where else has he/she lived?
10. What does he/she do for hobbies and recreation?
11. Where are his/her favorite places to vacation?
12. What passions does he/she have?
13. What are his/her core values and beliefs?

Business Questions

14. Where was he/she employed prior to his/her present job?
15. Why did he/she leave his/her last job?

16. What are his/her responsibilities?

17. How much does he/she earn?

18. For what portion of the company's earnings is he/she responsible?

19. Who reports to him/her and to whom does he/she report?

20. How much influence does he/she appear to have in the company?

21. Is he/she inside or outside the "magic circle" at the top of the organization?

22. Are his/her position and his/her job solidified?

23. How good is he/she at what he/she does?

24. Is he/she looking for or considering a position elsewhere?

25. Is he/she really concerned about how well your product will work or is there another motive for bringing you in?

26. Will he/she be the person you'll work with once the sale is closed?

27. How personally important is it to him/her that the best possible solution is found?

▬ ▬ ▬

58 Twenty-One Questions to Ask about the Buyer's Decision-Making Process

Decisions rise to the management level where the person making them is least qualified to do so.

— Laurence J. Peters and Raymond Hull

Amateurs believe they've succeeded when they win over the buyer. Professionals understand that a sale is not a sale until someone signs a contract or a check. Someone, somewhere in the organization, has final authority to purchase your product or service and it may not be the person with the big smile sitting across from you. You need to know where that final authority resides as well as the process that can give you what you need. These questions help you uncover the people and the process behind the buying decision. You may not get answers to every question you ask. The answers you can get will tell you what action is needed to obtain a decision in your favor.

With Regard to People

1. Who are the key players involved in making the buying decision?

2. Who in that group will be most influential?

3. Who are most in agreement about the process to use in making this decision?

4. Who are most in disagreement?

5. Who has the biggest stake in the decision?

6. What does each key player want out of the decision?

7. Who from the outside will be involved—lawyers, consultants, accountants, or others—and how much influence will they have?

8. How much influence will the CEO or CFO have?

9. Who will make the final decision?

With Regard to Process

10. What criteria will be used to make the decision? What is the single most important one?

11. What internal political issues may affect how this decision is made?

12. What procedures will be followed? Face-to-face meetings? Teleconferencing?

13. Are serious questioning and debate likely to occur? Will there be a vote? Will voting be private or public?

14. What can I do to provide the information people need to make the decision as soundly and as quickly as possible?

15. What other companies are bidding for the business?

16. Is anyone already leaning toward a particular supplier?

17. In the past why have bids typically been rejected?

18. If we are not chosen, what other supplier is likely to get the business?

19. Will a single supplier be chosen or will the winners be splitting up your business with other suppliers?

20. When will the decision be made?

21. When do you hope to achieve a final solution to your problem?

Bond and Build Rapport

Dartnell Research found that 9 out of 10 salespeople arrive at the end of their sales process before 80% of their customers are ready to buy. One reason for this is that those salespeople don't take the time to bond and build rapport. Chapter 5 showed you how to analyze and understand your buyer. The lists that follow show you how to use that knowledge to create emotional bonds and build personal rapport with a buyer. People prefer to buy from someone they feel good about and can identify with. Use the advice in this chapter to connect with people so that they'll want to give you the sale.

▬ ▬ ▬

59 Eleven Reasons Up-front Contracts Help You and the Buyer

> *Nothing sets a person up more than having something turn out just the way it's supposed to be.*
> — Claud Cockburn

The level of a child's fear about going to a dentist has everything to do with the dentist. In one office the dentist abruptly examines the child, pronounces the presence of a cavity, and yanks a drill into position. The child is gripped by fear—not knowing what's going to happen or when the pain will begin. A second dentist's waiting room is filled with children's books and toys. After the dentist introduces herself, she offers the parent and child a tour of the office, meanwhile getting to know the child. When a cavity is found, the dentist explains what that means, and brings out a model of a tooth to illustrate. The dentist reassures the child in going over each step of how she'll fill the cavity. In the same way, the contracts you make with buyers at the beginning of the sales process contain a clear understanding of the steps you will take. This reduces their resistance and encourages them to listen rather than defend against pressure and a pushy close. Up-front contracts benefit you as well by clarifying expectations for buyer behavior during the meeting. Here's why they work.

1. **Up-front contracts give both you and the buyer the opportunity to ask questions.**

"Pat, let's set some ground rules for our meeting. I'd like to be able to ask you some questions about your business, and I want you to be able to ask me anything you'd like about my service. Is that fair?"

2. **They give both you and the buyer the right to say no if there isn't a fit.**

"As we ask and answer each other's questions, we may decide there isn't a fit between what you need and my service. We may realize it doesn't make sense to spend any more time together. If we reach that point, are you comfortable with telling me that?"

3. **They enable the buyer to say yes if there is a fit.**

"On the other hand, if you see that my service makes sense to you, we can decide to move forward. OK?"

4. **They provide an end result to your sales call.**

"And when we finish today we'll agree to a plan as to how you and I will proceed. Does that make sense?" You want to come away from every sales call with a clear and concise agreement as to what happens next. If this is a one-call close, you want agreement to keep moving in your selling process. If you're in a multiple-call cycle, you want to be invited back for another meeting after outlining your selling cycle to the buyer.

5. **Up-front contracts allow for enough time.**

"How much time have you set aside for this meeting? Your time and mine are valuable, and I want to make sure we make the best use of it." You've undoubtedly been on a sales call where you bonded instantly with a buyer. You talked about everything but business, and suddenly the buyer said, "Look, sorry to rush you, but I have only five minutes left. What do you have for me to look at?"

6. They make sure there are no interruptions.

"Pat, I don't know if this has ever happened to you, but there have been times when right in the middle of an important issue a phone will ring or people start walking in and out of the office. This can be very distracting. Can we make sure this will not happen during our visit?"

7. They establish an agenda for the meeting.

"Pat, what are some of the things you would like to accomplish today?" or "Pat, when we were on the telephone, I asked you to write down three of the biggest problems you were having in the areas we discussed. Can you share those with me?" or "Pat, I've been in sales long enough to know there are no accidents. I believe there is a purpose for us being together. What motivated you to invite me in?"

8. Up-front contracts give you the opportunity to manage your biggest weaknesses up front.

Use this step only for genuine fears you have about how you sell. For purpose of illustration, assume you have difficulty dealing with money. "Pat, before I tell you about my service, let me share something with you. My concern is that when we get to the end of my presentation, you're going to like what you see and hear, and I'm going to have difficulty asking you for money. This has always been a problem for me. So that I can give your problem my full attention, are you OK dealing with the money up front?"

9. They enable you to be "invited" in to a meeting set up by a telephone call.

Have you ever arranged a meeting on the telephone, but were caught off guard by the buyer's defensiveness or antagonism when you met? Buyers will say one thing over the telephone and another thing when they get you face-to-face. You enable that to happen when you fail to use appropriate ideas from this list to establish an up-front contract during your telephone call.

10. They help you handle the dreaded request for literature. (38)

- A time-proven way to get rid of a salesperson is for the buyer to say, "Send me some literature." Next time, use this response: "Pat, I'll be happy to send literature, but before I can do that, I need to ask you a question, OK? Sometimes when people ask for literature, as opposed to meeting with me, what they are really saying is that they just don't have any interest, but they are too nice to tell me because they don't want to hurt my feelings. Is that the case here, Pat?"

- If you decide to send the literature, ask a question that ensures you will send the right material and that allows you to try again for an appointment. Say this: "Pat, I have a tremendous amount of literature, which may or may not be of interest to you. Do you mind if I ask you a few questions to make sure you will be receiving the right material before I send it?"

- Before you actually send material, get agreement on what will happen next. "Pat, I'm going to send you the literature. It's probably going to get there Thursday. How much time are you going to need to review it?" [Buyer responds.] "Let's assume you've gone over it by next Tuesday. I'll call you on Wednesday, and here's what I would like to have happen, if you can be comfortable. I'd like for you to be able to say you have some questions or that you see absolutely nothing in the literature you can use. If you have some interest, I would like you to invite me in for a face-to-face meeting. Is that fair?" (39)

11. They help you control the proposal process.

Here are four up-front contracts to set when you do a proposal:

- The *Rough Draft*. Ask to do a rough draft for the buyer's review based on what you know now, with a commitment to sit down with the buyer to make revisions before you submit the final proposal.

- The *Last Look*. If you're in a competitive situation, you want to be the last person in front of the buyer. Try to get a "last look" promise.

- The *Confidentiality Commitment*. How many times have you lost a bid only to learn that the winning proposal had incorporated some of your ideas? Submit proposals with a stated agreement from the buyer that none of the information in your proposal will be revealed to any of your competitors.

- The *Price Promise*. When you suspect you won't be the low bidder on a proposal, say this: "Pat, just so you understand, we're never the low bidder. In putting this proposal together for you,

I'm assuming you're looking for the highest value and not the lowest price. Am I right on that, or will you be forced to choose the least expensive supplier regardless of quality?"

▬ ▬ ▬

60 Ten Ways to Increase Sales Effectiveness Through Vocals

Let your conversation be always full of grace, seasoned with salt, so that you may know how to answer everyone. —Colossians 4:6

Over one-third of the messages you exchange with buyers are conveyed through *vocals*. These aren't the actual words you use, but what you do with your voice to clothe words with meaning. Vocals include your tone, pitch, emphasis, accent, inflection, pronunciation, volume, rate, and tempo. They provide you with great opportunity to reinforce your words. Vocals also give you a tool to increase your buyers' comfort with you. By understanding and reflecting their vocal patterns, you give them the feeling that you are congruent with them.

To Communicate with Greater Impact

1. Vary your vocals.

You'll bore most any buyer with either a monotone or a singsong vocal pattern. Salespeople with a monotone speak with little if any variety in pitch, emphasis, or inflection. They drone on like robots. Salespeople caught in a singsong voice monotonously go up and down with inflection or tone, typically ending sentences on the upswing. Don't be imprisoned by either of these patterns. Vary your vocals to emphasize your critical ideas and liven your speech. (10)

2. Drop your tone at the end of critical assertions.

When you drop the tone of your voice, *not your volume*, at the end of a sentence, you signal the importance of the idea in that sentence. You also indicate a transition to a new idea to be started by the next sentence. This technique is an effective way to signal the end of your part of the dialogue and your desire for the buyer to speak next.

3. **Don't substitute question marks for periods or exclamation points.**

When we're not sure of ourselves, we tend to raise our inflection at the end of a sentence? This is particularly noticeable when we answer a buyer's question? The result is that it sounds as though we're answering a question with a question, when we really mean for it to be a statement? (Hear what we mean by reading the previous three sentences out loud.)

4. **Show friendliness through a relaxed tone.**

This is particularly important when you first meet a buyer. Put a relaxed tone into your voice, and you'll help the rest of your otherwise nervous body to calm down.

5. **Improve your pronunciation.**

There are few surer ways to make a bad impression than to mispronounce a word that your buyer knows how to pronounce correctly. The best way to check yourself is to ask colleagues to listen to you during a presentation for words that you slur or misspeak. When meeting with buyers from other cities, listen to how they pronounce the names of their city and surrounding areas. Use the same pronunciation. Here are a few names of cities that most out-of-towners don't pronounce the way natives do.

- Detroit, MI
- Gettysburg, PA
- Louisville, KY
- New Orleans, LA
- Norfolk, VA
- Rochester, NY
- Worcester, MA (11)

To Increase Buyer Comfort

6. **Temper your accent.**

You may be from a part of the country where folks speak English with a distinctive accent. There is nothing wrong with having an accent, but it could cost you some rapport with buyers from other parts of the country. It may be wise to learn how to water down your accent in settings where the majority of people don't share it, and perhaps don't value it. (5)

7. Echo the buyer's volume.

Speak louder than your buyers and you'll come across as pushy, overbearing, or rude. Speak softer and your honesty, openness, or decisiveness may come into question.

8. Reflect the buyer's speaking rate.

Speak much faster than your buyers and you'll be seen as slick or hard to understand. Speak much slower and they'll conclude you're inconsiderate for wasting their time or you're not honest enough to get to the point more quickly. It'll be difficult at first to vary the rate at which you speak. Once you begin to pay more attention to rate, you'll have more luck controlling it.

9. Reflect the buyer's tone.

Does the buyer in front of you have a high and squeaky voice or speak in a rich baritone? If your voice is at the opposite end of the scale, it will be tougher to establish rapport. Record your voice in different speaking situations to learn your tonal comfort zone. Practice ranging around that comfort zone. Eventually, you'll learn how to get closer to the differing tonal patterns of buyers more naturally.

10. Reflect the buyer's tempo.

Some speakers start off very slowly and relaxed, building up to an emotional ending. Other speakers expend their emotions near the beginning of their remarks, and end more subdued. Watch for the rhythm your buyers and customers use. It may take a meeting or two for you to get in synch with their tempo. A greater sense of mutuality in your exchanges will result.

▬ ▬ ▬

61 Fifteen Ways to Increase Sales Effectiveness Through Body Language

> *The body says what words cannot.*
> *—Martha Graham*

Every moment you are in the presence of a buyer you communicate, even when your mouth is shut. Research suggests that over half of the messages your buyer receives comes from your body language: gestures, eyes, facial expression, touch, grooming, clothing, movement, posture, breathing, and use of space. The first section on this list offers do's and don'ts for making sure your body works for you and not against you. Since buyers feel most comfortable with salespeople whose communication styles match their own, the second section calls for you to be consistent with your buyer's body language.

Do's and Don'ts

1. Do maintain eye contact.

Look in the buyer's eyes, without staring or leering, when either one of you is speaking. Many buyers will trace an absence of eye contact to an absence of honesty, trustworthiness, or reliability.

2. Don't point.

Pointing at things is OK. Pointing at people is a controlling, condemning, and demeaning gesture.

3. Do take care of your shoes.

If buyers notice your unkempt shoes, they will wonder how much they can count on you to match the product or service quality they need. (2)

4. Do control body odors.

Before you make your next sales call, get some honest feedback about your potential to offend buyers with bad breath or body smells. Here's the best way to ask a colleague for such feedback: "If I were to do one thing to remove the slightest possibility of offending others with my breath or body odor, what would you suggest I do?" (5)

5. Don't touch things without permission.

Don't move things around on the buyer's desk or touch anything in his or her office without consent. Some people are oversensitive about their possessions. If you do touch or move something, be sure to return it to its original position and condition. If you accidentally break anything, replace it within 24 hours.

6. Do sit next to — not across from — the buyer.

It's tough to bond with someone sitting on the other side of a table or desk. Do your best to avoid physical obstructions between the buyer and you.

Reflecting Body Language

7. Reflect handshake.

Instantly fit your handshake to the buyer's in these qualities:

- Force of outward thrust
- Firmness of grip
- Number of pumps
- Release (3)

8. Reflect body position.

You should both be standing or sitting at the same level. When you're both sitting, in what position is the buyer? Arms folded or down? Hands clasped, on the face, on the table, or in pockets? Is one leg crossed over the other? Without striving to exactly mirror the buyer's pose, get as much congruence between the two of you as possible. And don't worry about being caught. It is rare for people to consciously note the relationship between your body language and theirs.

9. Reflect posture.

Is the buyer relaxed or tense? Upright or hunched? Leaning forward or leaning backwards? Don't do just the opposite.

10. Reflect eye contact.

When you or the buyer is speaking, you should look at the buyer. There will be other times that neither of you is speaking—perhaps when a third party is present. For those times do a careful analysis of the buyer's gaze and blinking pattern. Look away when the buyer looks away; connect visually when the buyer wants to connect.

11. Reflect facial expressions.

Respond to a smile with a smile. Respond to a "neutral face" with one of your own. Should you frown when the buyer frowns? Yes, if the match is appropriate and does not covey a condescending or judgmental message.

12. Reflect hand gestures.

Does the buyer use his or her hands a lot when speaking? Does the buyer emphasize statements by wagging a finger? Does the buyer pound one hand into an open fist? Are there any other hand gestures you should mirror?

13. Do not reflect idiosyncratic, nervous habits.

The buyer may have a nervous habit (e.g., constantly pulling on an earlobe, scratching the forehead or chin, picking nails, or biting the lip). Matching such behaviors is condescending, rude, and unnecessary. Reflect only those behaviors that are "normal"— those which do not draw attention to themselves.

14. Reflect only the body language you feel comfortable with.

Any discomfort you feel in mirroring behaviors is likely to be detected by the buyer. Match as much as you can within the limits of your own personal comfort. Subtlety and naturalness are two keys to the success of matching.

15. Oppose the buyer's body language to emphasize autonomy or disagreement.

There will be times in the selling process when you don't want to bond with or appear in synch with the buyer. For example, if the buyer demeans your company or your product, you would, in addition to your spoken words, convey your umbrage through your body language. You might stand up or change your seated position dramatically as you set the record straight.

— — —

62 Fourteen Statements That Help Buyers Maintain Their Self-Esteem

No passion so effectually robs the mind of all its powers of acting and reasoning as fear.

— Edmund Burke

As you take buyers through the sale, you are dealing with people experiencing varying degrees of fear. First, they know they have a problem, which itself is discomforting. Second, they know they may have to invest considerable time and money to fix it, which adds another level of anxiety. Third, they may not be expert at solving the problem they have been charged with solving. And finally, they risk their ego, their esteem in the eyes of their family and friends, their stature in the company, and maybe even their job if your proposed solution doesn't work. Most buyers need comfort, encouragement, and reassurance. Depending on the particular inadequacies or pain your buyers feel, one or more of these statements could bolster their self-esteem and make them feel good about putting their fate in your hands. (53, 70)

1. "What you're feeling is normal and rational. Your reaction makes perfect sense."

2. "Your concerns are typical of my customers."

3. "If you weren't this worried or concerned, you wouldn't be earning your salary."

4. "I have a suggestion for how we can make this a no-risk decision for you."

5. "Why don't we do a small pilot program first to make sure it will work for you?"

6. "What do you need from me to make you comfortable with this deal?"

7. "You didn't create this problem. It resulted from changing [technology/regulations/competition/demand]. Everyone is facing it in one way or another."

8. "I'm glad you're not asking me to describe the troubles *I'm* going through this week."

9. "I sense that you're feeling uncomfortable right now, and maybe even doubting yourself. That's an uncomfortable position to be in."

10. "Well, if you *weren't* feeling uptight and insecure about your problem, I'd question your judgment."

11. "It may be hard for you to believe this, but your problems are not at all unusual. Neither are they more serious than what I typically see. So what we can offer you should work quite well."

12. "Don't worry about understanding this part of the system right now. It usually takes a while for people new to the product to grasp it."

13. "That's a really important question you asked."

14. "I appreciate your honesty and candor."

63 Ten Suggestions for Selling to a "Dominant" Type

Don't fight the wind — adjust your sails.
                        —Author unknown

Dominant buyers try to maintain control and walk away with most (if not all) of the marbles. During negotiations they seek to control the agenda. They get to where they want to go because they lead, not because they follow. Nonverbally, they are likely to project a forceful, domineering posture and stance. When frustrated or angry they may pound fists and point fingers. Vocally they emphasize their position by increasing volume and maybe even using profanity for impact. Follow these tips when the buyer in front of you fits this profile. (50)

1. Never convey to a Dominant that you are hungry for the sale.

Sure, you want the sale. But don't beg or plead for it. Giving the impression that your next meal depends on this sale will trigger this buyer's predatory instincts.

2. Go to the bottom line and work backwards.

A good opening line with a Dominant is "Can we fast-forward to the end of the movie and then work backwards? What exactly will you need to close a deal that will make you happy?"

3. Match nonverbal behavior.

Return the Dominant's gaze. Move forward in your chair when the Dominant moves forward. Use your voice and your body to emphasize key points. Come across as passive and meek and the Dominant will turn you into "road kill."

4. Limit small talk.

Dominants want to get down to business quickly. As soon as you sense that the buyer is ready for business, switch from your social manner to your business mode.

5. Draw lines in the sand.

What is negotiable and what is not? What is a fixed, unequivocal policy and what is flexible? Without clear answers to these questions before the negotiation, the Dominant may kick the sand in your face.

6. Probe assertions.

Dominants will try to structure the sale to conform to their wishes. They'll assert their requirements up front. Move beyond those assertions to uncover underlying issues with statements like these:

- "Yes, I understand you clearly. Why do you believe that?"
- "Why is that so important to you?"
- "What do you mean when you say . . . ?"
- "I wonder if we could examine this issue further."

7. Limit your answering of questions with questions.

Answering questions with questions is a reliable way to keep pressure on the buyer, but this strategy will alienate the Dominant. Provide specific answers when asked specific questions. Follow up with questions *after* you present your information. "Sure, I'll be happy to answer that. The number of overseas facilities using this equipment is four. But let me ask you this: how does that information help you?" (73, 81)

8. If you're feeling pressure, identify it as an obstacle to crafting the best possible deal.

Dominants want to win. Your feelings are inconsequential unless they get in the way of shaping a good deal. Consider this as a response to pressure tactics: "I'm feeling pressured right now and a little uncomfortable. Because of this pressure I'm afraid we might not end up with the kind of deal best for you. Could we take a deep breath, sit back, and focus on how we can best solve your problem?" (90)

9. Offer choices.

Dominants need control. Limit their alternatives to what will work for you, but offer choices within those alternatives. You win, but Dominants feel as if they had won.

10. Ask for a summary of any agreements.

Dominants are not the greatest listeners. Ask them to tell you what they heard. If there are any misunderstandings, clarify them on the spot. In order to verify that Dominants view agreements in the same way you do, let them, not you, do the summary.

64 Eight Suggestions for Selling to an "Influencer" Type

Baloney is flattery laid on so thick it cannot be true, and blarney is flattery so thin we love it.

— Fulton J. Sheen

Influencers have a high need for approval and recognition. They love to talk. They want to know about you and they want you to know about them. They are likable and trusting. They will offer you refreshments and inquire about your comfort. In turn they want to be accepted and trusted. In negotiations, they are likely to act quickly, take risks, and rely on intuition. After the negotiation, however, they may second-guess the decision. Nonverbally, they project an overall image of being open and approachable. They smile, nod in agreement when appropriate, and may even touch you on the shoulder, back, or arm when introduced. Follow these tips when the buyer in front of you fits this description. (50)

1. Reflect the buyer's communication behavior.

Return smiles with smiles, eye contact with eye contact, and nods of agreement with nods of agreement. Portray as much openness in your posture and gestures as the Influencer shows.

2. Create a personal relationship during the bonding stage.

Show that you want to develop a long-term association that's mutually rewarding. "I'm not in this for the quick sale. My main interest is in seeing us build a relationship that will be rewarding and satisfying for years to come."

3. Acknowledge personal pictures, photographs, or certificates in the office.

Influencers create working spaces that are personally fulfilling and meant to reach out to others. Noticing the personal touches will earn points.

4. Emphasize the intangibles of your product or service.

Highlight whatever prestige, distinction, or esteem comes with your solution. Pinpoint its high caliber, reliability, and quality.

Focus on intangible attributes as much as those that directly solve the buyer's problem. (80)

5. **Demonstrate how purchasing your product or service will satisfy others who depend on this purchase.**

The Influencer is making a decision that will affect other people throughout the organization. Acknowledge these people. Help the buyer see how much they will appreciate the decision.

6. **Listen for underlying feelings and motives.**

Influencers are in tune with feelings. Recognize those feelings through your responses to buyer statements.

- "It seems that what you're saying is . . . "
- "The reason you feel that way is because . . ." (Let the buyer finish your sentence.)
- "How much help would you like to see them get?"
- "What you just said shows concern for the people who will use the product." (74)

7. **Bring in third-party endorsements.**

Influencers are reassured by learning that others are happy with your products. Offer testimonials and stories about how lives have been improved.

8. **Get a commitment for every decision.**

You want to guard against buyer's remorse. Ask the Influencer questions to head off second thoughts. The answers to these three questions will tell you what it will take to solidify the buyer's commitment.

- "I'm not saying this will happen. But suppose a week from now you rethink the wisdom of this decision. What will you do?"
- "Tell me again . . . what convinced you to buy?"
- "What will you do if next week one of my competitors calls asking you to switch?"

▬ ▬ ▬

65 Six Suggestions for Selling to a "Steady Relater" Type

Don't think there are no crocodiles because the water is calm.   —*Malayan proverb*

Steady Relaters have a passive approach to problems. This does not mean they are weak, uninterested, or martyrs. They do take a position, but they are neither forceful nor demanding in expressing it. As the term "steady" implies, these buyers take a measured and balanced approach to conflict and negotiation. They project an unassuming and amiable style. What they may lack in passion they make up for in diligence. They are patient and persistent. Nonverbally, they project an openness and nonjudgmental quality. If the buyer sitting across from you fits this profile, follow these tips. (50)

1. Reflect the buyer's communication style.

Steady Relaters listen attentively and focus on what you have to say. Their body posture and gestures convey an openness and willingness to discuss. Show them the same. Maintain eye contact. Position your body to see and hear as much as you can.

2. Demonstrate a sincere interest.

Social bonding is important to Steady Relaters. They care and want to know you do the same. Ask about hobbies, family, and personal interests. Listen to the answers and comment. Share your own personal data, but only after attending to theirs.

3. Be patient.

If you give the impression of trying to impose your agenda or close the sale, Steady Relaters will back off. They need to set a measured pace based on their own internal clock. Synchronize your clock to theirs. (53)

4. Demonstrate how you and your product can be trusted.

The instincts of Steady Relaters are to be loyal to you. Give them reasons to see you as a worthy person and to judge your product as dependable. (21)

5. Limit the focus of analysis.

Steady Relaters like to focus their attention on one particular aspect of your product. Help them gain this focus and at the same time control the agenda by saying something like this: "Given your concerns and your analytical approach to buying, I think you'd be most interested in focusing on [aspect]. Is that accurate?"

6. Don't mistake passivity for weakness.

Steady Relaters are not wimps. They will be as thorough as other buyers. You'll have to be as sharp with them as with anyone else. They simply call for a different communication style.

▬▬ ▬▬ ▬▬

66 Eight Suggestions for Selling to a "Compliant" Type

The man who looks for security, even in the mind, is like a man who would chop off his limbs in order to have artificial ones which will give him no pain or trouble. —Henry Miller

Compliants have a strong need for security and are risk-averse. They tend to focus excessively on details, procedures, and policies. The resulting behavior is often manifested in perfectionism. In buying situations they need constant reassurance that they are making the right decision. They are much more interested in hearing what you have to say than in telling you what they want. Their nonverbal cues are cautious, controlled, and guarded. If the buyer sitting across from you fits this description, follow these tips. (50)

1. Reflect the buyer's communication style.

Compliants project caution, concern, and focus. They position their bodies to listen intently and to take in as much information as possible. Do the same. Through steady eye contact, a sincere tone of voice, and attentive posture, communicate your desire to serve.

2. Uncover organizational factors that might increase insecurity.

Consider these questions that get at the risk felt by the buyer.

- "Has your company regretted similar purchasing decisions in the past?"
- "Why did you regret that decision?"

- "Are you under any special pressure regarding this decision? Why?" (53)

3. Emphasize your willingness and ability to diminish risk.

Show how you can reduce the uncertainty associated with making the buying decision. Consider building a "safety net" for Compliants, without bending so far that you create an unprofitable customer. For example:

- Creating a money-back guarantee.
- Expanding the usual after-sales service.
- Lengthening the repair warranty.
- Negotiating the contract obligation for a shorter time period than normal.
- Building scheduled points into the project for when it can be terminated by the customer. (53)

4. Highlight your referrals and satisfied customers.

Compliants seek safety in numbers. If they see that others have signed on and are satisfied, they too may make the leap. Provide as many endorsements as possible.

5. Show how your product or service will reduce pain.

Pain reduction is especially important to Compliants. Whereas other types of buyers are concerned with the "what," Compliants are more interested in the "how." If you lack the technical details of exactly how and why your product relieves pain, bring in support personnel to do a reassuring dog and pony show. (75)

6. Validate cautious approaches.

Although Compliants may not explicitly seek your approval, they nonetheless respond well to it. Compliment them on an approach that will ensure that the right decision is made. "I think your idea to shorten the length of your obligation on the contract is sensible given the uncertainties you face."

7. Use the best-case/worst-case scenario question.

Ask these questions: "Describe the best-case scenario that might result from purchasing this product." [Wait for a response.] "Describe the worst-case scenario that might result from purchasing this product." [Wait for a response.] Demonstrate that the worst-case scenario is highly unlikely and that the best-case scenario is highly probable.

8. Bring out the data.

Compliants crave proof. Bring plenty of catalogs, bulletins, brochures, and circulars. Point to numbers, statistics, specifications, blueprints, and any other comforting details.

▬▬ ▬▬ ▬▬

67 Twelve Ways to Identify and Sell to a Visual Buyer

Vision is the art of seeing things invisible.
—Jonathan Swift

Visual buyers "see" the world. They make sense of it through pictures. Their words and phrases convey visual images. They don't think a lot about the words they use. Their minds work like a VCR. They capture images and then program their minds to rewind, edit, or fast-forward the tape. Over half of the buyers you call on fit this description. Here's how to identify and sell to a visual.

Identifying a Visual Buyer

1. Visuals talk quickly.

Visuals need to keep up with the pictures speeding through their heads. They're sometimes skipping over the four or five frames they're behind.

2. Visuals are not careful about what they say.

Visuals sometimes mispronounce or garble their words because they speak so quickly. They don't particularly care about what is said or how it is said, as long as they believe their "picture" is conveyed. Visuals often stop their sentences and begin again. They frequently find themselves having to say, "That's not what I meant to say."

3. Visuals speak in viewable language.

They use phrases like these: "I don't see that as a problem." "Do you have a clear picture of what I'm saying?" "It looks like ..." "This appears to be ..." "Let me focus in on what you're saying."

4. **Visuals use their bodies to communicate.**

They look you straight in the eyes. They make the "OK" sign with their fingers. They use thumbs-up to say everything is "GO." They rotate their palms upward to ask, "What's going on?" They shrug their shoulders to signal indifference or ignorance and nod their heads to demonstrate agreement.

Selling to a Visual Buyer

5. **Make a positive first impression.**

Groom yourself well. Dress appropriately according to the buyer's business and expectations. Don't wear your finest attire to a construction site or a sweater to call on a Fortune 1000 CEO. (3)

6. **Let the buyer control the pace of the call.**

Visuals are in a hurry to get information. Keep up with them without going so fast that they fail to recognize the pain you can relieve for them.

7. **Use audiovisual aids.**

Bring your brochures, and show them the product. Use overheads, flip charts, white boards, and any other graphic aids you can get your hands on. Show them charts, graphs, cartoons, plans, and memos to give them a clear image of what you want them to buy. When you make a point, draw it somewhere. (87, 109)

8. **Urge note taking.**

Visuals take in information so quickly that they don't stop to write things down. If your visual buyer is true to form and doesn't take notes, encourage him or her to do so. When you come to an important point, say, "You might want to write this down." If your request appears to make the buyer uncomfortable, you take the notes and leave them behind.

9. **Give good eye contact.**

The visual buyer may judge anything less as a sign of your disinterest or your dishonesty. (61)

10. **Paint a picture.**

Use visual metaphors such as these:

- "Your project will take off like a jet."
- "This will brighten up their day."
- "I can see what that means to you."
- "I'm glad we see eye to eye."
- "That image is etched in my memory."
- "You're moving in the right direction."
- "How did they look when you rolled that idea out?"
- "There is no doubt in my mind."

11. Use the spoken imagery of each visual you meet.

Each visual buyer you call on and each visual customer you serve has favorite words and pet phrases (e.g., "Do you see what I mean?"). Write these down as you hear them and incorporate them into your future conversation with that person.

12. Follow up in writing.

Record everything that the two of you discussed. Send the buyer a summary letter composed in visual language. (48)

▬▬ ▬▬ ▬▬

68 Twelve Ways to Identify and Sell to an Auditory Buyer

> *For by your words you will be acquitted, and by your words you will be condemned.*
> *—Matthew 12:37*

Auditory people "hear" the world. They experience it through sound. They hear their internal dialogue first before they speak out loud. Words are very important to auditory people; they select them thoughtfully and listen to yours carefully. Auditory buyers need to talk things out at length in order to get their thoughts in order. Over one-third of the buyers you call on fit this description. Here's how to identify and sell to an auditory.

Identifying an Auditory Buyer

1. Auditories speak at a moderate pace.

They don't speak especially fast or slow, but at an even pace. They may delay a bit before responding to you while they think to themselves internally before committing to their carefully crafted words.

2. Auditories pronounce words carefully.

They care both about the words they use and how they say them.

3. Auditories speak in aural language.

They use phrases like these: "How does my situation sound to you?" "You and I speak the same language." "Well, let me understand this." "You've made it clear as a bell."

4. Auditories make little use of their bodies to communicate.

They place their chins in their hands when they talk to themselves without moving their lips. Auditories think they can hear better if their eyes are closed in order to fight outside distractions. To compensate for the lack of eye contact, they lean forward and tilt their ears toward you to indicate they're listening. They make a limited amount of eye contact, looking to the side to avoid confusion while they listen. They do smile to show approval, knit their brows to show confusion, and even stare at the floor to show disagreement.

Selling to an Auditory Buyer

5. Vary your vocals.

When you speak to an auditory buyer, emphasize the words you hope will stick with that person. Vary your tone, pitch, inflection, emphasis, volume, and rate to reveal the true feelings behind your words. Slow down and drop your tone to store critical points in the buyer's memory bank. (60)

6. Keep them talking.

Auditory buyers need to talk to make sense out of the world. Don't interfere with their train of thought. Let them talk their ideas through without interruption. Build rapport by listening attentively and responding with "uh-huh" or "yes." Paraphrase what you hear and ask lots of questions to keep them on a roll. Take notes. When they give you the signal to speak, ask for clarifying explanations to be sure they have satisfied their need to talk. (74)

7. Speak in the auditory buyer's language.

Use auditory metaphors such as these:

- "Listen to this."
- "How does this sound to you?"

- "I hear you're talking about changing your supplier."
- "Tell me more about that."
- "Let me suggest another reason."
- "How willing are you to give me your ear on this?"
- "There's a hidden message in all of this that we need to hear."
- "I'm speechless about what you just told me."

8. Reflect the preferred language of each auditory you meet.

Auditory buyers you call on and auditory customers you serve have favorite words and pet phrases (e.g., "That's music to my ears"). Write these down as you hear them and incorporate them into your future conversations with them.

9. Use testimonials.

Auditories like to hear what other people say about your product. Read or show quotes from newspapers or other authoritative sources. Share endorsements from other satisfied customers. Tell a third-party story. "I want to tell you about a situation you might find interesting."

10. Expose them to spoken advertising.

If you buy radio advertising, give your auditory buyers a schedule of upcoming spots. Offer them copies of any audiotapes that have been produced for your product.

11. Spot their buying signal.

When auditory buyers begin to ask questions, they're hooked.

12. Use parting statements.

A postscript is the most memorable portion of a letter. In the same way, your final statement as you walk out of the auditory buyer's office will reverberate. Choose those final words carefully. Don't waste them on "Good-bye."

▬ ▬ ▬

69 Twelve Ways to Identify and Sell to a Kinesthetic Buyer

Some people feel with their heads and think with their hearts. —G. C. Lichtenberg

Kinesthetic buyers "touch" and "feel" the world. They make sense of it through tactile and emotional data. They look for harmony in your words, vocals, and body language. Everything you do or say, as well as everything you *do not* do or say, tells them whether or not you are reliable and believable. Feeling is as important to kinesthetics as seeing is to visuals and hearing is to auditories. Less than one-fourth of the buyers you encounter fit this description, but here's how to identify and sell to a kinesthetic.

1. Kinesthetics speak slowly.

They are careful not to reveal what they're thinking, but watch and listen to others before speaking. They often look down, think about what they are about to say, and check with their inner feelings about a particular issue before declaring themselves.

2. Kinesthetics are great listeners.

They make you feel comfortable and reinforce what you say by slightly smiling their approval.

3. Kinesthetics speak in physical language.

They use phrases like these: "Do you have a grasp of our situation here?" "Are you comfortable with that?" "You seem to have all the figures at your fingertips." "I have a great sense of relief that we understand each other."

4. Kinesthetics are "touchy-feely."

Often they not only shake your hand for several seconds, but also grab your elbow with the other hand. When you really bond with kinesthetics, they reveal their sincerity and acceptance by leaning in toward you and giving you a touch on the forearm to show you're OK.

Selling to a Kinesthetic

5. Connect physically.

Provide immediate and direct eye contact to kinesthetic buyers. Give a firm handshake with your palm fully bonded to theirs. Furnish them with your undivided attention. (3)

6. Start selling immediately.

Kinesthetics can spot discomfort instantly. So get past social chitchat and onto what you feel best about—your product or service. Show your belief in it and the conviction you have that the buyer will profit from it.

7. Speak in physical metaphors.

Use phrases like these:

- "Can you feel the down-to-earth reality of this service?"
- "Do you feel comfortable with what I've just walked you through?"
- "Do you believe you can hang in there any longer without handling the problem?"
- "We'll work hand in hand with you to make sure that does not happen."
- "My intuition tells me that you're not ready for any more."
- "Right now, who's being hurt by that?"
- "I get the sense you're considering changing your supplier."
- "That hassle must be unbearable for employees who encounter it every day."

8. Emulate the preferred language of each kinesthetic you meet.

Kinesthetic buyers you call and kinesthetic customers you serve have favorite words and pet phrases (e.g., "It feels right to me"). Write these down as you hear them and incorporate them into future conversations with them.

9. Speak slowly.

Give kinesthetic buyers a chance to get a feeling about each benefit of your product or service. Allow them to "feel" your words and thereby experience what you're saying.

10. Show your honesty.

Honesty is important to all buyers, but especially kinesthetics. Don't give them any reason to question your integrity. Answer all questions candidly without hesitation. If you don't have the answer to a question, say so, and get it for them as soon as you can. (21)

11. Share the physical part of the selling process.

Allow kinesthetic buyers to touch and use your product. If it's a service, hand them the brochure.

12. Make kinesthetic buyers feel good.

Tell emotional stories and testimonials about the experiences of satisfied customers. Show how your product has dramatically enriched the lives of others.

Determine the Pain

Buyers become your customers when they gain confidence in you as a "doctor" who can ease, if not altogether eliminate, their pain—that is, the roadblocks to their success. In order to demonstrate how your product or service removes a roadblock, you need to learn what a particular buyer's roadblocks are. You require an inner ear. As you hear the buyer's words you need to listen for the buyer's pain. Once you and the buyer understand the nature and scope of that pain, the two of you can work together to find a solution—your product or service—that will relieve it. This chapter will help you develop the inner ear that listens for pain and responds to it with the right medicine.

70 Seven Motives Your Buyer May Have

The art of life is the art of avoiding pain; and he is the best pilot, who steers clearest of the rocks and shoals with which it is beset. —Thomas Jefferson

The traditional selling system focuses on the notion of selling benefits to the buyer. This approach glosses over the reality that people make decisions for two reasons: one is to move toward pleasure, the other is to move away from *pain*. People buy emotionally, and the strongest emotion buyers experience is pain. The best formula for selling is to find someone who believes he or she is well. Next, get that buyer to feel his or her "hurt" by asking probing questions such as those in List 76. If you can help your buyer uncover a number of hurts, these hurts will quickly appear to both of you as a full-fledged "illness." Then you can do what you are paid to do—perform a healing miracle. The exact buying motive you uncover with your questions will fall into one of these seven categories.

1. Pain in the present.

This is the most important pain to elicit. It is also the one to go after first. "How much money are you losing as we speak?" (75, 76)

2. Pain in the future.

Fear of an impending outcome is also a motivator to buy, but isn't as strong as pain in the present. "How much do you expect this problem to grow once your staff doubles in size?" (75, 76)

3. Pleasure in the present.

In third place on the selling hierarchy is your buyer's desire for gain right now. "How much further ahead of your competitors do you wish you were?"

4. Pleasure in the future.

Delayed gratification is less compelling than immediate gratification. In order to sell to this emotion, you need a proven track record with the buyer. "What kind of an increase in ROI are you looking for next year?"

5. Pain in the past.

Buyers may want to avoid repetition of an earlier mistake. "How would you like to never have to worry about that happening again?"

6. Pleasure in the past.

Buyers may want to return to past greatness. "How important is it for you to regain the prominence you've lost?"

7. Interest, arousal, or curiosity.

These are the weakest motives to connect with. Unfortunately, many salespeople place great stock in them. "Would you like to see something that will knock your socks off?"

▬ ▬ ▬

71 Nine Reasons Why Questions Are Your Most Powerful Sales Tools

> *Questions are never discreet. Answers sometimes are.* —Oscar Wilde

Professional salespeople learn and apply a secret that amateurs never learn or never fully understand. The secret to successful selling is not remembering what to say, but rather remembering what to ask. Questions are magic.

1. Questions focus on the buyer, not you or your product.

Questions take the pressure off you and put it on the buyer, where it belongs. (78)

2. Questions uncover pain.

There is only one reason you will sell anything: your ability to reduce a buyer's pain. You can't reduce pain if you don't know what it is. Buyers will tell you if you ask correctly. (76)

3. Questions represent positive psychological strokes.

When buyers speak and you follow with a question, buyers know they are being heard and feel important. Being listened to meets needs for self-importance and individuality.

4. Questions are more conversational, natural, and less manipulative than a prepared presentation.

Buyers expect a "smooth-talking" salesperson with a flashy, bells-and-whistles presentation. Buyers are pleasantly surprised by a salesperson who instead shows interest in their problems and concerns.

5. Questions relieve your pressure and stress.

When you approach the buyer with memorized scripts, you're naturally worried about remembering what to say and when to say it. Rather than memorizing scripts and specific counters to objections, just listen attentively and ask questions about what you hear. Give the buyer the lead. (77)

6. Questions ensure that the buyer does most of the talking.

The rule of thumb is 70–30. Successful salespeople talk only 30% of the time. They give buyers 70% of the airwaves. (74)

7. Questions give you a chance to think.

While the buyer is talking, you have an opportunity to think. The words you hear also tell you what you need to do to make the sale.

8. Questions minimize the risk you will say something you might later regret.

When you're not talking, you can't say anything stupid.

9. Questions commit the buyer.

People feel manipulated when they're sold something. When it's *their* choice, buyers remain committed to a purchase decision. When they conclude that they want to buy because of how they answer your questions, buyers feel ownership of their decisions and are less likely to back away from them.

▬ ▬ ▬

72   Eight Types of Questions and When to Ask Them

The wise man doesn't give the right answers, he poses the right questions. — Claude Lévi-Strauss

Professional service technicians typically have multiple variations of the same tool in their tool kits. For example, they might have a wide selection of drill bits, screwdriver heads, wrenches, and saw blades. Each variant has its own unique characteristics appropriate for a given situation. Similarly, professional salespeople require a variety of questions depending on the specific situation. Put these types of questions in your tool kit.

1. The broad, open-ended question.

Break the ice and get the buyer talking. *Example:* "What qualities are you looking for in a supplier?"

2. The factual probe.

Follow up the buyer's statement to get specific, detailed information of a factual nature. Factual probes are effective for qualifying the buyer. *Example:* "What other problems have you had with that equipment?"

3. The attitudinal probe.

Follow up a buyer's statement to learn attitudes and feelings. Attitudinal probes are effective for uncovering underlying emotions. *Example:* "How did you feel when your customers complained about the product?"

4. The mirror probe.

Restate the buyer's preceding comment with your voice trailing up at the end, implying a question. *Example:*

Buyer: "All of the bids we have received so far are way too high."
You: "All the bids are way too high?"

Your implied question subtly probes for further information. This is a good way to get more data without coming off as aggressive.

5. The summary question.

Summarize what you just heard to validate your understanding. This is a powerful technique used to move from one stage of the sales call to another. *Example:* "Are you saying that you're looking for a supplier that has a great track record and will go above and beyond the call of duty to satisfy you?"

6. The dummy, or Columbo, question.

Dummy, or Columbo, questions derive their name from the television detective portrayed by Peter Falk. These questions allow you to suggest that the buyer or customer is contradictory, or otherwise deceiving you, without saying so directly. You convey puzzlement and bewilderment while asking the person to help you understand the apparent contradiction. *Example:* "Earlier you said you want to solve your problems next week. Now I hear you saying you can afford to wait. I'm confused . . . what did I miss?" (78)

7. The reverse question.

Reverses get buyers to overcome their own objections. This question turns the tables by forcing buyers or customers to change perspective and become your partners. The question "reverses" the buyer from an offensive position to a defensive position. *Example:*

Buyer: "I can't understand why anyone would pay the price you're asking."

You: "You're right. We never have the lowest price. Why do you think we have the sales success we have with our prices so high?"

No matter how buyers answer this question, they will overcome the objection for you. (77)

8. The implication question.

As you near the close of the sale, the implication question confirms the benefits of your product through a question rather than an assertion. *Example:* "If we could reduce your problem of employee turnover within the budget you allocated—and I'm not saying we can, but if we could—what would happen next?"

▬ ▬ ▬

73 Nine Ways to Ask Questions Without Sounding Alienating or Manipulative

It is not every question that deserves an answer.
— Publilius Syrus

A tool is only as effective as the person using it. Similarly, questions are only as effective as the salesperson posing them. Achieve the full power and magic of questions by guarding against alienating the buyer or sounding manipulative. The tips in this list will help you realize the benefits of questions without raising a buyer's or customer's suspicions.

1. Listen with every ounce of concentration you can muster.

Your goal is to understand this person as fully as possible. Listen carefully to the answers your questions evoke. Good listening also tells you what question to ask next. (74)

2. Listen with your eyes as well as your ears.

The buyer or customer is always talking, even when his or her mouth is closed. Monitor physical signs of discomfort, nervousness, and anxiety. Your questions will put some pressure on buyers and customers, but you don't want to go too far. (61)

3. **Assume the role of a coach/consultant, not inquisitor/prosecutor.**

If your questions are judgmental ("Why would you make a statement like *that*?") or accusatory ("How do I know you aren't just giving me the run-around?"), you can expect to be asked to leave. Ask questions to help, not indict.

4. **Nurture buyers and customers.**

And then nurture them again. Head off any discomfort they may have with your questions. Convey the impression that you want to help them reduce pain. Say things like this before or during your questioning:

- "The more we talk about your need, the sooner we'll resolve it."
- "I'll be asking you some questions today to understand your needs. Is that OK?"
- "If any of my questions trouble you, let me know so we can talk about it."
- "The more I understand your business, the more I can help."
- "I think a few questions might help us clarify some issues." (53, 62)

5. **Monitor and control your body language.**

Coaches and consultants project a supportive, nonthreatening demeanor. They put the respondent at ease. Inquisitors and prosecutors, on the other hand, project superiority and moral certitude. They make the respondent uncomfortable. Project the former style, not the latter. (61)

6. **Use softening statements.**

Take the edge off your questions with lead-ins like these:

- "I wonder if I might ask you a question."
- "I'd like to probe that a little further."
- "I'm a little confused. Do you mean . . . ?"
- "Could you please help me out?"
- "What you just said raises an important question." (77)

7. Aim for a 70–30 split.

You will raise suspicions if you only ask questions. Talk about 30% of the time, leaving the rest of the time for the buyer to respond to you.

8. When the buyer or customer feels you're answering too many questions with questions and wants a specific response, give it.

Answering questions with questions (e.g., "That's a great question, why are you interested in . . . ?") is a powerful technique as long as it doesn't frustrate the questioner. When your gut tells you the buyer or customer wants specific information *now*, give it.

9. Thank the person for answering your questions.

Just as you are not obligated to answer every question buyers and customers pose, neither are they obligated to answer each of your questions. Periodically, thank the person for candor and responsiveness (e.g., "Thanks, I appreciate your honesty").

74 Fifteen Steps to Better Listening

The greatest compliment that was ever paid me was when someone asked what I thought, and attended to my answer. —Henry David Thoreau

The ability, the desire, and the patience to listen are prerequisites to success in sales. You'll pay the highest compliment to the buyer. You'll choose just the right reverse in tough situations, and you'll get to the bottom of the buyer's pain. But few sales professionals are naturally good listeners. They believe they need to immerse the buyer in information about their products. They grow impatient when the buyer rattles on about nothing. They get defensive at challenges or criticisms. They don't want to hear about the competition. They listen to what they *expect* the buyer to say rather than what is actually said. Their minds race and wander off the speaker. Here's the best advice we know to overcome these distractions and improve your listening.

Improve Your Listening Overall

1. Get determined.

In order to adopt any new behavior, you need to make a personal development commitment to it. You'll become a better listener when you become disgusted with the results you get by not listening. Can you say these words out loud right now? "I *will* become a better listener!"

2. Value people over things.

David Schwartz once said, "Big people monopolize the listening; small people monopolize the talking." This quote can be paraphrased as, "People who value other people are good listeners; people who value things are poor listeners." When things and people compete for time in your life, who, or what, typically wins? Can you stop what you're doing or thinking to give your attention to someone who is speaking?

3. Value feedback.

Every new piece of information you get from others increases your knowledge, even when that information is critical of your behavior or challenging to your beliefs.

4. Value the benefits.

Good listeners gain enormous advantages.

- They avoid saying the wrong thing at the wrong time; they let their ears tell them what to say and when to say it.
- They learn the motives of people around them.
- Armed with greater knowledge of others, they become more capable of persuading them.
- They look more intelligent because they let *others* put their feet in their mouths.
- They win the respect of those they listen to.
- They defuse anger in others by allowing them to vent their frustrations.
- They increase the self-esteem of others when they give up their precious time to hear them out.
- They demonstrate caring to those they listen to.

5. Strike an accountability contract.

Find a family member, friend, or colleague who will give you ongoing feedback on the quality of your listening and on your progress toward betterment. Offer the same deal in return.

Listen Better on a Sales Call

6. Prepare in advance.

As you wait for the meeting, think about the buyer and the company. Don't allow yourself to focus on other issues right before you enter the buyer's office. Pledge to yourself that you will give this person the best listening-to he or she has ever received.

7. Set a goal.

Vow that in the time allotted to you for the call, you will get to know this buyer's values, beliefs, goals, desires, dreams, fears, and pain better than anyone ever has. Muster all the concentration you can. Listen to understand the buyer, not to plan a counterattack.

8. Get into a listening posture.

Give steady eye contact; resist the temptation to let your eyes shift around as you think. Sit slightly forward when the buyer speaks, lean back when you speak. Nod occasionally. Smile and lift your eyebrows slightly.

9. Take notes.

It's polite to ask permission to do so, but you'll almost never be denied. Taking notes shows your interest in the buyer's message, helps you stay in control of the call, and provides valuable data to review later or share with your sales team.

10. Screen out distractions.

Don't glance around the office while the buyer speaks. Pay no mind to noise filtering into the room. Don't be thrown off by people who may walk by. Imagine you and the buyer are in a tunnel alone and all you can see or hear is each other. Think only about the message.

11. Limit your talking.

You can't listen and speak at the same time. Hold your fire. Hear the buyer out completely on every topic. Don't interrupt even if you have a pat answer to a point the buyer makes. Judge the meaning of the buyer's message only after all the words are spoken.

12. Listen for content.

Listen to the words. Don't respond to your stereotype of, or past history with, the buyer. Stop judging the style of delivery.

13. Check for nonverbals.

Monitor the buyer's voice, including intonation, inflection, emphasis, rate, and volume. What do these reveal about the true meaning of the spoken words? What does the buyer's body language tell you? (51, 61)

14. Keep the buyer talking.

Put one of these ideas to work when the buyer winds down but you want to hear more.

- Repeat the final words from the buyer's last sentence, possibly as a question. "You don't believe the problem is all that serious?"
- If the buyer is talking about a particularly emotional experience, keep him or her ventilating by saying, "That must be [exciting/an inspiration/challenging/difficult/painful] for you."
- Use a nondirective probe: "Really?" "And?" "What else?" "Who else?" "How do you feel about that?"

15. Prove that you listened.

Once you believe the buyer has said everything, paraphrase what you heard. ("What I hear you saying is . . .") Think of this technique as the price that you pay for the right to speak. It demonstrates that you cared enough to listen. It also confirms that what you are about to say responds to what the buyer really said.

■■ ■■ ■■

75 Thirty-Four Pains Your Product or Service Might Reduce

When written in Chinese, the word "crisis" is composed of two characters. One represents danger, and the other represents opportunity.

—John F. Kennedy

Every pain your buyer feels is an opportunity for you. Your task is to uncover that pain and help the buyer see how your product eases it. This list contains the most common pains buyers are likely to be experiencing. Convince buyers you'll reduce one or more of these pains and you'll increase your sales.

Pain Felt in the Form of Declining . . .

1. Revenues

2. Market share

3. Profit

4. Stock price

5. Shareholder value

6. Credit rating

7. Customer satisfaction

8. Raw materials quality

9. Maintenance quality

10. Product quality

11. Employee quality

12. Employee morale

13. Employee productivity

14. Employee accountability

15. Teamwork and coordination

16. Quality of facility management

17. Employee involvement and commitment

Pain Felt in the Form of Increased . . .

18. Raw material costs

19. Facility management costs

20. Maintenance costs

21. Labor costs

22. Employee grievances

23. Staff turnover

24. Interpersonal conflict

25. Inter-team conflict

26. Employee accident/injury rate

27. Resistance to change

28. Product rework, rejects, and returns

29. Deadlines missed

30. Inventory management costs

31. Inventory shrinkage

32. Competitor capability

33. Customer defections

34. Legal complications

▬ ▬ ▬

76 Thirty Questions That Probe for Pain

> *Pain is real when you get other people to believe in it. If no one believes in it but you, your pain is madness or hysteria.* —Naomi Wolf

Once buyers feel comfortable with you and confident in your ability to help them, they'll speak more freely about their needs. As their tongues loosen they'll grow more candid about the problems you can help them solve. Use questions to pinpoint their troubles and woes. The first group of questions below works to keep buyers talking and connect them with the reality of their pain. The second group reveals the extent and the nature of the pain. Use the pain-evoking questions most in line with your style and more likely to yield fruitful answers with your buyers.

Keep Buyers Talking

1. "And?"

2. "What happened next?"

3. "What else?"

4. "How many?"

5. "Can you tell me more about that?"

6. "And how did that work?"

7. "How do you feel about that?"

8. "What tells you that?"

9. "What makes you sure?"

10. "How do you measure that?"

Determine Pain and Its Extent

11. "Is there anything about your current situation you don't like?"

12. "Does that mean you're completely happy with your current situation?"

13. "In the industry we've noticed problems with [name a difficulty you've overcome for customers]. Have you experienced any problems in this area?"

14. "Which of those concerns you more?"

15. "If you could change one thing, what would it be?"

16. "And you've never had a problem with [name a difficulty you've overcome for customers]?"

17. "Can you be more specific about the [problem alluded to by the buyer]?"

18. "What recent example of that comes to mind?"

19. "How long has that been a problem?"

20. "What have you tried in the past to fix the problem?"

21. "What's worked for you and what hasn't?"

22. "Why do you think you got the results you did?"

23. "Is it getting worse or better, and how fast?"

24. "How much do you figure that has cost you?"

25. "What is the most recent action you've taken to correct it?"

26. "What do you hope to achieve with a solution that you don't have now?"

27. "If you could wave a magic wand in this situation, what would it do?"

28. "What personal distress is this causing you?"

29. "How much are you willing to invest to solve the problem?"

30. "How do you see me helping you?"

▬ ▬ ▬

77 Nineteen Reverses That Clarify the Buyer's Position

Never answer a question, other than an offer of marriage, by saying "yes" or "no."
—Susan Chitty

Reversing is the strategy of shifting back onto buyers the pressure they place on you with challenging questions and statements. The buyer uses these questions and statements to mask deep levels of emotion and pain. Reversing often involves asking a question in response to a buyer's question. One reason to reverse is to keep buyers talking. Another is to get them to redefine their original question or statement to something that is closer to their real intent, which they almost never reveal without help. To keep from antagonizing buyers with your reverses, remember two things: (1) when buyers repeat a question, answer it, and (2) precede most reverses with softening statements spoken in a gentle and friendly voice. Examples of softening statements include "That's important . . . ," "I appreciate that . . . ," "Help me to understand . . . ,"

"I'm not sure, but...," "Good point...," "I'm glad you asked...," "A lot of people ask that...," "That's a critical issue...," "Makes sense...," "Off the record...," and "First, let me ask you this...." Use reverses in these challenging situations. (62)

1. Pinned down.

Buyer: "What's this going to cost me?"
You: "Good question. Why do you ask?"

2. Off the record.

Buyer: "What's the price?"
You: "Off the record, Pat, what price were you looking for?"

Obviously, none of this discussion is off the record, but the pressure it relieves will many times open up buyers.

3. A trap is laid.

Buyer: "Do you have more than one of these?"
You: "How would more than one help you?" or "Is having more than one critical to your situation?"

4. Controlling the interview.

Buyer: "What about [topic you don't want to discuss yet]?"
You: "That's an important question. Could we back up for just a moment, first?"

5. Pressure-packed moment.

Buyer: "Why is it that you won't give me a price?" (Buyer is bearing down on you, maybe even attacking.)
You: "Pat, is there some reason why you're putting all this pressure on me?"

6. Situations you can't handle.

When presented with a situation beyond your control—perhaps an objection you cannot easily overcome—say, "We have a problem." When the buyer asks what it is, repeat the objection and your difficulty resolving it. End with, "Do you see a way to overcome it?" This is often an effective way to get the buyer to help you overcome his or her objection.

7. Lull in the interview.

When things get bogged down, try, "Pat, ask me a question." Wait for a response. Then reply, "Good question. Why did you choose that one just now?"

8. The "magic wand" reverse.

This reverse helps buyers paint the picture of their needs and wants. You ask, "If you had a magic wand that could produce the ideal solution to your problem, what would it be?"

9. The "you start" reverse.

You: "Pat, is it fair to say that we need to discuss all aspects of your problem?"
Buyer: "Yes."
You: "Fine! You start."

This reverse helps the buyer feel freer to tell you what's going on.

10. Complete the sentence.

When you need to hear more, but your buyer is getting impatient with questions, start a sentence and pretend you're searching your mind for an answer to let the buyer finish it. *Example:* "Let me see if I have this straight. . . ."

11. What?

When buyers say something that is in your best interest, say, "What?" This allows them to hear it a second time and is a powerful way to make them more positive about your product.

12. Buyer has a problem.

Buyer: "I have a problem with signing a contract today."
You: "May I ask you something?"
Buyer: "Sure."
You: "Why is that a problem?"

13. Buyer poses a dilemma.

When the buyer presents a choice that you'd rather not make, say, "If you were me, what would you do?" or, "Why do you see that as a choice that needs to be made at this point?"

14. Buyer expresses mistrust or anger.

Your best reverse is, "There must be a reason you feel that way." Take great care not to get angry back.

15. A question you can't answer.

When you don't know the answer to a buyer's question, say, "I'm not sure. What do you think?" Never answer a question dishonestly.

16. You need more information before you respond.

Buyer: "How reliable is your delivery?"
You: "Please help me with something. What does reliable mean?"

17. Your price is under fire.

Buyer: "Here's what I'm paying my present supplier. Can you beat it?"
You: "No. That's a good price. [pause] Let me ask you a question. Can you guess why we do so much volume in this market, and yet we never have the lowest price?"
Buyer: "Service?"
You: "That's it! [Say this no matter what the buyer picked.] Now why do you think our customers are willing to pay extra for service?" (89)

18. Your delivery is under fire.

Buyer: "Can you do it for us in March?"
You: "I don't know. March could be a problem. By the way, why March?" (89)

19. The unasked question.

We often hear a question when, in fact, the buyer is making a statement. For example, the objection "The price is too high" is a statement, not a question. Get the pressure off you, and find out what the buyer really means, by helping the buyer convert the statement into a question. Check these examples.

Buyer: "The price is too high."
You: "Which means . . . ?"

Buyer: "Your deliveries are too slow."
You (softer): "And . . . ?"

Buyer: "You people always do this to me."
You: " 'Do this to me' means . . . ?"

Buyer: "I'm really unhappy about this situation."
You: "When you say 'unhappy,' Pat, what do you mean?"

Buyer: "This problem needs to be settled before we can go any further."
You: "Settled means . . . ?"

▬▬ ▬▬ ▬▬

78 Fifteen Dummy-up Reverses That Keep You in Charge

A closed mouth catches no flies.

—Italian proverb

It can be dangerous to reveal too much product knowledge during a presentation. A point you make to clinch the deal may actually kill it if you talk the buyer out of a sale. (Can you imagine ever "listening" yourself out of a sale?) In the list immediately preceding, you learned how to use reverses to get buyers to discover their pain and make their positions more clearly known. The dummy-up reverses in this list serve three additional purposes. First, they keep you from prematurely dumping product knowledge that may in fact hurt the sale. Second, they enable you to test the waters regarding the value of a particular feature or benefit before sharing it with the buyer. Third, the more you appear to struggle as you dummy up, the more you disarm buyers, decrease their resistance, and make them feel better about themselves. Dummy-up reverses can do for you what they did for the bumbling detective played by Peter Falk on the television program *Columbo*.

Avoid Dumping Product Knowledge

1. Delivery.

Buyer: "How soon can we get this?"
You: "I'll check. Is there a specific requirement?"

2. Choices.

Buyer: "Is this available in blue?"
You: "I'll have to inquire. Did you need any other colors?"

3. Capability.

Buyer: "What is the maximum capacity of this system?"
You: "That's a good question. I'll check if it's important. Is it?"

4. Price.

Buyer: "Your competition is cheaper than you."
You: "Oh. I guess I won't be getting the order then, huh?"

5. Not convinced.

Buyer: "I'm not convinced yet."
You: "Oh, I see. Uhm, what should I have shown you?"

Test the Waters Regarding the Value of a Feature or Benefit

If the buyer answers any of the following reverses in the affirmative, respond with, "Oh? Why is that?" For negative answers say, "I didn't think so."

6. "I don't suppose."

You: "I don't suppose [name a major benefit of your product or service] would be of interest to you."

7. The "take away."

You: "It's probably not the case here, but sometimes I'm asked if we can [name a popular customization request you receive]. You didn't want us to do that, did you?"

8. The "third-party story."

You: "Last week I had a customer who was asking for [name a popular customization request] because it would help the company [name a bottom-line benefit the request provides]. Would that be relevant here?"

9. "Do I have it straight?"

You: "So let me see if I have this straight. What you're hoping we can do is [summarize the pain relief you hear this buyer asking for]. Is that right?"

10. "It's probably not important."

You: "Pat, it's probably not important for this to have [name something you're convinced is important to this buyer], is it?"

Learn These General Dummy-Ups

11. "I'm not sure."

You: "When you say [put anything here], I'm not sure I understand what you mean."

12. "I'm confused."

You: "I'm confused, Pat. Help me with that."

13. "I need help."

You: "I have a problem that I need your help with."
Buyer: "What's the problem?"
You: "The problem is [this might be an unreasonable stance the buyer is taking]. Can you help me?"

14. "I'm slow."

You: "I'm not as quick as you guys. I just need a little more help. Can you tell me again what you're hoping we'll do for you?"

15. "I'm getting lost."

You: "I'm getting lost. OK if I ask you a few questions?"

▬ ▬ ▬

79 Nine Ways to Remain Third-Party During a Sales Call

> When a man is wrapped up in himself he makes a
> pretty small package.   —John Ruskin

Imagine how much more effective you could be with an objective, analytical coach whispering in your ear during a sales call. The coach would tell you what you're doing well and what you should change. The coach would, above all, keep you from getting emotionally bound up in the sale you're hoping to make. You could critically and objectively assess the interactions between you and buyers. Good news! You don't need a coach to "remain third-party" during a sales call.

1. **Recognize that all buyers are human, acting out psychological "scripts" reflecting their needs, desires, biases, and defense mechanisms.**

The very best salespeople are amateur psychologists. They understand that everything a buyer says or does is a reflection of scripts they carry in their heads. These scripts reflect various degrees of psychological maturity. Buyers are prisoners to their scripts. Therefore, there is no reason to be upset by their "readings." (49–52)

2. **Take a close look at your own psychological maturity.**

Do you whine, complain, and manipulate like a child? Do you control, smother, nurture, and criticize like a parent? Or do you behave like a composed, confident adult? The very best salespeople have egos and personas that reflect more of the adult than the parent or the child. The more time you spend in the adult state, the more objectively you can observe what happens during your sales call from a dispassionate viewpoint. (5)

3. **Probe, probe, probe.**

Respond to buyer statements with probing questions. This increases your ability to remain third-party because:

- The buyer does most of the talking.
- You can listen, think, and reflect during the answers.
- The buyer's underlying pain will eventually emerge.
- You can identify the buyer's logic and reasoning. (73)

4. **Listen with your eyes and inner ear.**

Buyers will always tell you how they feel about you, your company, and the product. But they may not tell you directly. Instead they will convey their true feelings through tone of voice, body movement, and composure. Tune in to these subtle cues. (74)

5. **When attacked, respond from your head, not your gut.**

If the buyer is manipulative, sarcastic, and aggressive, do not respond in kind. Take a deep breath, exhale slowly, and ask this question: "Can you please tell me what happened to make you feel this way?" (103)

6. Talk about your feelings; don't bury them.

You and the buyer are engaged in a psychological drama where each is trying to maintain security and control. If you feel manipulated, stressed, or uncomfortable, bring it out in the open. If you think the buyer is feeling pressured, bring that out in the open. After clearing the air you can move toward closing the sale.

7. Get into the buyer's shoes.

Reverse your perspective. What might the buyer be feeling and why? What emotions is the buyer revealing? If you were the buyer and had to deal with a salesperson like you, how would you feel? Empathize with these feelings. (71, 73)

8. Listen to your "coach."

Listen to your inner voice of reason and objectivity—your coach. Your coach wants you to make the sale, and doesn't want you to waste time and energy protecting your ego. Listen empathetically to the buyer and respond nondefensively.

9. Disengage.

Imagine that there is a third person in the room observing this interaction in silence. When the going gets tough for you, become that third person. In your detached state, ask yourself what you are seeing and hearing. What advice would you give to the salesperson (you)?

■■ ■■ ■■

80 Fourteen Intangibles Buyers Will Buy

When you care enough to send the very best.
—Hallmark Cards slogan

For years IBM sold mainframes, PCs, and laptops with a compelling message: "You'll never have to apologize for purchasing an

IBM." The power of this slogan was based on IBM's dominant position in the computer industry. Corporate customers were buying more than computers. They were buying the IBM logo—an intangible. Similarly, when you sell intangibles, you increase the value (and purchase price) of your product. This list contains 14 types of intangibles buyers may find irresistible.

1. Prestige.

Luxury-branded perfumes, watches, clothing, and cars can be marketed for a premium price simply because markets value their prestige. Do most people buy Tommy Hilfiger clothing because of its style and quality?

2. Distinctiveness.

Companies like Volkswagen and Apple promote the idea that buying their products signals that one is somewhat countercultural, out of the mainstream, not your average Joe.

3. Reliability.

Maytag created a marketing icon with a repairman who never had to answer his phone. If you can prove Maytag repairers are *overworked* compared to your repairers, you've got an intangible people will buy.

4. Guaranteed satisfaction.

"If you don't like it, you don't pay for it" has sold everything from automobiles to zoom lenses.

5. Service.

The Zippo Company repairs lighters mailed in to corporate headquarters 30 years after they were purchased. How much is that worth to a Zippo customer? How much would it be worth to yours? (95, 97–99)

6. Aesthetics.

If it glistens, gleams, glows, shines, and takes your breath away, you've got an intangible worth money. One reason Harley-Davidson dealers are forced to maintain waiting lists for their motorcycles is because so many purchasers believe they are buying a work of art.

7. Safety.

If what you sell has a long track record of safety, you've got a product with significant intangible value. Car manufacturers scramble to outdo one another in reporting favorable results of crash tests.

8. Simplicity.

A product that is easy to understand and use has significant intangible value, especially if the product is technical or complex. America Online brought millions to the Internet because its software is so easy to navigate.

9. Technical support.

Car dealers who employ professionally certified mechanics can charge more for car repairs than dealerships with "street" mechanics.

10. Personally customized.

Why does a retailer add a significant markup to the cost of monogramming a shirt? Why can state bureaus of motor vehicles get more for personalized (vanity) auto license plates? Why will you invest more in house plans from an architect than in similar plans from a book of generic blueprints? (95)

11. Environmentally friendly.

If everything else about two products is equal and one is manufactured from recyclable materials and creates less toxic by-products than the other, which would you buy?

12. Socially responsive.

If everything about two products is identical and one is manufactured in a politically repressive country while the other is not, which would you buy?

13. Philanthropic.

If two products were identical and the manufacturer of one donated a portion of all profits to charity and the other did not, which would you buy? Some consumers frequent McDonald's simply to support the Ronald McDonald House.

14. Nostalgia.

Every Christmas, Coca-Cola displays its classic picture of Santa holding up a bottle of Coke. Isn't this company selling far more than a beverage? Images of Clark Gable, Marilyn Monroe, Humphrey Bogart, James Dean, W. C. Fields, and Mae West are still used to market products. Elvis lives.

✓ 8 Get the Sale

The essence of selling is helping buyers choose your product without feeling pressured or manipulated to do so. You'll not achieve this goal by memorizing scripts or closings, burdening the buyer with stacks of product literature, or troubling the buyer with follow-up phone calls. Rather, the key to nonmanipulative selling is using questions, reverses, and supportive presentations that lead the buyer to an inevitable decision: Sign the contract. And not only do the lists in this chapter work. They also relieve you of the enormous pressure that traditional sellers feel to say the right thing at the right time.

■■ ■■ ■■

81   Thirteen Uses of Negative Reverse Selling

> Overemphatic negatives always suggest that what is being denied may be what is really being asserted.   —Jonathan Raban

An amateur fisherman feeling a slight tug on the line would reel it in, and most of the time find nothing on it. In most cases, a tug means the fish is checking out the bait and maybe nibbling on it. Knowing this, you learn to strip some line off your reel ("striplining"), letting go a little slack. The fish pulls the bait deeper in the water and, feeling secure, gobbles up hook and all. When the line tightens, you jerk it to set the hook. Negative reverse selling works in the same way. Instead of moving in for what appears to be an obvious close, you back away gently. When the buyer responds to your reverses, the line tightens. The buyer, not you, closes the sale. You can also think of negative reverse selling as pushing on a buyer who is connected to the end of a pendulum. Shove the buyer away from you, inducing the negative reaction to you the buyer might have had anyway, and let gravity swing the buyer back toward you in a positive direction. In the scenarios below, notice how each negative reverse moves the buyer closer to a favorable decision.

Caution: Many sales professionals get great results with negative reverse selling; others have had it backfire on them. When you use it, take great care not to sound sarcastic or confrontational. If you observe a buyer being antagonized by a negative reverse, back off. If negative reverse selling isn't a good fit with your personality and communication style, avoid it altogether.

1. A complimentary buyer.

Buyer: "I like what you're saying."
You: "Interesting. Based on what you've been saying up to now, I would not have guessed you were interested in this. What did I miss?"
Buyer: "Well, maybe what you missed was how I see it solving my problem."
You: "Fine. I'm still a little confused. Could you tell me more specifically just how you see the fit?"
Buyer: "Yes, I'll use it to . . ."

2. An enthusiastic buyer.

Buyer: "Boy, our company is really going to love the . . . !"
You: "Fine. However, are you sure you have given this enough thought?
Buyer: "Well, I thought so, but maybe not."
You: "Maybe there is something else you would like to ask before you decide to make this investment. For, example, you could have asked me . . ." Pose those questions that highlight your knowledge of the buyer's pain and your product's strengths in order to close the sale.

3. Ready to sign on the dotted line.

Buyer: "I think we're ready to start."
You: "OK, but you're not sure." (Warm tone with slightly rising inflection on "sure.")

4. The "build up and take away."

You: "Most of our clients in your industry find that their problems concerning [. . .] are solved by our [. . .]. From our discussion, I'm getting the feeling that wouldn't be of interest to you, Pat."

Buyer: "That's not necessarily true."

5. The neutral buyer.

Buyer: "We might eventually do business."

You: "I'm surprised to hear you say that. If I were to guess, it would be that we'd never do business."

Buyer: "Well, I would never say never when it comes to business."

You: "Maybe I shouldn't either. However, in my experience, when someone says, 'We might eventually do business,' they never buy. Isn't that likely to happen here?"

Buyer: "It's true we're still studying our options, but we're serious about improving our situation."

You: "I appreciate that. I just got the feeling it wasn't a high priority."

Buyer: "Well, it may not be at the top of the list, but it's up there."

You: "But it won't make number one any time soon?"

Buyer: "I'm not prepared to do anything right at this moment."

You: "Probably not this month?"

Buyer: "No, but why don't we set up something for the first of next month to get the ball rolling?"

You: "Are you sure that's what you want to do?"

Buyer: "Absolutely."

6. The lethargic buyer.

Buyer: "Well, I guess we've had this problem for a while now."

You: "And you've officially decided to give up on fixing it?"

7. The buyer who asks for help.

Buyer: "Do you have a solution for me?"

You: "Well, we have one that's worked for other clients, but it may not work in your case."

8. Probing the buyer.

You: "Pat, it's probably not important for this to have [one of your features the buyer hasn't mentioned], is it?"

9. You blew the last order.

Buyer: "I don't know how you had the nerve to show up today.

You don't think we're going to put ourselves through another horribly botched order again, do you?"

You: "You shouldn't. If I were you, I wouldn't even do business with me."

Buyer: "I'm glad you agree."

You: "And that's because you're convinced you would have the same problems. I mean, that's the decision you've made, right?"

Buyer: "Well, I don't know if I've actually made that decision."

You: "I appreciate that, but you probably should have. I'm guessing that even when I tell you what we've done to make sure that doesn't happen again, you still won't use us. Probably never!"

Buyer: "I'm not sure I'd say never."

You: "Oh? What would you say?"

Buyer: "I'd have to be reassured."

You: "I probably couldn't do that."

Buyer: "Maybe you can't, but it's up to you whether or not you want to try."

You: "Suppose I did try. What would you have to see or hear?"

Buyer: "You'd have to prove to me that . . ." (103)

10. Is it over?

Buyer: "We're not getting anywhere."

You: "Pat, I get the feeling it's over."

Buyer: "No, I didn't say that."

You: "Good. What did you say?"

11. It's over.

Buyer: "Yes, it's over."

You: "Now that it's over, before I leave, may I ask you one last question?"

Buyer: "Sure."

You (struggling): "I guess I'm confused. Did something change between now and the day you asked for this meeting?"

Get the buyer to talk about the pain that originally triggered the meeting.

12. It's really over.

Buyer: "Look, it's really over now. I have to get back to work."

You: "Now that it's really over, can I stop being a salesperson for a minute and be a consultant? [pause] You're about to make a mistake on this, Pat. Even if you don't use us, you need to . . ." Here's where you throw your "Hail Mary" pass into the end zone with two seconds left on the clock and your team down by a touchdown.

13. Selected situations.

Negative reverses will work to make your buyer more positive in the following situations.

Buyer: "We're pretty happy with our current supplier."

You: "And you've made up your mind not to talk to another supplier [pause] for any reason?"

Buyer: "I'm not sure you can do better than our current supplier."

You: "I'm not sure either, but what would 'better' look like?"

Buyer: "I'm not sure we even need a [. . .] at this time."

You: "Hearing you, I tend to agree. [pause] I guess I should go?"

Buyer: "I see how this will help us."

You: "Appreciate you saying that, Pat, but how exactly do you see it fitting in?"

▬ ▬ ▬

82 Sixteen Tough Questions to Build Your Product Knowledge

> I keep six honest serving men
> (they taught me all I knew):
> Their names were What and Why and When
> and How and Where and Who.
> — Rudyard Kipling

The best way to get product knowledge is not by studying manuals, interviewing engineers, or watching videos of the manufacturing practice or service process. Yet this is typically the training most new salespeople receive. To gain and maintain product knowledge, ask the *toughest* questions about your product. Use the answers to position your product favorably in the minds of buyers.

1. What do your competitors fear most about your product?

2. What do competitors claim to buyers is the major weakness of your product?

3. How do competitors try to differentiate their products from yours?

4. What are the most common complaints customers have about your product?

5. What do customers like best about your product?

6. Who are the customers who have gotten the greatest value out of your product and what distinguishes them from others?

7. Why do your best customers continue to do business with you?

8. Where was your most recent customer defection, and why did it occur?

9. When your coworkers candidly critique your product, what problems do they identify?

10. When people in engineering, manufacturing, customer service, or other departments candidly critique your product, what problems do they identify?

11. What is top management or your research and development department working on right now to improve your product?

12. What improvements would you make in your product if you had the budget and resources?

13. What cutting-edge technology might make your product obsolete?

14. What changing demographic or cultural trends will have significant impact on your sales?

15. What product intangibles are your toughest sell (e.g., reliability, prestige, service, technical support)? (80)

16. What's the one question about your product you hope buyers never ask?

83   Eight Ways to Communicate Product Knowledge

Oh Lord, please fill my mouth with worthwhile stuff, and nudge me when I've said enough.

— A speaker's prayer

The best technical experts often make the worst salespeople. They care too much about the intricacies of the product and too little about the intricacies of the mind and heart. They believe products sell because of their features and benefits rather than because of the hope they give to the buyer. This list shows you how to use your words to sell your product, rather than conduct a free seminar about it.

1.   Demonstrate how the product reduces the buyer's pain.

Product features, technical specifications, and other bells and whistles are meaningless unless they help a buyer reduce pain. The buyer doesn't want to ring every bell or blow every whistle. Focus on the buyer's pain, not your product. Remember, Black and Decker and Craftsman don't sell drills, they sell holes. Disneyland and the *Delta Queen* don't sell rides, they sell dreams. Dentists don't sell fillings and root canals, they sell smiles. (75)

2.   Sell today, educate tomorrow.

Educating the buyer on your product before the sale may not result in a new customer. You may simply raise more questions and even talk the buyer out of the sale. Don't give free consulting. Wait until after you get paid.

3.   Control your need to prove how much you know.

You're a product expert. Unfortunately, experts are sometimes tempted to prove how smart they are and how much they know. When you succumb to that temptation, you start giving free consulting.

4.   Become an expert on what your product does, not how it does it.

Obviously you need to intelligently discuss the mechanics and specs of your products. It is, however, the *performance* of your product that buyers really care about.

5. Use questions to connect product benefits with buyer needs.

Your buyer has a mental image of his or her needs before you begin the presentation. Ask questions like these to lead the buyer to discover how your product addresses those needs:

- "I don't suppose you would be interested in [one your product's top benefits], would you?"
- "Did you say [one of your product's top benefits] was important to you?"
- "I don't suppose you have a problem with [a common problem that your product solves]?" (71–73, 76)

6. Wave your "magic wand."

You might choose to build your presentation around the answer to the following challenge: "Pat, assume you had a magic wand and could design a product that would solve all your problems. Describe the product." Then show how much your product looks like the buyer's picture.

7. Delete technical jargon.

Many buyers would rather fake understanding than admit they don't understand. They don't want to come across as being "not-OK." Anticipate their ignorance of your company's special vocabulary and modify those parts of your presentation containing unfamiliar terminology. Speak in the buyer's language. (84)

8. Define technical terms with empathy.

Never come across as smug. That will only reinforce your buyers' feelings of inadequacy, and make them not feel very good about dealing with you. Say something like, "Most people don't know what this terms means. It means . . ." (83)

■■ ■■ ■■

84 Seven Tips for Translating Your Jargon

Eschew obfuscation. — *Author unknown*

Buyers aren't impressed by terms they don't understand. They are made uncomfortable by them. Can you describe your product with clarity and impact to someone who lacks your formal training, experience, and familiarity with the product? If you can't, you're probably relying too much on technical jargon. The tips in this list will transform you from a product expert to a product salesperson.

1. Increase your sensitivity to jargon.

You can't change a problem until you realize a problem exists. Tape-record your next presentation to see if you're guilty.

2. Identify your jargon.

Here are two tests for jargon: If your mother, father, aunt, uncle, or any family member who has never worked for your company doesn't understand a term, then it's jargon. If the word is not in the thesaurus tool of your word processor, it's probably jargon.

3. Ask nonthreatening questions to validate the buyer's comprehension.

Simple, nonthreatening questions or statements signify your concern and provide the information you need to clarify and simplify.

- "What I just described can be very confusing. Is there anything you'd like me to go over?"
- "Most people have trouble with this concept. Would you like me to spend more time on it?"
- "If there's one thing I need to go back over for better clarity, what is it?"
- "If I were in your chair right now, I'd probably be totally confused. Are you where I'd be?"
- "I know this sounds like a $100 word but it really has a 10-cent meaning: . . ."
- "Wow, how's that for gobbledygook? What it really means is . . ." (53, 73)

4. Publish a product jargon glossary.

Here's a project for your engineering and production staffs: Develop a glossary of all technical terms related to the product. Publish the glossary and give a copy to all buyers and customers. This value-added service will help you stand out from your competition.

5. Use analogies to simplify the jargon.

An analogy is a comparison that relates the unknown and unfamiliar with the known and familiar. "A computer's CPU is like the human brain, processing information." "How fast is a nanosecond? If you could put one foot in front of the other each nanosecond, you could walk around the equator in about three seconds."

6. Use examples based on the buyer's business.

Assume you sell industrial cleaning compounds to a company that manufactures plastic moldings. In describing the antiseptic properties of your solvents you could say, "You're in the business of producing plastic parts that are clean, neat, and safe. This new bacteria-destroying compound will do the exact same thing in all your restrooms." (83, 94)

7. Translate company-specific jargon for buyers and customers.

Instructing coworkers about "Form 90-9" is fine. Just don't ask customers to complete Form 90-9. Instead ask them, "Complete the yellow form that we need for . . ." (Better yet, complete it yourself.)

▬ ▬ ▬

85   Fourteen Ingredients of a Winning Proposal

In preparing for battle I have always found that plans are useless, but that planning is essential.
— Dwight D. Eisenhower

"Send me a proposal." These words can strike dread into the heart of a sales professional, but they needn't. Proposals and presentations are a vital part of the sales process. When they reach the right audience at the right time with the right message, they improve your ability to close more sales. The success of your proposals depends on finding the right buyer, being timely and thorough with your proposal, and clearly positioning your company's competitive advantage.

Find the Right Buyer

1. Make sure there's a good fit between this potential customer and your company's core competencies.

You have something valuable to sell to the right buyers. It is the core competency of your company expressed through products and services. When you see a written RFP (Request for Proposal), hear about an opportunity, or are asked to submit a proposal, consider the fit between the buyer's needs and your company's ability to meet those needs. Pursue only "good-fit" buyers. (29, 94)

2. **Look for opportunities to submit fresh proposals to existing customers.**

The best potential customer is an existing customer with a new need closely linked to goods and services you already provide. The second best potential customer is an existing customer with a need in a department not previously serviced by your company, but with needs related to your core competencies. (115)

3. **Favor buyers with potential for increasing business beyond the immediate sale.**

Lean toward buyers who have the potential to give you additional business in the future. However, reject the thought of breaking into a company with a low bid in order to do more profitable jobs later. If the first job isn't profitable, the second one usually isn't either.

4. **Find the "pain" described in the RFP.**

Identify the pain behind the needs described in the RFP. You'll find those needs described in logical, cognitive terms (e.g., a need for sales training). Pain, on the other hand, exists in fervent, emotional terms (e.g., we're "bleeding" because we can't close promising sales). Prepare to focus your proposal on the pain caused by the need. (75, 76)

5. **Research the competition.**

Find out who else will put in a bid on this job. What does your investigation tell you about whether you want to compete? What will it take to have the winning bid? (27)

6. **Compare the cost of the proposal to the potential benefits.**

The profit you can expect from a given sale is apparent. Less obvious are the costs associated with submitting a proposal to get that sale. These costs include the time and expenses of carrying out the other 13 steps in this list. Add to this the time and cost of actually writing, producing, and presenting the proposal. Take these costs into account to judge if it's smart to submit a proposal.

Respond in a Timely and Thorough Manner

7. Verify the buyer's budget.

Make sure that the target budget revealed by the buyer is consistent with a profitable solution developed by your company. (56)

8. Develop an up-front contract.

Agree to submit a proposal only when you and the buyer both agree about what will happen once the proposal is delivered. (59)

9. Identify decision makers.

It is the personal "pain" of these decision makers, in the context of their company's needs, that will shape your response to their situation. (58, 86)

10. Choose the steps you will follow to create your proposal.

These steps begin with identifying the problem and end with making a presentation. Be sure to fit the stages of your proposal development process within the timing of the buyer's decision.

11. Follow the steps carefully.

Do not take shortcuts in your proposal development process to meet the time demands of your buyer. The competition won't submit a slipshod bid; why would you? Speed is better achieved through increased effort and staffing.

Position Your Company Favorably Relative to the Competition

12. Link solutions to your core competencies.

In your proposal, develop a detailed statement of the buyer's problem. Connect that problem inextricably to your core competencies. Show how your solution takes advantage of your products and services relative to the competition.

13. Sharpen your proposal.

Make as many preliminary presentations to the buyer as you need before developing the final proposal. (Be sure to include these dry runs in your cost analysis in step #6, above.) Get feedback from key decision makers in the company. Incorporate this feedback into the final proposal.

14. Deliver a professional presentation.

Talk to your contact person about the final presentation. Make sure you have an agreement about what will happen at the end of the meeting. Confirm that the primary decision maker will be there. Learn what you can about the needs of the people who will attend and about the kind of presentation they're looking for. Give it to them. (86, 87)

▬▬ ▬▬ ▬▬

86 Fourteen Steps to Ensure Successful Sales Presentations to Groups and Committees

> Committee—a group of men who individually can do nothing but as a group decide that nothing can be done. —Fred Allen

Presentations to groups or committees add even more challenges to those you face in the sales call on a single buyer. At the same time, this special presentation context offers certain advantages not present in the one-on-one setting. Follow the advice in this list to surmount the challenges and exploit the advantages of sales presentations to groups of buyers.

Before the Sales Presentation

1. Identify the decision makers—the "cast of characters."

In a meeting with your contact person, take out a sheet of paper. Rotate it to the horizontal and draw a two-inch square at the top. Ask, "Does the CEO have any input into the decision making for this project?" Take note of the answer inside the box. Ask, "Who else is involved?" Draw boxes for each person mentioned in proper relationship to the CEO box. Learn everyone's involvement in the decision and note this in his or her box. Let your contact person help by writing on the paper if so inclined. This helps to bond the two of you. Finally, revisit each box and ask, "What do you think [person's name] wants out of this? How come?" Ask other questions to learn more about the cast of characters. One good one is, "Which of these players is pushing hardest for one of our competitors?" (58, 84)

Cast of Characters

CEO

> Not part of decision, but must approve it.

(Wants to smash competition.)

CFO

> Ultimate decision maker. Has most influence over CEO.

(Wants to slash costs.)

Plant Manager

> Ultimate user. Has veto power but not ability to contract.

(Wants to make money and keep the CEO happy.)

Quality Manager

> Should have major say, but lacks power.

(Wants to win the Baldrige National Quality Award.)

Shift Supervisors

> Consulted by Plant Manager.

(Want job security and a smooth-running operation.)

Chief Engineer

> Looked up to by Plant Manager for supplier advice.

(Wants to keep supervisors out of the decision.)

2. Speak one-on-one with as many group members as possible as many times as you need.

Establish relationships before the sales presentation and identify your White Knights (those favorable to your cause) and the Black Knights (those antagonistic to your cause). Say something like this as you set up each appointment: "Pat, I've received some information on which I'd like your feedback. I understand you may be the best person to evaluate it." At the meetings uncover both personal pain and corporate pain. Ask, "What's the one thing you'd most like to see come out of this?" Go down the list of committee members and ask what the person you're interviewing believes each of them wants. This information is critical to a successful presentation.

At the Sales Presentation

3. Introduce yourself and any members of your team.

Go beyond job titles and responsibilities. Focus on the particular talents and special interests that bring each member of your team to the presentation. Give a brief overview of the presentation.

4. Set up-front contracts concerning time and agenda.

Check your understanding of the ending time for the meeting and find out if everyone can stay throughout. Verify the roles of all members of the buyer committee and their positions relative to your proposal. (59)

5. Set expectations and outcomes.

What will you need from group members? What can they count on from you? Where do you expect the group to be at the end of the meeting? Does everyone have the same expectations for the end result?

6. Turn the meeting over to your contact person for a "pain review."

Introduce your principal contact to review his or her understanding of the problem and how your product or service solves the problem. *Example:* "We've had an opportunity to meet with Terry Young prior to today's presentation. Terry, before we start, can you give an overview of some of the situations and problems we've uncovered and how we might be able to solve them?" Meet with Terry before the meeting to rehearse what Terry's going to say.

7. **Watch the group as your contact person speaks.**

What kind of respect do they appear to give Terry? What does their body language suggest about how they accept Terry's analysis? Does their response alert you to any Black Knights who'll need to be won over and White Knights who'll back you up?

8. **Validate.**

Confirm Terry's understanding of the problem. Add your own helpful comments. Go around the room to have each person offer one or two descriptions of their understanding of the problem and about how it affects their department. List these on a flip chart in the front of the room.

9. **Enlist key helpers.**

One way to co-opt your Black Knights is to get them involved physically in your presentation. You can ask them to pass out materials, plug in equipment, or tape paper on the wall from the flip chart you use to record participants' problem descriptions.

10. **Present.**

Show how your proposal addresses the most important pain. Open the meeting up to questions. After you answer each one, go from person to person with this question: "Are you 100% satisfied with the way our solution addresses the need?" If any are less than 100% satisfied, ask what it would take to make them 100% comfortable. Write these discoveries on the flip chart. Respond to each request. For difficult requests ask other team members for their ideas on how to address them. (For example, someone asks, "How much sooner will we get a job done using your equipment?" You answer, "That's an important question. Based on some of the things we talked about today, can anyone take a stab at that?") If there's anything you can't handle now, use it as a pretext to come back. Don't move on until you are confident that each request is handled or is going to be handled. Remember that successful presentations are interactive. If they're not asking questions, they're probably not buying. (87)

11. **Stroke.**

Compliment the committee for their progress to date. (Even if it has been made without you!) Thank meeting participants for the contributions to your presentation both as the contributions are made and at the end of the presentation. Be careful not to come across as patronizing or ingratiating when you stroke team members.

12. Don't rescue anyone.

Let committee members work out their own questions and answers as much as possible. The conclusions they reach as a group will have more potency than ones you make for them.

13. Manage disagreement.

When two committee members have divergent views, align yourself gently with the opinion closer to your own. Ask the other person for a reaction to what's happening: "Mr. Smith, I realize it doesn't look like the two of you see eye to eye on this. How do you feel about this particular situation?" Stay out of it now if you can, and let the two of them work it out.

14. Assure closure.

If you've done your job up to this point, the committee should close the deal themselves. If, however, you reach the end of the meeting and no decisions have been made, ask, "So what happens now?" Depending on the answer to this question, you may need to draw everyone's attention back to the up-front contract for expectations and outcomes. Hold them to their agreement.

▬ ▬ ▬

87 Twenty Steps to a Successful Presentation to a Large Audience

> The Christopher Columbus Award for presentations goes to the speaker who starts out not knowing where he's going, returns not knowing where he's been, and takes a lot of other people's time getting there. —Author unknown

This list is for anyone who makes presentations in front of large groups. Use it as a step-by-step guide the next time you lead professional meetings, seminars, workshops, classroom training, briefings to upper management, updates to committees and boards, public relations presentations to community groups, or motivational speeches to large audiences.

Organize Your Presentation

1. **Analyze and adapt to your audience.**

Learn your audience's goals, attitudes, values, beliefs, mood, needs, pain, dreams, ambitions, and concerns. Tailor your presentation to ensure you meet them. (53, 57)

2. **Determine your purpose.**

What do you want the audience to *know*, *feel*, *say*, and *do* after your speech? These ultimate purposes for speaking determine the strategy you follow, the organization you adopt, and the materials and content you choose.

3. **Generate the three to five main points that sell your ideas best.**

Most people can't remember any more than about five central ideas shared with them on a topic. Cluster and organize your ideas into the three to five most important concepts or statements that do the best job of revealing and achieving your speech purpose. Each assertion you'll make in the presentation will fall under one of these main points.

4. **Create compelling content.**

Use as many of these and other schemes of organization and rhetorical devices as will help you achieve your speech purpose.

- Logical appeals: Rational arguments intellectually support your position.
- Emotional appeals: Passionate arguments tug at the heart or conscience.
- Quotations: Notice the persuasive impact they have in this book.
- Stories: Storytelling is a powerful means of moving images from one person's mind to another.
- Examples: Bring your ideas alive with illustrations.
- Definitions: They attach greater clarity and strength to your claims.
- Transitions: Weave your ideas together smoothly as you move from one section of your presentation to another.

5. Plan and control the setting.

Coordinate with everyone involved to ensure everything at the site of your presentation will be just as you expect.

Connect with Your Audience

6. Open decisively.

Know what the first few lines of your opening will be. Let the first words out of your mouth be well-planned, decisive, and attention-getting. Cause people to think: "I'm glad I'm here." Choose openings like these:

- Quote someone famous or knowledgeable on the topic.
- Cite a startling statistic relevant to your content.
- Make a strong or surprising statement.
- Ask a rhetorical question.
- Tell a story.
- Connect to a current or historical event.
- Connect to a previous speaker.

7. Tell your audience where they're headed.

Reveal the main points you'll cover.

8. Build credibility.

Win the trust of your audience by treating them respectfully and thoughtfully, establishing your credentials, involving them in the presentation, and showing your human side.

Send Powerful Messages

9. Free your language of sexism, racism, profanity, and other forms of offense.

10. Speak correctly.

Minimize mistakes of usage and grammar. (10, 11)

11. Speak forcefully.

Rid your presentations of apologies, especially during the opening. Stay away from vague words and phrases. Shun clichés and repetitive pet phrases. Avoid euphemisms, jargon, long unfamiliar words, passive voice, long complex sentences, and foreign words and phrases. (84)

12. Speak clearly, distinctly, and eloquently.

Check your diction, pronunciation, and eloquence, using your voice mail system or a tape recorder. Get feedback from others on what you can improve.

13. Avoid unnecessary utterances.

Watch "aah," "uhm," "okay," "like," and "you know."

14. Vary your vocals.

Check for troublesome vocal patterns, using your voice mail system or a tape recorder. Listen for a droning monotone, a predictably up-and-down singsong pattern, and question marks substituted for emphatic periods at sentence ends. Vary your tone, pitch, inflection, emphasis, volume, and rate to reveal the true feelings behind your words. (60)

15. Harness your body language.

Look into the eyes of your audience. Smile and keep your eyebrows up. Maintain an erect posture. Keep your hands at your side or on the lectern, not in your pockets; natural hand movement is fine. Avoid any repetitive actions such as playing with markers, adjusting the microphone, pacing predictably, fingering a mustache, twiddling clothing, or adjusting glasses. (2, 61)

Master the Finishing Touches

16. Use notes that do the job.

Choose a size of paper that works for you. Write trigger phrases, not sentences, to keep your eyes up most of the time. Keep your notes far forward on the lectern to minimize head movement when you need to see them.

17. Use audiovisual aids to advantage.

Choose the ideas you want to simplify and make more memorable. Decide where you need to spice things up to keep your audience engaged. Choose the transparencies, handouts, models, and board writing that best accomplish these goals. (109)

18. Defeat stage fright.

Accept moderate nervousness as a good thing. Look forward to the opportunity you have to shine. Prepare thoroughly and rehearse extensively. Get familiar in advance with the setting where you'll present. Release excess energy with exercise just before you begin. If necessary, memorize the first minute. Involve the audience in some action to relieve your pressure.

19. Manage the audience.

Handle questions with aplomb. Deal decisively yet tactfully with disruptive audience members. Defuse hostility. Resolve audience objections to your assertions.

20. Close with a bang.

Summarize your three to five main points. Issue a call to action— tell your audience what you want them to do.

— — —

88 Eight Questions to Ask When the Buyer Is Considering Someone Else's Offer

I don't seem to do my best unless I'm behind or in trouble. — Mildred "Babe" Didrikson

At the point where you hope to get a decision, the buyer may tell you that while your presentation was impressive he or she is considering another offer. This may be a statement of fact, or it may be a ploy to get you to come down in price. Don't mistake this statement, true or false, for a question. You don't have to respond to it with anything more than "That's fine. Where do we go from here?" But if you have the need to determine the nature of a competing offer, try one or more of these questions. (105)

1. **"If we weren't in the running, who would be getting this business?"**

Find out what competition you're up against.

2. **"If you accept the competitor's offer, will you come out ahead in the long run?"**

If your offer is in the buyer's best long-term interests, show how and why.

3. **"I don't suppose that offer includes [a benefit only your company offers]?"**

Tout benefits that you know this buyer values.

4. **"If you reject our offer, what will take its place that's any better than what you're assured of receiving from me?"**

In the discussion following this question, emphasize your guarantees.

5. **"What guarantees come with that offer?"**

If the buyer tells you what they are, follow up with this question and statement: "When you told the other salesperson about your concern that that firm will actually stand behind that guarantee when things turn sour, what was the response?"

6. **"How can you be sure you'll get a better deal elsewhere?"**

Use this question with a buyer who has not yet investigated the competition.

7. **"What additional information do you need from me in order to choose between the two offers?"**

Don't offer any concessions until you've verified the competing offer and unless you absolutely have to come down in price or go up in value in order to get the sale.

8. **"Am I right in feeling you don't believe our offer is a fair one?"**

If the answer is "Yes, it's not fair," ask what the buyer believes would be fair. Either move closer to it without changing the basic parameters of your offer or explain why you cannot. If the answer is no, say, "I'm glad you're with me. Now, what's the next step?" If the competing offer doesn't exist, you're likely to close the sale with this question.

89 Eight Questions to Ask When Pressured to Respond to an Unreasonable Deadline or Price Offer

Let us never negotiate out of fear, but let us never fear to negotiate. —John F. Kennedy

Buyers want your products and services as quickly and as cheaply as you can provide them. They will often push you to the wall with unreasonable expectations on delivery and on price. Here are some questions you can use to stay in control when they do.

When They Ask for an Impossible Delivery Date

1. **"What keeps us from being able to negotiate that date?"**

This question will lead the two of you directly into problem solving unless the buyer refuses to give you an answer. If you get stonewalled, say that the refusal puts unnecessary pressure on the negotiation.

2. **"If you're under pressure to meet that deadline, how can I be a relief valve for you?"**

Someone else may have dictated the deadline. Regardless of who ordered it, if you can learn the reason behind it, you may be able to provide a solution to the buyer without having to meet the impossible deadline.

3. **"How about we deliver on [promise the earliest realistic time], and we'll also [make an attractive concession you can afford]?"**

You don't want to lose the sale because you can't meet an imposed delivery date. Some extra product—or perhaps a reduction in price—may be an acceptable price for you to pay to keep it.

When They Argue for an Unreasonably Low Price

4. **"What's the reasoning behind this offer?"**

The buyer will either give you a reason or decline to do so. You hope for a reason so the two of you can problem solve together. If the buyer refuses to cooperate, your best option may be to follow with a counteroffer and the reasons behind it.

5. **"What do you think I see as a fair offer?"**

With this question you're hoping to get the buyer to use empathy. If you see the buyer getting into the spirit of this question, state why you believe it's in *both* your interests to have you walk away satisfied.

6. **"If I accepted that offer and thereby failed to make a fair profit on the sale, where do you think that would put us?"**

This is better than the question you *really* want to ask: "Do you think we're running a charity here?" It encourages the buyer to assume responsibility.

7. **"What criteria do you believe our final agreement should meet?"**

Whatever answer you get, this question achieves two goals. First, the answer should reveal why the buyer is pushing so hard. Second, regardless of the answer, the way will be opened for you to give equal weight to the criteria important to you.

8. **"What are you hoping to accomplish with that price?"**

This is a more direct way than the previous question to get the conversation to the point where you can justify the need for a fair price. If you reach a price impasse, leave the sale on the table. Hang on to your dignity, and you'll have it for the next price negotiation.

■ ■ ■

90 Eleven Questions to Ask When the Buyer Says, "Take It or Leave It"

> *Where force is necessary, there it must be applied boldly, decisively and completely. But one must know the limitations of force; one must know when to blend force with a maneuver, a blow with an agreement.* — Leon Trotsky

Whether negotiating a delivery date, a price, or a contract, the principles are the same. In all cases you search for an agreement in which both you and the buyer walk away winners. One of the best ways to achieve a win-win solution is to carefully balance assertiveness with a desire to gain equal value for both sides.

Unfortunately, buyers often play by a different set of rules. They may negotiate aggressively—not assertively—and try to get all the value for themselves. When buyers play "hard ball" with you, you need to catch every speeding pitch they fire at you without backing away, and rely on good control rather than speed when you return the throw. In other words, you need to protect your interests while helping them meet theirs. One of the best ways to do this in negotiations is to ask questions—questions that keep you in a position of power without overpowering the buyer. One of the following questions will work best for you when the buyer attempts to close off negotiations by saying, "Take it or leave it."

1. "What's your preference?"

This question may throw the buyer off balance. If the buyer answers that you "take it," say, "And I'd love to take it—what can you offer to help me do so?" If the answer is something like "that's up to you to decide," say, "Well, I'd like to *take* it—what can you offer to help me do so?" In the unlikely case the answer is "leave it," say, "Why would you want me not to accept your offer?"

2. "If I could suggest an alternative more attractive to you than the one just proposed, would you still ask me to take it or leave it?"

By suggesting that further discussion might benefit both of you, you encourage the buyer to listen to your alternative.

3. "Do you want me to take it or leave it right now, or can I take some time to think over the possibility of taking it?"

This stall tactic buys you the time you'll need to make a decision without pressure. When you come back to the table, you'll be able to respond without the threat hanging over your head.

4. "Can you take a few more minutes to explain the benefits of taking it?"

This approach transfers the pressure from you to the buyer and may reveal information that'll help you make a better decision.

5. "Are you under pressure to bring this discussion to a close?"

If you get a denial, simply say something like, "I guess I misread you." You'll have done your job of putting the buyer on notice to let up a bit. If you get an admission that the buyer feels pressure, win him or her over by empathizing with that plight.

6. **"How would you respond if the roles were reversed and you had to respond to the pressures of a 'take it or leave it' demand?"**

This question calls it like it is, and gives the buyer cause to rethink his or her stridency. If the buyer's answer is, "It wouldn't bother me," ask, "Why not?" If the answer is, "It would bother me," say, "Well, that's what it does to me. How can we change that?"

7. **"If I take it, will you agree to [name a concession]?"**

What incentive do you need in order to meet the buyer's demands?

When the Result of Your First Question Is an Impasse . . .

8. **"Do you have any ideas that might close the gap between our two positions?"**

You'll be amazed at how often this question will stir a constructive idea in someone who hitherto has been closed-mouth and unyielding.

9. **"If six weeks into the future we were to look back at this discussion, what might we wish we'd have brought to the table?"**

Be ready to answer this yourself if the buyer fails to respond. Make a small concession with the hope that the buyer reciprocates. This may open the way to a solution.

10. **"Assuming I could push this—and I don't know if I can—what concession do you need from me to close the deal right now?"**

The answer to this question tells you exactly what movement you'll need to make to get a favorable decision.

11. **"On a scale from 0 to 10, with 0 meaning there's no chance to come to terms, and 10 meaning you're ready to sign on the dotted line, where are you?"**

If the answer is 6 to 9, ask the follow-up question: "What will it take to make it a 10?" If the answer is 0 to 5, you either need to redesign your total approach or walk away from the sale. If you accept a deal that is not a win for you and your company, you've just signed up a "bad-fit" buyer who doesn't belong on your customer rolls.

▬ ▬ ▬

91 Fourteen Strategies for Creating Win-Win Negotiations

Make sure you leave some fat for the other side.
— Chinese proverb

The best strategy for building repeat business and referrals is to approach every sale with a win-win orientation. In other words, both you and the buyer should walk away from the negotiation feeling as if you succeeded. Implement the following strategies to join the ranks of sales professionals who create win-win outcomes with their buyers and customers.

1. Develop a negotiation perspective of long-term mutual gain versus short-term personal gain.

The essence of win-win negotiation is shared benefit. Stop thinking of making a killing on each sale. You and the buyer benefit from a deal that makes you both happy.

2. Set a trusting, cooperative tone at the outset.

Win-win negotiations are built on a foundation of trust and mutual respect. You'll build this foundation when you:

- State your desire to achieve mutual benefit.
- State your desire for a long-term relationship.
- Insert the phrase "win-win" into your sales call vocabulary, without overusing it.
- Give evidence of your honesty and of a servant attitude.

3. Do your homework.

Flipping coins, shooting from the hip, jumping to conclusions, and pulling figures out of the air will hurt both you and the buyer. Enter the negotiation with as much information as is available. Before you sit down with the buyer to discuss specifics, answer these questions:

- What do I want and why?
- What does the buyer want and why?
- What is the minimum I am willing to walk away with and still feel satisfied?
- What is the minimum the buyer is willing to walk away with and still feel satisfied?

4. Discuss the issues using first person plural pronouns.

First person plural pronouns (we, our, us) highlight mutual benefits and interdependence. First person singular (me, mine, my, I) or second person (you, your) pronouns suggest independence, personal gain, and even confrontation. There's a place for both sets of pronouns during a sales call, depending on your goals at the moment. Talking about "our" needs establishes a tone for win-win outcomes and teamwork when that's your goal.

5. Focus on interests, not positions.

Positions are what you want; interests are why you want them. When you move from the "what" to the "why," you move from a discussion of demands to a discussion of mutual needs. You move from focusing on requirements of the sale to focusing on buyer pain.

6. Increase the number of issues you negotiate.

You increase the chance for win-win outcomes by increasing the number of issues you can resolve. If you focus strictly on price, you set the stage for win-lose. But if you negotiate price along with delivery date, support services, volume purchases, or guaranteed right of first refusal, you increase the opportunities to trade off so that both of you will win something of value.

7. Avoid ultimatums.

Take-it-or-leave-it dictates create pressures and limit options. The only possible outcome of a demand is win-lose. Don't paint yourself or the buyer into a corner.

8. Give to get.

If you give on one issue (e.g., price), ask the buyer to give on another (e.g., order size). Show your willingness to give and take as long as the buyer shares this same willingness.

9. Don't get caught up in the emotion of the negotiation.

Maintain your composure, objectivity, and analytical powers. If you become angry, you lose. When your patience is tested, ask yourself this question: Am I looking for the best solution to this dilemma or am I struggling to protect my ego? (79)

10. Engage in creative problem solving.

The problem you and the buyer are trying to solve can be stated very simply: How can we arrive at a deal that (a) maximizes our individual benefits, (b) minimizes our individual losses, and (c) is fair for both? Brainstorm all the possible alternatives that might achieve these three criteria. Choose an alternative you can both live with.

11. Keep searching for ways to add value.

Leave no stone unturned to find ways to increase the value the buyer receives while maintaining the profitability of your sale. (94)

12. Make concessions incrementally and gradually.

Small, incremental moves over the course of negotiations are preferable to large, drastic moves. You can make more minor concessions than major concessions and thereby provide more opportunities for the buyer to respond in kind. Smaller compromises also have the advantage of not raising suspicions. If you make a major concession, the buyer might think, "If she could give that up, she was asking for far too much to begin with!"

13. Document deals.

Record agreements as they are made. Avoid any possibility of misunderstandings that might change the tone of your negotiation to win-lose and the actuality of your negotiation to lose-lose.

14. When the buyer assumes a win-lose posture, test the limits.

Some buyers will give you ultimatums or other threats designed to force your hand. Rather than counterattacking or accepting the resulting pressure, use the "broken record" tactic. ("I hear that you have to have that price or it's over, but I don't believe you heard that that price is impossible for me.") Each time the buyer pushes, repeat the phrase verbatim. If it's really over, the buyer will walk away. If it's not over, you've established your limits successfully.

━━ ━━ ━━

92　Eight Times to Walk Away from a Sale

> *The proverb says that "You should not bite the hand that feeds you." But maybe you should if it prevents you from feeding yourself.*
>
> — Thomas Szasz

Salespeople have "war" stories—anecdotes about the toughest, easiest, funniest, or most profitable sales they ever made. They also have another story. The one about the sale they turned down. Any person who devotes a career to sales will at some point leave a deal on the table. Even though this is a book about smart moves for *making* sales, you need to stay alert for those times when the smartest move is to walk away.

1.　When the buyer asks for a bribe or kickback.

Buy the sale with service, quality, and performance, not your ethics or integrity. You can be sure that the short-term gain you realize from compromising your principles will extract an exorbitant price later.

2.　When the buyer asks you to break the law or act unethically or immorally.

If you would rather not tell your loved ones what you had to do to get a sale, give it up. (21, 119)

3.　When the buyer continually abuses or demeans you or your coworkers.

Abrasive personalities and difficult people come with the territory. However, limit your tolerance for anyone who harasses, belittles, or demeans. (55)

4.　When a cost-benefit analysis suggests that the time and energy needed to satisfy this customer is not justified by the probable gain.

One of our friends, a manufacturer's rep, has a saying: "Fire any customer who costs twice as much in heartache as he produces in cash flow."

5. **When the buyer asks you to modify your product or service to the degree that you can no longer deliver the very best.**

You need to stand ready to modify and customize your product to get a sale. But don't allow modifications to take you beyond your level of expertise.

6. **When the buyer's stipulations put too many demands on your fulfillment team.**

Maintain goodwill with the manufacturing and service departments of your company. They have to deliver on your sales. Don't ask them to jump through more hoops than is reasonable. (89)

7. **When your buyer asks for modifications that eliminate your profits.**

Make expensive changes in your business solutions only if buyers are willing to underwrite their cost.

8. **When you realize that your solutions really won't work fully for a buyer.**

Never get so hungry that you're willing to close a sale that will not produce a satisfied customer along with a satisfactory profit.

9 ✓ Manage the Post-Sell

Professional salespeople realize that a signed contract is not the end of the sale but the beginning of it. From the moment buyers commit to the purchase you must commit to delivering exactly what you promised. Better yet, buyers should feel that you under-promised and overdelivered. This is how you turn them into raving fans and walking billboards. This is where the referrals come from. This is how to keep those commissions flowing.

93 Twenty Questions That Help You Debrief Your Sales Call

The best never rest. — Ford Motor Company slogan

Regardless of how well you performed on the last appointment, you can always do better. In order to do better, you need to know how you did on that call. Ask these questions of yourself, of a teammate who witnessed the call, or of the buyer you called on.

1. Did I establish an up-front contract with the buyer, specifying mutual expectations and an agenda? (59)

2. Was I mentally and physically prepared? (2, 3)

3. Was I focused on my goals for the call?

4. Was I more concerned about ensuring success or preventing failure?

5. Did I accurately assess the screens through which the buyer views the world? (52)

6. Did I accurately assess the communication style of the buyer? (51, 67–69)

7. Did I adapt my communication style to the buyer's screens and communication style? (63–69)

8. Did I probe for the buyer's pain? (75–76)

9. Did I accurately summarize the buyer's pain to the buyer's satisfaction?

10. Did the buyer commit to recognizing the financial cost of his or her pain?

11. Did I accurately probe for information regarding the buyer's budget? (56)

12. Did I find out exactly when, where, how, and who would make the buying decision? (58, 86)

13. Did I focus my presentation on the buyer's pain? (70, 75)

14. Did I translate all the jargon in my presentation? (83)

15. Did I obtain a definitive (yes or no) answer from the buyer?

16. If the answer was no, did I probe reasons?

17. Did I follow the 70–30 rule? Did I ask questions and lead the buyer to speak most (70%) of the time? (71–74)

18. Did I maintain my composure and respond to stress with questions and reverses? (77–79, 81)

19. Did I lead by letting the buyer control the process?

20. What did I learn about this particular call that will help me in my next call?

▬ ▬ ▬

94 Six Ways to Add Value to a Client's Business

No one can long make a profit producing anything unless the customer makes a profit using it.

— Samuel Pettingill

As the saying goes, it costs five times as much to win a new customer as it does to retain an existing one. Are you doing enough to keep your customers so happy that they wouldn't dream of going anywhere else? Have you convinced your customers that by turning to another supplier their business would suffer? You'll answer yes to this question after you focus your attention away from traditional selling goals. Once you raise your aim from providing your customers with the very best products and services to adding value to their businesses, you'll become indispensable. Here's how to do it.

1. Increase their revenues, decrease their costs, and if possible, do both.

Business decisions are driven by bottom-line consequences. Document your contribution to the client's bottom line.

2. Improve profitability.

Financial ratios are the language of business. Do your homework and show how in the past 12 months, or over the past 12 years, you have increased one or more of these ratios:

- ROA (Return on Assets)
- ROE (Return on Equity)
- ROI (Return on Investment)

3. Advance strategic operational goals.

Every successful organization has a strategy for long-term success. Which of these elements of strategy can you prove you have influenced?

- Increased market share
- Increased customer share
- Increased ability to adapt to competitive pressure
- Improved internal operating efficiency
- Improved products
- Improved customer service
- Achievement of TQM (Total Quality Management) goals

4. Advance strategic human resource goals.

Regardless of what you sell, you have the potential to:

- Increase job security
- Reduce grievances
- Decrease turnover
- Increase the ability to attract high-quality recruits

- Improve employee skills
- Enhance employee productivity
- Increase job satisfaction and morale

5. Improve intangibles.

When you enhance the intangible attributes of a client's product, you accomplish one or more of the preceding goals on this list. Examples of intangibles include aesthetics, prestige of ownership, and reliability. (80)

6. Perform a traditionally in-house operation better, faster, and cheaper.

Outsourcing is the practice of relinquishing an internal business operation to an outside individual or firm. For instance, some companies outsource design and printing, training, audiovisuals, payroll, warehousing, distribution, sales, and certain human resource functions. Do something your client is doing better than the client can do it and you have truly added value. (95)

---

95 Five Ways Customers Want Your Product or Service

Expectations are critical when you serve customers. Meet them to satisfy the customer. Exceed them to make the customer love you. Set unrealistic expectations—promises you can never hope to keep—and your customers will hold you beneath contempt. —Robert A. Peterson

Customers can have up to five expectations for the products and services they receive. Your customers probably differ on the relative importance of these expectations. Know your customers so that you and your service representatives will meet, and even exceed, the particular expectations they hold most dear.

1. Quick.

People don't want to be kept waiting. Their time is precious and they don't want to waste it. Their needs exist now. Certain customers might actually incur a cost each hour or day that your response is slowed. Even customers who do not lose money by your delays will be inconvenienced and angered. The culture in which we live does not support the value of delayed gratification.

2. Right.

Customers expect your products to perform as promised. They count on your services causing the end result you predict. They want quality, reliability, and functionality. They expect you to stand behind your warranties and guarantees. They don't want to have to make return trips or experience multiple deliveries before they get a product that works.

3. Cheap.

We are a nation of bargain hunters and sale seekers. However, sophisticated customers want to minimize total cost and not necessarily price. They don't want to pay a low initial price for products that cost them dearly in the long run because of constant repairs. In the same way, they won't select inexpensive services that dollar for dollar don't deliver the same value as higher-priced, but higher-valued, services. (31)

4. Easy.

Customers don't want to have to jump through hoops to get your product or service. They're not happy about filling out long forms. They don't appreciate being bounced around from one employee to another to get what they need. They'd rather not have to travel across town. They can't afford to study for a Ph.D. in order to use your product or service effectively. Your special credit card or service card makes their wallet bulge.

5. Personalized.

These days more and more customers are willing to pay a little more to receive better attention and more personalized service. They like having their ego soothed by a hotel front desk clerk who remembers their name. They enjoy the ability to revise the standard plans to a home they're building. They see value in custom-fitted clothing. They'll pay more to avoid walking a few extra steps from a remote parking lot. They want you to make them feel special.

━━ ━━ ━━

96 Fifteen Questions to Answer to Ensure Major Account Penetration

> *We must not stay as we are, doing always what was done last time, or we shall stick in the mud.*
>
> —George Bernard Shaw

One of the best targets of opportunity for increased sales is your existing client base. Don't make the mistake of becoming too quickly satisfied with the volume of business your customers provide. Ask and answer the following questions to uncover additional possibilities for revenue with each of your major accounts.

1. **Given the size of the account, what is the sales potential for each product or service sold?**

How potentially lucrative is this account? Is there room for growth? How much? The answers tell you how much effort is justified to devote to growing the account and your offerings to it.

2. **What is your share of the business in each category?**

To what extent might you already be achieving your potential within the account?

3. **What is the cost of this account?**

How much time and expense does it typically take to deal with this account? Is the amount of time spent with the account consistent with the profits generated? Will expanding this account require above-average or below-average resources? The answers indicate how much true return you're likely to receive from focusing greater attention on the account.

4. **How profitable is this account for you?**

Does this account tend to use your highest- or lowest-profit products and services? Can the product mix be made more profitable?

5. **How successful is this account in its marketplace?**

A client making high profits at the moment is ripe for expanding and upgrading its purchases. (28)

6. How healthy is the relationship?

The more White Knights you have and the better the relationship, the easier it is to exploit growth opportunities.

7. Why or how did you get the business?

Did the customer come to you as a result of a referral, or did you develop the sale from a prospect list? How long did it take to get the sale, and did it involve team selling or the efforts of a single salesperson?

8. What factors influence how this account buys?

Is this a *price-sensitive* client swayed mostly by purchase price and maintenance costs? Is this a *service-sensitive* client looking more closely at availability of the product, reliability of service and maintenance, customer service, and the like? Or is this a *technology-sensitive* client needing to stay on the cutting edge? (56, 95)

9. Who's on the decision-making team—buyers, users, influencers, and decision makers?

These groups are not necessarily mutually exclusive, and although one person may make the decision, all parties can influence sales. What role does each person play, and what does each person need from you to play the role favorably? (58, 86)

10. How will the account's short-term and long-term goals affect demand for your products or services?

Are they about to experience restructuring, downsizing, or reengineering? Are they acquiring other businesses or being merged into a larger enterprise? Are they looking for ways to reduce personnel costs through outsourcing? Do they anticipate a major retooling effort? Take advantage of your knowledge of current and future priorities to partner with the account.

11. What are your strengths and weaknesses in relation to the account's goals and priorities?

How good a fit do you appear to have? Where will you need to change, improve, or grow in order to support a long-term partnership? Should you consider such changes or are they too profound to make for any one account? (82)

12. How much business is the account doing with your competition?

With which of your competitors is this account active and for what products and services? Is the competition outdistancing you with stronger products or services? Where can't they touch your competencies? Are they making inroads on business you want through better selling efforts than yours? Do you see these same trends across other accounts? How should you respond? (27)

13. Where do you outdistance the competition?

Where are you distinctly stronger? What do you need to do to stay in the lead? Is the competition neglecting markets that you serve for reasons that should be a lesson to you?

14. What will you do to fend off a competitive raid?

For this account what will your precise response be to attempts by the competition to increase account penetration at your expense? (105)

15. How can you get more of your competitor's business?

The first question is, do you *want* to? If the answer is yes, how hard will it be to take more of this account's business? How lucrative is this account compared to others? What is your plan for getting more of its business? (115)

▬ ▬ ▬

97 Fifteen Customer Service Visions

If you can dream it, you can do it. — Walt Disney

An old-time slogan of General Electric was "We don't desert you after we deliver it." Once you succeed in getting the sale, you want your service representatives to treat customers as well as you did when you courted them. This is more likely to happen once your company creates a customer service vision—a mandate to employees and a pledge to customers of the treatment they will receive. In the book *The Discipline of Market Leaders*, Michael Treacy and Fred Wiersema recommend a focus on one of three "market disciplines." Under the *operational excellence* discipline, companies strive to provide low prices for high value, dependability, on-time delivery, and convenience. Under the *product leadership* discipline, companies provide the highest-performing products or services through a focus on invention and product development. Companies favoring a *customer intimacy* discipline worry less about having efficient operations and advanced products; they are more concerned about gaining a thorough knowledge of their customers' needs and doing whatever it takes to meet those needs. Your sales approach must be consistent with the company's vision in order to retain customers over the long haul. Which of the following sample customer service visions is closest to yours?

Visions within the Operational Excellence Discipline

1. To provide the best value in our industry.

2. To have the lowest price in our market.

3. To be the low-cost provider of choice in our field.

4. To get it there quicker than the competition.

5. To have a waiting line no more than three minutes long.

Visions within the Product Leadership Discipline

6. To offer the most innovative products in our field.

7. To provide state-of-the-art solutions to our customers' problems.

8. To exceed the expectations of our clients.

9. To have the lowest return rate in our product line.

10. To be recognized as having the highest quality in our product line.

Visions within the Customer Intimacy Discipline

11. To partner with our clients to provide customized solutions to the problems they need to solve today.

12. To empower our clients to meet their customers' needs more fully.

13. To give responsive service and personalized advice.

14. To be seen as a trusted business advisor.

15. To be known as the company that cares.

■■ ■■ ■■

98 Eighteen Categories of Questions to Focus Your Customer Service

> *From our customers' point of view, if they can see it, walk on it, hold it, hear it, step in it, smell it, carry it, step over it, touch it, use it, even taste it — if they can feel it or sense it — it's customer service.*
>
> —SuperAmerica gasoline and food chain

How does your customer service stack up? Does it beat the pants off the competition, or are you left holding the pants? Does it delight and dazzle your customers, or does it disappoint and discourage them? You need to know. Here are some questions to ask yourself in order to find out. How many of them can you answer with an unqualified yes?

1. Vision.

Do you have an ambitious and inspiring customer service vision statement that makes a bold declaration of how much you value customers as well as how you pledge to serve them? Do your employees know what that vision is? Have they embraced it? (97)

2. Leadership.

Are your employees treated so well and led with such thoughtfulness, inspiration, and compassion that they act as *partners* with management to provide exceptional customer service? Or do they act more as *hired hands* going through the motions to earn their pay? In other words, do employees have good reason to feel emotional ownership for your quality service goals? (116)

3. Management actions.

Does management walk the customer service talk? Does it act consistent with the customer service vision? Does it fully support employee efforts to provide quality care? Do employees get the resources they need to excel?

4. Recruitment and selection.

Do you go out of your way to hire employees who are emotionally, culturally, and intellectually prepared to provide the quality of service your customers expect and deserve?

5. Performance expectations.

Do your employees know exactly how you expect them to behave in the various customer service situations they encounter, from answering the telephone to resolving customer complaints? Do they have those expectations in writing?

6. Orientation and training.

Are your new employees thoroughly immersed into your quality service culture? Do you baptize them with the waters of the customer service vision before you ever turn them loose on customers? Do you keep that vision constantly in front of them? Do you empower them to meet your customer service expectations by training them fully in all aspects of their work?

7. Accountability.

Are your employees held responsible for embracing the customer service vision and achieving performance expectations? Do they receive periodic performance reviews and other forms of feedback—both positive and negative—to help them stay on track? (116)

8. Continuous improvement.

Are you on an endless customer service improvement journey? Does management practically beg your employees for their ideas on how to serve customers better and faster? Does someone listen to these ideas and make sure the workable ones are used?

9. Bonding communication.

Whether on the telephone or in person, do your employees use language and behavior that bond them to customers? Do they avoid language and behavior that might offend customers or put them off? (101)

10. Being up front.

Are you honest with your customers? Do you keep them informed? Do you empower them to make good decisions? Do you avoid misleading, manipulating, or deceiving them? Do you give your customers complete information and full disclosures, or do they sometimes get burned because they didn't read the fine print or heeded the wrong sign?

11. Quick and complete response.

Do customers ever have to ask more than once for what they want before your team swings into action? As soon as any employee learns of a customer need, does that employee feel personally responsible to see that it is met? Do your customers ever have to lift a finger to get quality service? Will you make the call, fill out the form, check the records, correct the mistake, and otherwise go the extra mile to keep them happy? (95)

12. Making it right.

Are customer complaints resolved quickly, responsively, competently, happily, generously, and remorsefully? When you don't get it right the first time, are you sure to get it right—even *more* than right—the second time? (103)

13. Not products or services.

Do your employees both recognize and act with the understanding that customers do not buy your products and services? (They buy solutions to their problems, reduction of their pain, chances for personal gain, gratification of their needs, fulfillment of their hearts' desires, achievement of their goals, or expansion of their profits.) Therefore, do your employees not allow themselves to be satisfied until the customer is? (95)

14. Taking care of each other.

Do your employees serve their internal customers as professionally, as responsively, and as faithfully as they serve their external customers? Do your various departments and divisions meet each other's needs quickly and fully? (112)

15. Remaining paranoid.

Do you act every day as though you are one day closer to losing every one of your customers? Do you treat them warmly, friendly, sympathetically, courteously, attentively, sensitively, responsively, thoughtfully, and appreciatively? Is there enough evidence to convict your employees of treasuring their clients?

16. Dazzling customers.

Do you underpromise and overdeliver? Do you exceed customer expectations at every opportunity by doing the little things that mean a lot? Do you personalize and customize your service? Do your customers believe that you meet their unique needs? (99)

17. Feedback.

Do you listen to your customers in every way possible in order to understand what they want from you and how well you're providing it? Do you act on what you hear in order to improve the experiences customers have with you? (100)

18. Partnering.

Do you "partner" with your customers? Are you "client-centered" and "customer intimate"? Rather than pushing your products and services on them, do you learn where they're headed and help them get there? (94)

▬▬ ▬▬ ▬▬

99 Ten Commandments of Exceptional Customer Service

> *Natural talent, intelligence, a wonderful education—none of these guarantees success. Something else is needed: the sensitivity to understand what other people want and the willingness to give it to them.* —John Luther

As you and your customer service representatives meet the needs of your customers, 10 basic principles should guide your performance. Translate these principles into your behavior with customers and they would be foolish to desert you.

1. **Treat every customer as though he or she is your first customer of the day.**

Remain enthusiastic, energetic, and positive no matter what may have just transpired with another customer.

2. **Treat all customers equally well.**

Do not be influenced by dress, age, gender, race, accent, nationality, or size of account.

3. Learn the names of your customers.

Use their names when you greet them and when you thank them for their business. Be sure to use the preferred pronunciation and the correct spelling. Don't assume you can use first names. (41)

4. Be patient with customers.

Be especially tolerant of those who make mistakes, who are slow in their thinking or motions, or who do not immediately understand you. You may have been through the process they're experiencing dozens of time before. But each time is the *first* time for *this* customer.

5. Communicate thoughtfully.

Speak with graceful words and helpful tones. Put signs and written directions in places where customers will see them *at the time they need that information* rather than in places convenient to you at times convenient for you. (101)

6. Respond immediately.

Solve each customer's problem after it is first stated; make no customer have to restate a need to you or to another employee.

7. Be polite.

Display your best manners. When you must leave customers to serve them, ask permission to do so. Explain what service you will be providing for them after you depart. When you return, thank them for their patience. "Can you wait while I check this out for you? . . . Thank you for waiting."

8. Don't leave a customer you're with to serve another customer.

Keep the second customer waiting. Better yet, quickly give the second customer something to do while waiting, or have another employee help the second customer.

9. Use good judgment when serving a long line.

Show empathy and appreciation to each person who has waited. Be equally attentive to each person in line without rushing your service to those in front to get to those in back. Don't ask, "Who's next?"—keep track of that yourself.

10. Accept total responsibility for care of your customers.

Don't make customers have to work for exceptional customer service. You make the call, you check the records, you correct the mistake, and you go the extra mile to make them happy.

▬ ▬ ▬

100 Fourteen Steps to a Customer Satisfaction Survey

The best customer to have is the one you've already got. — Dick Shaaf

A number of years ago a White House Commission concluded that fewer than 5% of all unhappy customers voice their dissatisfaction. In other words, you don't hear nearly the number of complaints that you should. Ridiculous? Not when you consider what the mute malcontents do. On average each one says bad things about you to 10 other people, who repeat what they hear to five others. Ultimately, over 90% of dissatisfied customers will leave you for another supplier. It makes sense every day to measure how well your company is meeting customer expectations. This is the best way to dig up those unstated dissatisfactions.

Caution: The purpose of this survey is to gather customer satisfaction data that will enable you to solidify your standing with the customer. Do no selling during a customer satisfaction survey.

Prepare to Conduct the Survey

1. Choose the customers to survey.

This survey will work with any of your customers. You may want to focus first on your largest, most mature accounts.

2. Decide whether to conduct the survey in person or over the telephone.

The survey has the greatest impact when done face-to-face, but you may not have time to meet with every one of your customers. You will certainly want to survey your largest clients in person.

3. Draft your survey questions.

Use our recommendations on the next page to draft a script in your own words.

4. **Schedule a single-agenda meeting.**

Don't combine the survey with a sales call. Show your customers that your one purpose is to improve your service.

Conduct the Survey

5. **Ask the customer for information on what dimensions of customer service are most prized.**

You: "Pat, one of the most important things to us is to continue to build our relationship with you and to be sure you're getting everything you need from us. I have a question. What are the five most important things you look for from us? What are the five needs that we can meet fully to make you 100% satisfied?"

Customer: "I've never thought about it quite that way. Certainly your response time is important along with reliability and technical expertise." (Record the answers.) (95)

6. **Probe for more information as needed.**

You: "That's three, Pat. What else?"

Customer: "Well . . . I'd have to add low cost and personal attention to our needs." (Keep writing.)

7. **Summarize what you hear.**

"Let's see . . . You've given me response time, reliability, technical expertise, low cost, and personal attention."

8. **Ask the customer to prioritize the information.**

You: "How would you rank the importance of those five criteria?"

Customer: "That's tough. I'd have to say that response time is most important, followed by reliability, low cost, technical expertise, and then personal attention." (Record the priority rankings.)

9. **Ask for a fulfillment rating.**

"Pat, I'm going to read those five back to you in the order you gave them to me. On a scale from 0 to 5, where 0 means terrible and 5 means terrific, please give us a score on each one. Response time . . . ?" (Record your ratings.)

10. Ask for comparison ratings on your closest competitors.

"Pat, I want to be sure we're doing a better job for you than anyone else. You've told me that you do business from time to time with the ACME Company. May I ask you to rate ACME on each criterion? Response time . . . ?" (Record the ACME ratings.)

11. Respond to the comparative ratings.

"Pat, I'm pleased that we do so well on response time and technical expertise. You scored us a full point higher than ACME on both. But I'm not happy with how we're doing on reliability and personal attention."

12. Ask for improvement ideas.

"You gave us a four on reliability. What's one thing we can do to bring that score up to a five? And even though personal attention is your least important need, that three we earn there is unacceptable. How can we pull that score up to a five?" (Listen and take notes on the actions recommended by the customer.)

13. Thank the customer, and take immediate action.

"Pat, I really appreciate the time you've taken to give me this vital information. I'm going to get our drivers and order fulfillment people working on these problems right away."

14. Check back soon to verify that improvement actions are having the desired impact on the customer.

"Pat, based on our telephone conversation last month, our delivery team and service department implemented several ideas to improve both our reliability and our attentiveness. What improvements are you seeing on either of those two aspects of our service?" (Listen and respond appropriately to the customer's answer.)

▬ ▬ ▬

101 Seventeen Customer Encounters That Call for Gracious Responses

> Two important things are to have a genuine interest in people and to be kind to them. Kindness, I've discovered, is everything.
> —Isaac Bashevis Singer

Depending on your use of language, you can either build rapport with customers or offend them. When you are positive, upbeat, and considerate in service to your customers, you will often say the right thing in the right way. When you don't feel so enthusiastic and aren't so thoughtful, you run the risk of using language that alienates the people you serve. For each of the following customer actions there is at least one response to avoid in favor of one to try. Memorize them for those times when you might otherwise say the wrong thing.

1. **Greeting a customer.**

   - *Avoid* "Hi" or "Yes?" (The first is nonprofessional, the second is noncaring.)
   - *Try* "Hello," "Good morning," or "Good afternoon."

2. **Customer walks into your store.**

   - *Avoid* "May I help you?" (Bugs customers and typically evokes a "no thank you, I'm just looking.")
   - *Try* "Is this your first time in the store?" (If the answer is yes, you can ask, "What brought you in?" If the answer is no, you can ask, "Thank you for coming back; what brought you in this time?")

3. **Customer asks for help when you cannot immediately give it.**

   - *Avoid* ignoring the customer or saying, "You'll have to wait a minute."
   - *Try* "It will be my pleasure to have you as my next customer. Please make yourself comfortable, or feel free to look around, until then."

4. **Customer asks if you can help at a time when you are able to give it.**

   - *Avoid* "OK" or "Sure." (Although these nonprofessional responses may actually be appreciated in limited situations.)
   - *Try* "I'll be happy [or pleased] to take care of that for you."

5. **You have to leave a customer to check on something.**

   - *Avoid* leaving without saying anything or saying, "I'll be right back." (Too brusque and the customer has no idea if you're leaving to help the customer or grab a bite to eat.)
   - *Try* "Will you be able to wait a few minutes while I check on that for you?"

6. **You return after having checked on something for a customer.**

   - *Avoid* "Here's what I've learned."
   - *Try* "Thank you for your patience. Here's what I've learned."

7. **You need to ask a customer to fill out a form.**

   - *Avoid* "You need to fill out this form."
   - *Try* "I need to ask you to fill out this form for me in order that . . ." (Make it a personal request and give a reason.)

8. **You're asked why your company is out of a popular item.**

   - *Avoid* "They [meaning management] didn't anticipate such demand for that item." (Never use the word *they* when referring to your company.)
   - *Try* "That's proven to be a very popular item. I can show you something else that may do the trick, or I'll be pleased to make your order a priority on our next shipment."

9. **Customer asks for a service you don't provide or a product you don't stock.**

   - *Avoid* "No." (This is a word customers need not hear.)
   - *Try* asking the customer how he or she plans to use the product and then stating what you *can* provide that meets the same need, or stating why you can't meet the need.

10. **Customer wants to do something that isn't possible.**

    - *Avoid* "You can't do that."
    - *Try* "I have another idea for how we can make that happen for you." (A tactful way of saying "you're going to do it my way.")

11. **Customer is clearly wrong or lying.**

    - *Avoid* "You're wrong" or "I don't believe that."
    - *Try* "Please let me show you why that information may be inaccurate." (Let the data, not your words, convict the customer.)

12. **You need to have the customer do something he or she may not be prepared to do without your intervention.**

    - *Avoid* "You have to . . ."
    - *Try* "May I ask you to help me with something?" (The answer to this question is usually "Yes" or "What is it?" either of which opens the way for your request.)

13. **Customer asks you to do something that someone else in your office or store is assigned to do.**

   • *Avoid* "That's not my job" or "I don't handle that."
   • *Try* "If you wait here, I'll find just the person who can help you." (And *you* be the one to explain the customer's need, rather than making the customer restate it.)

14. **Customer asks you to speed up the processing of an order.**

   • *Avoid* "We're doing the best we can!" (Often said in exasperation.)
   • *Try* "You can be assured your order is receiving the highest possible priority" or "Because we have given it the highest possible priority, we should have it delivered to you by . . ."

15. **Customer is difficult for you to understand.**

   • *Avoid* "Can you speak more clearly?" or "It's difficult to understand you." (Don't blame the customer, even if that's where the problem lies.)
   • *Try* "I'm sorry, I didn't hear that. Please repeat what you said."

16. **The transaction comes to a close.**

   • *Avoid* saying nothing.
   • *Try* "We appreciate your business" or "Thank you for allowing us to serve you." (Say it with sincerity and not in rote fashion.)

17. **Customer thanks you or compliments you on your service.**

   • *Avoid* "No problem" or "It's my job."
   • *Try* "My pleasure," "You're welcome," or "It has been my pleasure to serve you." Add the customer's name to the end of each of these responses.

━━ ━━ ━━

102 Nine Strategies for Preventing Buyer's Remorse

> The foolish and the dead alone never change their opinion.   —James Russell Lowell

Salespeople soon discover a transcendent truth about human behavior: People are fickle. A customer may express undying loyalty to you and your product at the moment of purchase but curse you and your product a week later. This fickle mood swing, known as buyer's remorse, is a risk you face each time you close a sale. These strategies will help you minimize that risk.

1. Qualify, qualify, qualify.

Is the buyer in a position to buy what you're selling? Don't sell hang gliding lessons to people with vertigo, venison to vegetarians, or wool suits to executives in Bali. Make sure the buyer and the goods are a logical match. (28, 29, 56, 57, 76)

2. Sell the product, don't hype it.

Underpromise and overdeliver, not the other way around. It's OK to sing the praises of your product, but not in a falsetto voice. Better yet, follow the advice in this book so that the buyer does the singing.

3. Get objections out before the sale, not after it.

One of the reasons salespeople are afraid to make follow-up phone calls to new customers is fear of what they'll hear. Objections prior to the sale increase the likelihood of satisfaction after the sale. Before you close a sale, make sure that whatever might upset buyers later is aired and resolved.

4. Involve the buyer emotionally.

The more buyers are personally and emotionally involved in a purchase the less likely they'll regret their decision. Create emotional involvement by uncovering the buyer's pain and revealing how your product will reduce that pain. (70, 75, 76)

5. Get a commitment, not just an order.

A contract without a commitment is buyer's remorse in the making. Warn new customers not to sign on the dotted line unless they're sure they'll be happy with their decision. After the sale, ask questions focusing on commitment and what you can do to increase it. *Example:* "Pat, can you tell why you decided to buy and what if any second thoughts you were having at the time?" (77, 81)

6. Help buyers plan for remorse.

Rather than hiding from buyer's remorse, bring it out in the open. Help customers develop coping strategies. *Example:* "It's common to question a purchase once we've made it. That's just human nature. For both of our sakes I want to make sure we control any future regret with the contract you just signed. What will you do if you start questioning your decision and what can I do now to make sure that doesn't happen?" (102)

7. **Get agreement on actions in the case that buyer's remorse sets in.**

Make a contract with your customers about what they'll do if they begin to question their decision. At a minimum you want them to agree to call you the minute it happens.

8. **Describe what happens once the contract is signed.**

Buyers turned customers need to know exactly what's going to happen beginning the moment you walk out of the office. If you've done a good job up to this point, you've already described this, but that was to a "buyer." Now you have a "customer" in front of you, who may not remember much of what you said in the negotiation phase of your relationship. Make sure there will be no surprises or rude awakenings.

9. **Follow up.**

Use e-mail, phone calls, cards, letters, and visits. Remain visible and accessible. Let your experience with this product, and perhaps with this customer, guide you in anticipating problems before they occur.

━━ ━━ ━━

103 Eleven Responses to Heal the Customer Who Feels Betrayed

> *Satisfaction guaranteed or double your garbage back.* —Sign on garbage truck in Cambridge, Massachusetts

The most dreaded phone calls are from disgruntled customers who believe that their trust in you and your company has been violated. They counted on you to solve their problems, and you let them down. In fact, they now have two problems: the one they thought you would solve and the "disreputable, conniving, and lying" salesperson they now want to "fire." Here's how to handle that call and possibly even turn it into an advantage.

1. Let upset customers complain without interruption.

Angry customers need to vent and they want you to hear it. If you get hit with an emotional "explosion," so be it. Whether it takes one minute or 10 minutes, listen without interruption. When asked a question, refrain from answering directly. Instead, probe the feelings: "The most important thing right now is for me to hear how you feel and understand what went wrong." The more you probe, the more you learn. The more they speak, the faster they calm down. When customers wind down and you want to hear more, repeat a phrase at the end of their monologue as a statement or a question. To a customer complaining that a product isn't working, you might say, "Not working for you?" Expect to hear, "You bet it's not working! The red button is stuck, and . . ." Also use nondirective questions like "Really?," "And?," "What else?," "Who else?," and "What happened next?" (74)

2. Remain calm and in control of your emotions.

Don't let angry or attacking customers cause you to lose your cool. You can't reason with them if *you* get angry. You can't do your job if you drop into your stomach and feel the need to protect yourself. You *can* do your job if you rise into your head to become analytical and dispassionate about what's going on. It helps to remember that customers aren't really attacking you. Instead, they are behaving angrily for one of these five reasons:

- They feel attacked by you or by another employee.
- They believe you won't reason with them and that they must fire all their cannons to get through to you.
- They are interpersonally incompetent; anger is the only way they know how to express disappointment.
- They are hurt; they feel pain.
- They are fearful or deeply insecure. (79)

3. Thank the customer for calling you.

Express appreciation for the opportunity to make the correction. If you had established an up-front contract that you would be the first one to learn of problems, thank the customer for fulfilling that contract. No matter how negative the conversation has been to this point, begin to turn it around with your thanks and with a calm, unruffled voice.

4. Prove that you listened.

Once you believe the customer has vented fully, paraphrase what he or she said to show that you cared enough to listen and that you understand the problem well enough to resolve it. If your paraphrase is incorrect or if you missed something, ask the customer to help you out.

You: "Now let's see, Pat, you're saying that the software loaded onto your computer properly, but now does not appear on your program listing?"

Customer: "That's exactly what I'm saying."

5. Validate the customer.

Empathize: "I see why you feel that way" or "If I were in your shoes, I'd feel the same way." Note that this is not the same as agreeing with the customer's assertions. It shows you have listened and affirms that the customer's feelings are legitimate—which they always are. The purpose of this step is to fix the customer as you fix the problem. If the customer is talking about an especially emotional experience, statements of empathy sometimes work well both as validation and as an encouragement to say more. Try one like this: "That must be [challenging/painful/difficult/awful] for you!"

6. Apologize.

Apologize for the inconvenience, but don't feel the need to affix blame to anyone. Say something like "We really let you down on this one. Please give us a chance to make it right for you." Don't equivocate or look for scapegoats. You failed to deliver. Own up to it. There may be valid obstacles that prevented you from meeting expectations. However, the customer was paying you to overcome those obstacles. You were compensated for results, not excuses. Offering alibis could anger the customer even further.

7. Collect whatever additional information you need.

Some customers reveal the exact nature of their problem and others don't. Ask questions until you're sure you know what went wrong, the exact pain it caused, and what it will take to fix both the problem and the customer.

8. Deliver a solution.

When you have wronged the customer, make it right quickly, happily, and generously. Customers know that you won't get it right the first time, every time. But they do expect you to correct your errors immediately, without complaint, and possibly with some form of compensation for their inconvenience. Consider, for example, what happens when a diner complains of an inedible entree in a quality restaurant. Her reorder gets top priority in the kitchen, the waiter demonstrates pleasure at solving the problem, and the diner may receive a coupon to return for a free meal in the future. And of course, the customer receives a sincere apology from the manager of the establishment. (95, 99)

9. Be politely assertive with customers in error.

When you believe customer claims are mistaken or untrue, take one of these approaches:

- Double-check the facts in the presence of customers to allow the truth to settle the matter. ("Let's go over that invoice to see where it may have led you astray.")
- Get to the bottom of their assertions. If what the customer said sounds untrue, it may just be that he or she is not explaining the situation very well. ("You may be right about that, but I interpreted the message from your assistant differently. Please tell me again why the situation occurred.")
- Without being patronizing seize on a teaching opportunity. ("I'm glad you pointed that out to me. The information you needed was included on the third page. It's often difficult to find what you need in a manual when you read it for the first time.")

10. Be politely assertive with unreasonable customers.

When nothing you offer satisfies the customer, try one of these questions:

- "What would you like me to do?"
- "What will make you happy?"
- "If you had a magic wand that could produce the ideal solution to your problem, what would it be?"
- "If you had your druthers, what would you ask for here?"

If you can comply with the customer's answer to these questions, do so immediately. If you cannot comply with the request, say why you cannot, and tell the customer what you *will* do. When pressed, be a broken record: "I know you would like me to [customer's request], but I am able to [your solution], only."

11. Reestablish trust and loyalty.

Some married couples who experience betrayal move forward and heal the relationship. Others either tolerate the resulting mistrust or end up in divorce. Convince your customer that a "divorce" is mutually destructive. Solving the problem and asking for trust and forgiveness is a good start but not the total answer. Continue to act as if you deserve to be trusted and forgiven. Follow up often on recently healed relationships. Make sure your solution worked and that no hard feelings remain. (21)

▬ ▬ ▬

104 Twelve Strategies for Hanging on to Your Customers

> *Forsake not an old friend; for the new is not comparable to him: a new friend is as new wine; when it is old, thou shalt drink it with pleasure.*
>
> —*Ecclesiasticus 9:10*

The bad news is that every additional day you keep a customer puts you one day closer to losing that customer. The good news is that you can push that unhappy day further into the future, perhaps even beyond the date of your retirement. Here are a few ways to make that happen.

1. Treat every customer like a buyer.

Be as vigilant to the needs and peculiarities of your customers as you were the first day you called on them.

2. Start a "fuzzy file" for every one of your customers.

Keep a list of their major interests and hobbies. Whenever you run into an article or something that they would appreciate, send it to them. (57)

3. Stroke your customers.

Most people are stroke-deprived. Become a welcome source of attention and flattery for your customers: "Thanks for the business." "Really appreciate you, Sara." "Congratulations on your award; no one could have deserved it more." (62)

4. Keep plenty of White Knights.

In each company you serve, recruit and maintain at least two people who respect you and believe strongly in the value you provide. Build up your corps at every opportunity. No one stays in the same place forever.

5. Recognize the three stages new customers experience.

All new clients will go through three phases once they decide to buy from you.

- In the "new toy" phase they are excited about the future with you.
- During the "learning curve" they struggle with blending your product or service into their operation and their culture.
- Finally, they get it all together in the "results" phase and begin to experience a positive impact on the bottom line.

Boost your value to customers by exceeding the service they expect of you—especially while they labor through the learning curve.

6. Allow no mutual mystification.

Once you get the order, tell your customers exactly what they can expect of you and what you need from them to give knock-your-socks-off service. It's a good idea to put this statement of rights and responsibilities in writing.

7. Determine what it will take to lose the business.

At the beginning of your relationship with each client, ask this question at least once: "What would it take to cause you to take your business elsewhere?" You may need to add, "Would it most likely be because someone else offers you faster delivery, a lower price, more attentive service, a higher-quality product, or something else?"

8. Rehearse with customers how they will handle raids from the competition.

Teach them what questions to ask and what statements to make in response to incoming calls from the competition—especially from those trying to "lowball" your price. For example, rehearse them to ask whether the features critical to them—features you know price cutters can't afford to offer—are included in the price. (102, 105)

9. **Develop an up-front contract on how to handle future problems.**

Based on your experience, you know the likeliest problems to erupt with your product or service or in your relationships with customers. Get your customers to agree to behave in specified ways in each of the contingencies you can anticipate and overall if they encounter a problem. For instance, extract a pledge that they will call a particular phone number if any shipment is more than 15 minutes late. (59)

10. **Develop an up-front contract regarding backup.**

Get your customers to agree on a procedure to follow if they experience a problem and you're not around. Ensure that you have a colleague to back you up for every contingency. (59)

11. **Get an IOU for everything you do!**

Many salespeople do things for their customers above and beyond the call of duty, but fail to get an IOU. Imagine you get a call from a customer who asks for an early delivery of next week's shipment. Don't simply say, "No problem," and get the order processed—even if it's not a problem. Try this instead: "Carmen, I'd love to help you on this, but I think next week's deliveries have already been scheduled. [pause] Look, can I call you back in a few minutes? These people need to realize that we have to bend the rules once in a while for our best customers. Let me see what I can do." Thirty minutes later, call Carmen back to say that it's all been worked out. You have just deposited one favor in that customer's IOU account.

12. **Obey "Emerson's Law of Compensation."**

According to Emerson's Law of Compensation the way to get more from someone is to give them more. At the end of each week make a list of everything beyond the call of duty you've done for every one of your customers. Make sure each of your major clients appears at least once on the list. What will you add to the list next week?

▬▬ ▬▬ ▬▬

105 Six Steps to Ensure You Don't Lose an Endangered Customer

> When your customer is the most anxious, you need
> to be at your best—most competent, confident,
> calmest, and in control of yourself.
>
> —Chip R. Bell

What would you do if you learned that your competition was making a determined bid for one of your best customers? Many salespeople would make one of three mistakes. Mistake #1 is to have so much confidence in your relationship with that customer that you do nothing. Mistake #2 is to go on a fishing expedition with the customer using a question such as, "So how are we doing for you?" There are several problems with a question like this— the most obvious is that you may be doing just fine but your competitor proposes to do better. Mistake #3 is to make your customer uncomfortable by confronting him or her directly with your suspicion. Chances are your customer will deny any behind-the-scenes dealings. Let us suggest instead a process that makes it easy for your customer to level with you and gives you the opening you need to save the business.

1. Take your customer to lunch.

Breakfast or dinner works just as well. Do it at the customer's favorite restaurant.

2. Stroke your customer.

Start off with small talk on one of your customer's favorite topics—golf, professional sports, children, the stock market, or whatever floats the customer's boat. At the right opportunity say, "Pat, the purpose of this lunch is to tell you how much we appreciate your business, and how much I personally appreciate our personal and professional relationship." You may want to add a few more specifics, but don't get sickeningly sweet. (62)

3. Express empathy.

"Pat, I know that from time to time you hear from our competitors. I'm sure the claims and offers they make put you under lots of pressure. Other people in your company who are impressed by what others profess to offer may even be asking you to make a switch or give someone else a piece of your business."

4. Get your customer to talk.

"Pat, how do you handle it when other suppliers or your colleagues pressure you to switch?" When you put it this way, your customer is likely to be honest with you about what's going on. (74)

5. Reinforce the secure customer.

Pat: "Don't worry, I'm handling it very well."
You: "I'm glad to hear that, Pat. Now, if there's one thing I can do to make it even easier for you, what would that be?"

6. Save the slipping customer.

Customer: "Well, to be truthful, it's getting tougher each day to resist."
You: "Which means?"
Customer: "Which means I've given this a lot of thought and I'm going to give ACME 50% of the business just to see how they do."
You: "Suppose they do great. What happens next?"
[Pat responds.]
You: "And suppose they don't do so great. What happens then?"
[Pat responds.]
You: "Can I ask you a straight question, Pat? How did we get here?"
[Let Pat think and answer. Allow a pause to see if there's any more left.]
You: "Is that the real issue?"
[Pat responds.]
You: "I want to find a way to keep us in the most favored supplier position with you. I would like the chance to solve the problems you just revealed and retain that business. Rather than having you risk a throw of the dice with ACME, here's what I can do." [Get specific with concessions that you came to this meeting prepared to give if the news was this bad.] (77)

10 ✓ Selling in the New Millennium

In the first two chapters of this book we focused on physical, mental, emotional, professional, and spiritual preparation for selling. Then we concentrated on techniques that are useful throughout the selling process: finding buyers to sit down with, talking with them to learn about their pains, presenting your solutions, and making sure they received the service and support they deserved. In this final chapter we'll turn to a personally demanding sales arena: the global marketplace. The new millennium presents threats and opportunities never before presented. Implement the advice in this chapter and you will turn threats into opportunities and close the best deals you'll ever make.

■■■

106 Ten Personal Characteristics Required of Sellers in the New Millennium

A competitive world has two possibilities for you. You can lose. Or you can change.

— Lester Thurow

As is true of all major changes, the new century poses both threats and opportunities. Some salespeople see only the threats and build psychological walls against them. They may survive. Others see opportunities. They will thrive. The following personal characteristics distinguish the "thrivers" from the "survivors."

1. Opportunistically rather than fatalistically accepting change.

Anticipate, welcome, and embrace change. Avoid people who cling to the status quo, rationalize change as temporary discomfort, and long for the good old days. (107)

2. Appreciating cultural and demographic diversity.

Increasingly, your team members, buyers, and customers will be people whose race, values, and lifestyles don't match yours. Reject prejudice. Move beyond tolerance. Speed past acceptance. Learn from those not like you. Cherish diversity and thrive on its value to you, to your team, and to your clients.

3. Life-long learning.

Many lists in this book provide tips on keeping up with trends and learning new skills. Retooling, relearning, and reenergizing separate salespeople who simply get by from those who excel. (4, 12)

4. An unshakable ethical core.

Changes in technology, business alliances, product development, corporate loyalty, and competitive pressure put you in ethical minefields you never imagined a decade ago. Reject the increasingly popular notions of situational ethics and conditional morality. Unwavering integrity comes with a moral compass that directs you safely through the ethical minefields. (9, 21, 119)

5. Willingness to be a team player.

Team selling is no longer a fad. Complex sales require it. Tomorrow, even more than today, you'll be challenged to create consensus and cohesiveness within your sales team. (112)

6. Comfort with presentations to teams.

More and more buyers recognize the value of making team decisions. For major purchases, sales calls on individual buyers are becoming increasingly rare. Increasingly popular are "buying centers" used for corporate purchases involving multiple companies, sites, or departments. (86, 87)

7. Creative problem-solving skills.

You can't solve tomorrow's problems with yesterday's solutions. The new millennium tests your ability to solve new, complex, and unexpected problems for which past experience has no answers. You'll require more access to technical expertise and a broad range of resources to assist in the optimum decisions that your buyers demand.

8. Acting locally, thinking globally.

As the business world becomes increasingly interdependent, what happens halfway around the world can affect your customers at home. Although your decisions may be local decisions, they occur in the context of international forces. Remain knowledgeable of worldwide markets so that you understand those forces.

9. Adjusting to customer demands.

Each time the world turns, customers expect more. What was once quick enough, good enough, and cheap enough no longer is. Don't expect the people you serve to grow less discriminating or demanding than they are today. In the '80s they wanted *more for less*. In the '90s they wanted *even more for even less*. Starting with the year 2000 they'll want *everything for nothing*. (26)

10. Customer-oriented selling.

The new millennium dictates customer relations as a seamless process from finding the best-fit customers to serving those customers through unwavering attention to their evolving needs. The emphasis of customer-oriented selling is on the terms "best fit" and "unwavering attention." Reduced profit margins mean that making a bad customer choice will be more costly than ever. Intensifying competition means that more rivals will be out there to take your business away. (94)

▬ ▬ ▬

107 Nine Ways to Become More Resilient in Times of Change

> One of the best lessons children learn through video games is that standing still will get them killed quicker than anything else.
>
> —Jinx Milea and
> Pauline Little

Selling used to be a lot like fishing in a lake. When you weren't baiting your hook, casting your line, and pulling it in, there was time to relax. You knew the lake's challenges. The best fishing locations were predictable, the shoreline was familiar, and the water so clear you could almost see bottom. Navigating your boat was child's play. Then one day you encountered choppiness, which soon turned into scattered white caps. Without warning, you were trapped in rapids—rock-infested white water that buffeted your boat from side to side, threatening to beach it or sink it. Suddenly, fishing became a supreme challenge outweighed by the need to survive. The change buffeting you in sales may arise from technological breakthroughs, workforce diversity, corporate restructuring, government regulation, market shifts, customer demands, or cultural evolution. Whatever its source, you'll find several ideas below to help you deal with it effectively.

1. Anticipate the future.

By remaining educated on the future you'll be able to predict what it will look like and you'll be less shocked when it arrives. Stay current on the relevant literature (books, magazines, newsletters) in your field. If you work in a large company, find out what plans are being made by upper management. Memorize the strategic plan. Listen carefully to the speeches of higher-ups and read their writings in annual reports and other sources. (26)

2. Buy the future.

Remain on the technological cutting edge with your business tools. Be first among your colleagues to move up to the next version of the computer software you depend on. As soon as your computer processor has half the power of popular models, upgrade. (108)

3. Associate with those who welcome the future.

Talk to those in your company and in your profession who are "breaking down walls." Find out what they're up to. Spend more time with creative people and those who are on the cutting edge of new developments. Make friends with trend makers; shun naysayers.

4. Visualize future gains.

There may be a forthcoming change in your life that looks threatening to you. If so, play it through in your mind to a year down the road. Assume you've been living with it that long. Knowing that even the most initially unappealing change eventually offers some form of benefit, what do you anticipate the particular benefits of this change to be? How will these benefits improve your life? Is there anything you can do in the early stages of the change to make those ultimate benefits even greater?

5. Visualize future feared losses.

You resist something new or different when you fear it will result in a loss. Typically, you fear losing control, prestige, self-esteem, order, freedom, comfort, income, a prized possession, or a valued relationship. What loss do you fear in connection with a particular imminent change? Isn't it likely that a year into the change you'll look back and say the loss (a) didn't happen, (b) wasn't so bad, or (c) was more than made up for by an unanticipated gain?

6. Visualize future opportunity losses.

Identify the drawbacks of not changing. What future opportunities will not be realized if you refuse to adjust? What negative fallout will result if you fail to solve this problem or comply with this requirement? What's more costly, the change or the status quo?

7. Accept the future as inevitable.

Most actions we take, which we may not feel ready for right now, are necessary. They are essential building blocks of both personal growth and organizational renewal. Therefore, change is continual, natural, and indispensable if we plan to grow and improve.

8. Be less quick to judge the future.

One of the greatest sources of resistance is prematurely assuming the worst. Don't be quick to conclude that things or people are good or bad. Collect some data first. Curb your knee-jerk reactions. Give new things and new people a chance to reveal their true nature before you judge them. Give change a chance to prove its worth without prejudice.

9. Welcome the future.

Expand your comfort zone. Take one or more of these actions to start looking forward to the future.

- Sign up for a seminar in sales management.
- Audit a college philosophy course.
- Strike up a conversation with someone not in your family who is at least 20 years your junior or senior.
- Learn a foreign language or visit a foreign country.
- Plan your next vacation to a place you've never been.
- Watch a highly competent colleague make a sales call.

- Call on a buyer who could not possibly use your product.
- Rearrange your office.
- Go to a movie you believe is not your style of entertainment.
- Experience worship in a church or synagogue of another denomination.
- Experiment with a new toothpaste, shampoo, or soap.
- Change the newspaper, newsmagazine, and TV news channel that you depend on.
- Take your next five restaurant meals in places you've never eaten before.

108 Fifteen Ideas for Better Use of Information Technology

A computer will not make a good manager out of a bad manager. It makes a good manager better faster and a bad manager worse faster.

— Edward Esher

Willie Loman, the protagonist in *Death of a Salesman*, needed only a calendar, an order book, and a phone to conduct business. Modern Willie Lomans feel naked without laptops, cellular phones, beepers, and the Internet. Yet simply having access to the latest technology doesn't mean that you will be more successful than your competitors or even keep up with them. You must learn to *use* this technology to its greatest advantage and thereby leverage your selling skills.

1. Keep up with what's available.

New products are coming out all the time with greater power and more features. Scour airline magazines, PC publications, and professional journals for the latest technology. Before you buy anything, call the manufacturer to learn the schedule for the next product upgrade. Be wary of price specials. That's often a sign that a new and improved version is about to be unveiled.

2. Always buy the most advanced technology available.

Don't ever say to yourself or the sales clerk, "I don't need that much power." In the case of computer processors, their speed doubles every 18 months or so. If you don't buy the fastest, you'll soon have the slowest.

3. Buy an up-to-date laptop or palm-held PC now.

Don't wait any longer. A portable computer will carry all your information, give you access to the Internet and e-mail, and connect you to every other computer in your company's network. Be sure to choose a model that can share files with your desktop computer. Carry it with you everywhere and guard it with your life, particularly in airports.

4. Learn to use a contact management system.

A good computerized contact management system will organize your day, plan your week, signal you when to send personal cards for anniversaries, record critical notes on each buyer, maintain phone, fax, and e-mail addresses, help coordinate your efforts with others in your company, and more.

5. Record important ideas on a reliable notation system.

Insights, reminders, and creative ideas often come at a time when you're not ready to take advantage of them. Be sure to capture these cerebral gems. Whether you use a small notebook, palm computer, or a pocket recorder is up to you, as long as your system works. The one system not to rely on is your memory.

6. Learn a presentation software program.

Some clients will want to see and hear the bells and whistles of animated graphics and stereo sound. Others simply want the basic nuts and bolts on a sheet of legal pad. Develop the option of clicking the mouse through a slide show if that's what it takes to make the sale. (109)

7. Use voice mail to record personal reminders.

Voice mail systems are your personal secretary. Leave detailed messages, instructions, and reminders to yourself.

8. When you get into a customer's voice mail, play back your message before releasing it.

Voice mail systems often provide the option of listening to your message before sending or deleting. Once you develop the habit of listening to all your messages before sending them, you'll find yourself rerecording about half your messages and thereby improving your impact on clients.

9. Develop an electronic filing system that works for you.

For some people an electronic filing system simply means they can lose more files quicker. As the number of your contacts, proposals, and products increases, so too will your files. Develop a single system that provides you with immediate access to what you want when you want it.

10. If you are part of a sales team, explain your filing system to them.

Filing systems are reflections of the idiosyncrasies of the people who create them. If team members want to access one of your files in your absence, how would they do it? (112)

11. Make sure files prepared by others are compatible with the applications on your laptop or desktop.

You may have to "massage" files so that you can open them in your applications. You never want to be in the situation where an error message pops up on your screen in a buyer's office.

12. Distribute an agenda before a videoconference or teleconference.

An agenda is even more important for an electronic meeting than it is for a face-to-face meeting. Answer these questions:

- When will it begin?
- When will it end?
- Who will be the participants?
- What are their titles, organizational affiliations?
- What specific issues will be discussed?
- What is the order in which they will be discussed?
- What is the "bottom line" of the meeting? What is the action item the call or conference should produce? (86)

13. Don't tie up a buyer's or customer's fax machine with an unsolicited, lengthy fax.

If you have a long document, send it through courier services. The more paper you use up, the more patience you try.

14. Turn off anything that can beep when making a sales presentation.

The buyer should never be made to feel less important than the person making your beeper or telephone ring. Even if you don't answer the page, it's an unnecessary and annoying interruption.

15. Create a useful Web site.

Develop pages on the Internet that supply buyers and customers with attractive information about you and your products or services. Link the site to any archival or real-time information that will help you sell and service your customers. Give your customers valuable updates. Ask your customers what links they would like to see on your Web pages. (110)

▬ ▬ ▬

109 Eleven Hints for Using Presentation Software

We are all hungry and thirsty for concrete images.
— Salvador Dali

Presentation software is a marvelous audiovisual aid. With its help you can perk up a presentation by projecting information displays from your computer onto a screen. It adds excitement to what otherwise might be a lifeless list of items. It turns a monotonous table of figures into a multicolored bar chart. It relieves you of the worry that each slide is perfectly centered on the screen. It shows off your technological savvy. It can even ease your podium jitters by keeping people more focused on the screen than on you. Follow these hints to unleash the power of presentation software.

1. Make good use of the medium.

Follow these guidelines in preparing your slides.

- Orient them to the horizontal axis. This is the "landscape" option on your computer, and the only orientation choice offered for presentation software programs.
- Limit each slide to seven lines of text per page plus title; leave big margins.
- Use upper-case and lower-case letters—not all caps—in large (24-point or greater) sans serif fonts.

- For text use either clear or yellow lettering on a dark background, or black lettering on a light (preferably yellow) background.
- Favor bulleted lists over sentences and paragraphs.
- Favor bar charts and pie charts over tables of figures.
- Make use of graphic illustrations and cartoons.

2. Test your ideas.

Once you make your choices of color and layout, test two or three slides on the same equipment, and in the same room if possible, that you'll use for your presentation. Have a colleague there for an opinion. Is everything readable and pleasant to view? Do your choices complement the theme of your presentation?

3. Plan to keep the lights on.

The idea of a presentation is to enlighten your audience, not keep them in the dark. Make sure the projection system you're using and the room in which you'll present will allow you to project your transparencies with a good amount of room lighting. Strike a balance between readability and room illumination, rather than care only about readability.

4. Get organized.

Too many software-assisted presentations are delayed at the outset while their deliverers get the right wires in the right sockets and get their computers to speak to their projectors. Start setting up early and don't hesitate to scream for help.

5. Plan for disaster.

Have a hard copy and overhead transparency backup for crucial presentations. Murphy has more fun with laptops hooked up to projectors than with just about any technology you can imagine.

6. Don't throw away your notes.

Many people believe that presentation software takes the place of notes. So they stand off to one side of the screen with their eyes on it much of the time. Speak to your audience, not to the screen. The few times you look at the screen should be to influence people to focus there with you on a particular point of interest. (87)

7. Position the screen wisely.

Make sure that neither you nor anything else is blocking the audience's view of the screen. Position it so that it reflects a minimum of stray light.

8. Don't practice your pirouette.

Rehearse with your slides so that you know the exact order of slides. Then, *do not* turn around every time you change slides to make sure the next one is on the screen. You don't want to give your audience motion sickness.

9. Don't insult your audience.

They can read. You don't need to repeat every word on every slide. Trust that they'll read at least half of it without your help. Paraphrase, don't read, the rest.

10. Give them a break.

Too many people overuse presentation software. The end result is a slide show rather than a presentation. You *are* allowed to project nothing on the screen now and then so your audience can focus on listening to you speak, rather than being numbed by a parade of bulleted lists.

11. Remain in charge.

Too many speakers have allowed computer-assisted technology to relegate them to the shadows. It's almost as though they're the ventriloquists and the computers are their dummies. Stand up and speak!

━━ ━━ ━━

110　Eighteen Tips for Selling on the Internet

> To tour our factory, click on the door.
>
> —Message on a
> manufacturer's
> Web page

Gone are the days when merely having a site on the Internet gave you a competitive advantage. Today you need an Internet presence just to stay competitive. Moreover, some buyers won't deal with you unless you have that presence. Whether you have a significant presence in cyberspace or are just planning to enter, these tips will increase your site's earnings potential.

1. Set specific, strategic goals for the site.

Incorporate an Internet presence in your strategic marketing goals and plans. What exactly do you want the site to accomplish? Consider these possible strategic goals:

- Provide technical support services
- Provide in-depth product information
- Provide in-depth information about the company
- Provide product updates
- Display endorsements from current customers
- Solicit opinions, views, and questions from customers
- Answer customers' questions
- Build customer loyalty
- Generate leads
- Take sales orders
- Receive electronic payments
- Enhance prestige and image

2. Contract the services of a professional Web site developer.

Both the science and art of Web site development are changing at a dizzying pace. Invest in a consultant who understands the latest developments.

3. Contract the services of a professional ISP (Internet Service Provider).

An ISP provides the hardware and software to make it happen. This is a one-stop shop for your entire Internet needs. Get competitive bids and ask to talk to current customers.

4. Support the site with marketing material.

What good is having a site if no one knows it is there? An Internet site is only one component of your marketing effort. Support that site with printed materials. Include the site address on marketing materials, business cards, letterheads, proposal covers, invoices, fax cover sheets, newsletters, and annual reports.

5. Put your Web address in directories.

Your organization can be listed in the directories of trade associations, chambers of commerce, networking groups, and the like.

6. Link your site with search engines.

Search engines are like directory assistance for callers or card catalogs in libraries. They help customers (users) find what they are looking for. List your company, your Web site, and key words specific to your industry on all search engines you can find. Ask your Web consultant or ISP vendor for recommendations.

7. Connect hot links to your site.

Explore mutual interests with suppliers and trade associations in your field and in related fields. They may be open to linking their sites to yours if you can demonstrate some value that your site adds to theirs.

8. Design an interactive site.

Your Web page can allow for one-way communication, two-way communication, or real-time two-way communication. This last category includes chat rooms. Costs increase as the site increases in interactivity, but so does its appeal. Sites that solicit information from buyers and customers are more valuable than those that are little more than billboards in cyberspace.

9. Make it easy to use.

Once a buyer or customer hits your site, directions should be simple, clear, and self-evident. If anyone has to read extensive text or directions to either solicit or provide information, your site is probably doing you more harm than good.

10. Make it appealing.

Like almost no other advertising media the Internet allows you to be creative. Balance your need to instruct with the need to attract and rivet your customer's attention. A professional Web site developer will help you achieve this balance.

11. Make it secure and protected.

Having one's credit card number ripped off during Internet commerce is less likely than with paper receipts. Even so, many customers won't send payment or provide sensitive information if they believe your site is not secure. Build security into it, describe it, and then guarantee it. Your ISP has the software to provide security.

12. Make sure all copy is accurate and grammatically correct.

Once your message is in cyberspace, anyone in the world can see it. Check copy as diligently as if you were composing text for a billboard in Times Square. (11)

13. Monitor its use and its effect.

You can collect data from the site indicating who uses it, what they use it for, and how long they stay on. This information will help you modify and adapt your site to meet the unique needs of your buyers and customers. Be sure to follow privacy guidelines for using such information.

14. Offer value.

Don't just sell yourself on your Web site. It should contain more than information about you. Show buyers and customers how to use your products. Give them valuable advice they can use. Consider some of these ways to create a "hot" site:

- A customer newsletter
- A customer chat room
- Management tips
- Maintenance tips
- R&D developments affecting your products or services
- A customer bulletin board of industry-related news
- Contests, raffles, freebies, discounts
- Free products and services that will be more than paid for by the advertising value of your giveaways.

15. Make your site easy to get into.

A site that's full of color, animation, and long gouts of text can crash an older computer. Even buyers and customers with speedier processors will get impatient waiting for a complex site to download.

16. Don't let your Web site become a "cobWeb" site.

Limit the promises you make that new material will appear on your site by a certain date. It will be harder to keep up with your plans than you think. From time to time check the "last modified" dates at the bottoms of the pages of your site. Keep them all within six months of today's date to maintain a look of currency.

17. Constantly tinker with the site.

Add or delete links, improve the graphics, add or delete audio or video components, and change the value-added information. View your Web site as a work in progress rather than a finished product.

18. Prepare to fix it on a moment's notice.

Assume that the site will develop glitches, bugs, or other maladies of the electronic age. When that happens, fix it immediately. A Web site your customers can't access is worse than no Web site at all. Ask your ISP to build maintenance and repair guarantees into your contract.

━━ ━━ ━━

111 Eleven Principles of E-mail Etiquette

> We must learn which ceremonies may be breached occasionally at our convenience and which ones may never be if we are to live pleasantly with our fellow man.
>
> — Amy Vanderbilt

Isn't e-mail wonderful? You sit in front of your computer screen for a few moments, bang out a few words on your keyboard, hit the "send" button, and your message is in front of the recipient in minutes. You can transfer documents from your word processing clipboard right into the e-mail text or you can attach whole files to be downloaded at the other end. You can save time sending sales proposals, deliver the same message to multiple addressees in a flash, and stay in touch with your customers as never before. You can even highlight words in color. What a convenience! Except for one thing. E-mail is so convenient that it lulls us into careless and sloppy communication. Follow the advice below to avoid falling into the trap of electronic laziness.

1. Do not send an e-mail message when . . .

- A simple phone call can do the trick.
- You're disciplining someone or giving negative feedback.

- You're delegating work assignments.
- Your message contains a powerful emotional component that needs the reinforcement of appropriate voice tone or body language.
- You're afraid to say it face-to-face.

2. Write well.

Use both upper-case and lower-case letters. A message written entirely in upper case or lower case is difficult to read and speaks poorly of your professionalism. Use proper grammar and spelling. Some e-mail programs won't spell-check or grammar-check your documents. Limit paragraphs to five to seven lines. Organize your thoughts in advance so you can keep the message short. Watch those cutesy symbols known as "smileys" or "emoticons" that you make with colons, parentheses, and other symbols on the keyboard. They're not good substitutes for clear English in most professional communication. (48)

3. Be careful with format.

If you're sending a proposal, product prices, or pages full of sales figures, the format and layout you see on your screen will not necessarily be duplicated on the recipient's screen. Rows and columns may arrive at their destination out of kilter. Be sure to send format-sensitive documents as attached files, and make sure your recipient will be using the same version of software to retrieve those files. The standard format for sharing files in Windows word processing is "rich text" (.rtf).

4. Know your recipient.

People have different ideas for the uses and the style of e-mail. For all recipients, learn their preferences and respect their wishes. If you don't know the other person, be conservative rather than risk alienation. Unless you know your recipient appreciates such things, be careful about your use of slang, dialects, and other unusual forms of expression.

5. Respect your recipient.

Don't let the apparent anonymity of e-mail make you feel immune and protected from common standards of decency. Watch your language. Don't overuse capital letters for emphasis. The reader will feel shouted at.

6. Write for the world.

In composing your message assume that it will be widely circulated. Anything you say in an e-mail message can be saved, printed, or forwarded on to other people with a couple of clicks. In many companies e-mail is considered to be company property and subject to scrutiny. The bottom line is that e-mail is not secure. Don't write anything you'll regret later.

7. Don't send junk mail.

Many e-mail services allow you to send or forward copies of e-mails you receive to others. Don't overuse this feature. If you do send someone a copy of a message directed to a specific recipient, let that recipient know that others are receiving the same message.

8. Identify yourself and your subject.

Start off your e-mail with the reason for your message. Fill in the subject line. Provide a salutation at the beginning and sign-off at the end.

9. Respond helpfully.

When you're responding to a message, the recipient may have forgotten what he or she originally wrote. First, it helps to keep the subject heading the same or tag the words "my response" on to the end. Second, it helps to include critical portions of the original message immediately above your responses. Never answer questions yes or no without referencing the questions in your message. If your response to an e-mail is on a different matter, change the subject line.

10. Try not to use "receipt requested."

If your service allows you to ask for proof that your messages are actually read, use this feature only when you really do need verification. Many people will view it as a sign of mistrust.

11. Read your e-mail at least twice a day.

Most people count on messages getting to you the same day as sent. If you're going to subscribe to e-mail, accept the challenge to use this medium responsibly.

▬▬ ▬▬ ▬▬

112 Fourteen Tips for Successful Team Sales

When a team outgrows individual performance and learns team confidence, excellence becomes a reality. —Joe Paterno

Perhaps the greatest change in organizations today is the shift from independence to interdependence, from individual efforts to teaming. Teamwork is having a profound impact on selling. Many companies today leverage the synergy of teams by sending two or three team members to sell an account. This is especially true when accounts represent significant revenue or when the team will be cross-selling various products. If you're thinking about bringing in a selling partner, or if a sales team is about to be formed, consider these ideas.

Set Up the Team

1. Blend people with complementary skills and styles.

The primary value of a sales team is that regardless of the question asked, the problem posed, or the situation encountered, someone on the team will be able to handle it.

2. Select team members because of special talents or rapport with particular buyers.

You may choose a team member who is not in sales per se but has a degree in engineering from the same school as the buyer. Or you may select a team member who is a CPA because the buyer is also a CPA and bases all decisions on spreadsheet analyses. Or you may choose a team member who has firsthand knowledge of the buyer's problems from having worked in the same industry. Or you may load persevering people on a sales team for a deliberate buyer who will require a long sell cycle.

3. Exclude those who want to be stars.

You need a group of team players. The key to teamwork is orchestration with all players doing their part. Sales professionals unwilling to suppress their egos or their need for stardom will hurt the effort. Eagles do not fly in formation.

4. Select a leader.

Equality is admirable before and after the sales call but during the meeting one person leads. This should be the person who can best bring in the account and at the same time displays some leadership talent. The leader outlines the contracts established for the meeting and highlights the history of the account to date. The leader also presents possible what-if scenarios for discussion and team choices among alternative responses. The more empowered this sales team is to be, the more appropriate it is that members select the leader. (116)

5. Develop a clear set of rules.

Everyone on the team must agree to the following:

- There is only one leader.
- Only one person talks at a time.
- No deviations from the rehearsal, except as initiated by the team leader.
- Team members monitor and take their cues from the leader's nonverbal messages.
- Balanced participation—no clamming up and no hogging the airwaves.

Before the Call

6. Communicate expectations.

If you're partnering with someone for this particular sale, make sure you both have a clear understanding of expectations, roles, and responsibilities. It's especially important to agree as to how each person's part is to be played during the sales call. Set the ground rules. For instance, who is the team leader, who takes notes, who speaks to what topic, who answers what type of question, who asks what type of question, and so on.

7. Develop a single, unified sales "voice" and philosophy.

Don't bring in a partner who doesn't understand and respect your sales philosophy. For example, if only one of you buys into the selling system described in this book, the two of you will work at cross-purposes. The same thing is true for a larger team. The group must speak as one.

8. Build trust.

The most important outcome of steps #1 and #2 is to build confidence in each other. Be candid about your worries about team selling. One way to do this is to conduct a team-building session where you discuss the answers that each of you gives to this question: What's the one greatest misgiving you have about the success this group will have in team sales? Another strategy would be for each person on the team to tell the others one thing to do more of and one thing to do less of, compared to the past, in order to support the team effort. This feedback may sound like tough stuff, but tens of thousands of dollars may be hanging in the balance.

9. Rehearse.

Give new team members their assignments and review the particular sales techniques that the team has come to embrace. Practice how you will handle the greatest challenges you expect from the buyer.

During the Call

10. The team leader sets and guides the agenda.

The team leader is responsible for guiding the group toward its sales objective. At a minimum the leader will:

- Introduce team members.
- Ask the buyer to summarize any discussions of pain that preceded the meeting.
- Ask the buyer to describe the agreements and progress to date.
- Manage traffic (guide the discussion) during the call.
- Use the "verbal baton" to instruct a partner to take over: "Georgia, you brought up two questions about ACME as we were driving over here today. Would you mind sharing those now?"
- Use the "eye baton" by looking at team members who should respond to buyer questions or who should speak next.
- Summarize and conclude.

After the Call

11. The leader debriefs the call with team members.

Ask and answer these questions. Did the sales team achieve its goal for the call? Did the buyer get what he or she wanted? What could have gone better and why? What can happen immediately to capitalize on success or repair whatever damage was done? Who should follow up with whom and how? (93)

12. Assess the status of the account and the approach.

Are you where you want to be with the account? Should you continue with the team-selling approach for this buyer? What will we do differently on our next team call? Involve the entire team in this analysis.

13. The leader channels buyer questions and team responses.

Expect buyers to call team members directly without going through the team leader. The team member should clear the answer with the team leader before responding, unless the answer is innocuous or is one that was previously cleared.

14. The leader counteracts attempts to split the team.

Some buyers will try to play one team member off against another or otherwise attempt to create strife within the team. These buyers believe they can strengthen their position by weakening the cohesiveness of the team. The team leader must be prepared to defeat this divide-and-conquer strategy. This may mean exposing the trickery to warring team members or calling buyers on their actions and diplomatically insisting that they end. (92)

▬ ▬ ▬

113 Thirteen Rules for Selling Across Cultures

> *The Japanese have nineteen ways of saying no—suggestive of the extreme finesse with which their language navigates the shoals of conflict, avoiding it if possible.* —Richard Pascale

On his 1984 trip to China, President Reagan bought a souvenir, paid the shopkeeper in local currency, and said, "Keep the change." The shopkeeper ran after Reagan and with embarrassment and humiliation returned the money. At the time, tipping was officially outlawed in China. If the President of the United States can make mistakes in cross-cultural encounters, what chance does the salesperson have who is without access to state department experts and CIA briefings? This list may not transform you into a polished international ambassador, but it will prevent you from looking and sounding foolish as you sell around the globe.

1. Get a personal guide or coach.

Get up to speed on the culture as quickly as possible. You don't have the luxury of making mistakes and learning from experience. Get advice from someone who has firsthand experience with the culture. If no one in your company fits the bill, contact your embassy, a professional translation service, or the most cosmopolitan university nearby.

2. If you and the buyer do not speak a common language, work through an interpreter you trust.

Contact a professional interpreting/translating agency. Meet with the interpreter prior to the session to build trust, develop a feel for his or her "style," and allow that person to get accustomed to your speech patterns. (114)

3. Set realistic goals for the sales call.

An American selling to an American can get to the point and ask for the sale in the initial meeting. Selling in certain other cultures often requires considerably more time in bonding and establishing rapport. Be prepared for laying the groundwork over a series of meetings.

4. Understand the importance of context in affecting semantics across cultures.

Some cultures rely a great deal on nuance, subtlety, setting, and nonverbal communication in determining the meaning of words. These are *high-context* cultures. Others rely less heavily on these factors and are considered *low-context* cultures. The following list ranks 11 cultures along the context continuum from high to low:

- Japanese (context is most important)
- Arab
- Greek
- Spanish
- Italian
- English

- French
- American
- Scandinavian
- German
- Swiss (context is least important)

5. Speak simply, not simplemindedly.

You are speaking to foreign adults, not foreign children. Never give the impression that you are speaking down to them or that they are less sophisticated or intelligent than you.

6. Depending on the culture, "no" may not mean "no," "yes" may not mean "yes," and "maybe" may not mean "maybe."

In high-context cultures (Japanese, Arab, Greek) there is a reluctance to bluntly agree or disagree because of an aversion to displaying or hurting personal feelings. Validate your understanding so that you know exactly what has been accepted or rejected. Never interpret agreement or cordiality as unequivocal acceptance of your proposal. "We'll do all we can" may mean "This won't fly."

7. Don't trust someone just because he or she speaks English, nor mistrust someone because he or she doesn't.

Some buyers will speak English as a second or third language. Other buyers will speak only their native tongue. Never assume that because you and the other person speak the same language there should be greater trust. And never assume that because you don't speak the same language there must be mistrust. Lying occurs in every language.

8. Never assume more informality than is appropriate for the culture.

Taking off your coat, loosening your tie, rolling up your sleeves, and calling the person by his or her first name are taboos in certain cultures unless you have explicitly been told to do so. If you must err, err in favor of formality.

9. Limit negotiation to major issues and the spirit of the contract.

Save the details for your respective "lieutenants" or attorneys. Cross-cultural negotiations are fraught with geopolitical "ifs, ands, or buts." Let your assistants or counselors find a way to make the deal work once you and the buyer decide on the deal.

10. If you use graphics, make sure their content is appropriate for the culture.

You may want to translate all text to ensure cross-cultural understanding. Also consider the appropriateness of any drawings, cartoons, or graphics in proposals or on presentation software that may be funny to you but offensive in other cultures. The best test is to have an interpreter or native of that culture check your graphics and give you pre-meeting feedback.

11. Learn at least these three phrases in the buyer's language: "Hello," "Good-bye," and "Thank you."

These are bonding words conveying your attempt to honor that person's culture. Make sure your pronunciation is impeccable. The more of the buyer's language you learn, the more respect you show.

12. Watch your nonverbal language.

Match the tonality, volume, and rate of this culture's speech patterns. Make sure your body language (posture, movement, gestures, handshake, eye contact, selection of seats in offices and automobiles, clothing, and handling of business cards) is appropriate. (62)

13. Give the buyer your bilingual business card.

One side of your business card will be printed in English. The other side will be printed in the buyer's language. Hire a professional translator and use a printer with bilingual printing experience for the purpose. (37)

▬ ▬ ▬

114 Nine Tips for Selling Through an Interpreter

> *To work through an interpreter is like hacking one's way through a forest with a feather.*
>
> —James Evans

It's tough enough to sell when you and the buyer speak the same language. When you speak different languages, the problems are legion. Yet the new millennium is one where the "global village" replaces isolationism, and international trade reigns supreme.

Even mom-and-pop operations conduct business around the globe. When the person across the table from you speaks a different language, the tips on this list may make the difference between success and failure.

1. Decide on a single shared interpreter or a personal interpreter for each of you.

If you and the other party totally trust one another, and the negotiations are not complex, a joint interpreter is the way to go. If either of you believes that there may be tricky maneuvering, or if there is mutual distrust, you should each hire your own translator.

2. Use an objective, disinterested interpreter.

Would you want your buyer's secretary to act as interpreter? Do you think the buyer would have trouble if you chose your bilingual brother-in-law? An interpreter who has no vested interest in the outcome of the negotiation is best.

3. Hire a professional interpreter.

Although many multilingual people can paraphrase thoughts from one language to another, that doesn't mean they are professionals. In business negotiations, an interpreter who is accredited, certified, or referred by a professional agency best serves all parties. Check the phone book, local university, state department, or chamber of commerce for referrals.

4. If describing the product or service requires technical knowledge, hire an interpreter with that knowledge.

Professional agencies have access to interpreters with specialized expertise. Don't use an expert in eighteenth-century French literature to interpret the jargon of mechanical engineering.

5. Use the interpreter as a cultural coach.

The interpreter is an excellent source of cultural information. He or she should be able to give you a quick summary of cultural do's and don'ts.

6. Maintain eye contact with the buyer, not the interpreter.

You aren't selling to the interpreter; you're selling to the buyer. Make believe the interpreter isn't even there.

7. **Don't use idioms or slang.**

Regardless of the skill, acumen, and experience of the interpreter, phrases like the following will lose something in translation:

- We can *roll this out* for you in no time.
- He's *playing it close to the vest.*
- That project is a *no-brainer.*
- The competition *cleaned our clock* in that market.
- I need some *wiggle room* on this deal.

8. **Make sure that what you hear from the interpreter confirms what you see in the buyer's nonverbal behavior.**

Monitor the buyer's nonverbal cues: eye contact, facial expressions, gestures, posture, and tone of voice. In total these cues provide an overall impression. If this impression contradicts what the interpreter is saying, seek clarification.

9. **Allow for twice the time as normal to negotiate through an interpreter.**

The interpreter must repeat everything you and the buyer say. Build enough extra time into the agenda.

▬ ▬ ▬

115 Ten Ways to Increase Customer Share

> *Treat every customer as an appreciating asset.*
> —Tom Peters

Companies are constantly trying to increase market share. This means raising their percentage of the total volume of business in a particular market. The route most companies take to increase market share is to find new customers or take customers away from the competition. A more modern approach to the same goal stresses selling to current customers as opposed to focusing almost solely on acquiring new ones. This approach is called increasing customer share. When you adopt this approach, the cost of your sales effort is reduced. That's because of the rule of thumb suggesting that you'll spend five times more to acquire a new account than to sell to an existing one. Use these ideas to focus more intently on customer share.

1. **Move from a short-term sales approach to a long-term relationship approach.**

When your focus is on getting the sale today, you may suffer from a short-term view of customer value. Build customer relationships for long-term mutual benefit. Relationship selling views every customer as a valuable asset of the company to be nurtured and grown.

2. **Put customer needs to reduce pain above your need for financial gain.**

You get repeat business when customers believe you've delivered in the past and have put their needs above yours.

3. **Immerse yourself in your customers' industry and competitive pressures.**

The more you know about your customers' problems, the more empowered you'll be to suggest solutions to them. Walk a mile in their wing tips, loafers, sneakers, safety shoes, or two-inch pumps. (28, 94)

4. **Offer discounts, premiums, and special bonuses to valued customers.**

Here is a sure way to alienate your current customers: Continually tell them how special they are, but offer a sweeter deal to attract new customers than the one you offer to them. (32)

5. **Contact, contact, contact.**

Stay connected to your customers. Maintain constant, periodic contact with them, and not necessarily to discuss sales. Call just to say, "I've been thinking of you."

6. **Forget about merely satisfying your customers.**

From now on, completely, unequivocally, and passionately take their breath away with astounding service. Simply meeting their needs isn't going to keep them out of the clutches of the competition. (97–99)

7. **Ask them for a "wish list."**

If you could satisfy your customers' expectations beyond their wildest dreams, what would they have you do? Find out, and figure out a way to make it happen.

8. Put them on customer advisory boards.

Once customers start consulting with you on the health of your business, they have a vested interest in keeping you successful. (30)

9. Form strategic alliances.

Today's customers look to you as a resource for meeting the needs of their end users. Become a valuable cog in their production process and they will want to stengthen their partnership with you. (115)

10. Don't expect the relationship to stay the same.

Monitor the strength of the bonds with your customers and look for ways to reinforce them. Monitor the internal affairs of your customers. Search for ways to become an even more relevant supplier as those affairs change and evolve. (104, 105)

---

116 Fourteen Areas in Which to Become a Complete Sales Team Leader

The price of greatness is responsibility.

—Winston Churchill

The complete sales leader infuses direct reports with both accountability and ownership. *Accountability* means that team members accept full responsibility for the outcomes of their efforts. *Ownership* means that members of the sales team feel total emotional commitment to the goals and purposes of their organization. Your leadership performance can build accountability and build ownership on your sales team for each of these critical areas of sales management.

1. Vision.

Accountability: Create a clear and unequivocal vision—a desired future, ambition, or aspiration—for your sales team. (97)
Ownership: Share that vision with those who must help you achieve it and strive to gain their acceptance of it.

2. Expectations.

Accountability: State clearly and unequivocally your expectations for employee performance.
Ownership: Ask employees what expectations they have for your leadership.

3. Appraisals.

Accountability: Give employees a formal performance appraisal, based on your performance expectations, at least once a year.
Ownership: Ask employees for appraisals of your leadership performance and respond positively to what you hear.

4. Feedback and response.

Accountability: Constructively criticize employee failure to meet performance expectations and impose consequences when necessary.
Ownership: Praise, recognize, reward, and give full credit to those who meet performance expectations.

5. Communication.

Accountability: Speak precisely, powerfully, and positively. (10, 11, 60)
Ownership: Listen to the requests, questions, answers, reactions, concerns, fears, suggestions, interests, arguments, and ideas of employees. (74)

6. Managing by Wandering Around (MBWA).

Accountability: Keep your eyes and ears open so you can find out what's going on when you MBWA.
Ownership: Demonstrate support of employees and show interest in their work when you MBWA.

7. Staff development.

Accountability: Hold the members of your sales team responsible to plan their professional growth and development.
Ownership: Take every opportunity to train, coach, mentor, advise, and counsel sales team members. (4)

8. Change.

Accountability: Lead people through times of change and continually point to the opportunity created by organizational development and personal renewal. (107)

Ownership: Let your team help you decide upon and plan for change and help them deal with the threat they see in changes they have to make.

9. Continuous improvement.

Accountability: Demand excellence, total quality, and continuous improvement in all operations of your sales team.

Ownership: Admit your mistakes and embark on a continuous self-improvement journey.

10. Ideas.

Accountability: Sell your ideas effectively to superiors, peers, and subordinates. (19, 20)

Ownership: Ask others for their ideas; use them whenever possible and give them credit.

11. Meetings.

Accountability: Run a tight ship at meetings where important things get done and good decisions get made. (18)

Ownership: Run meetings where participants feel free to contribute honestly and constructively.

12. Conflict, anger, and hostility.

Accountability: Resolve conflict *with* others openly, directly, and constructively with continual focus on a solution that fixes the future. (103)

Ownership: Resolve conflict *between* others openly, directly, and constructively with continual focus on a solution that fixes the future.

13. Control.

Accountability: Remain confidently in charge and make necessary decisions with certainty. (6)

Ownership: Delegate responsibility, share power, and get others involved in decision making that affects them. (13)

14. Teamwork.

Accountability: Insist on team play and make your specific expectations for teamwork known. (112)
Ownership: Be a team player yourself.

— — —
117 Nine Guidelines for Sales Force Compensation

> *The will to win is worthless if you don't get paid for it.* — Reggie Jackson

Numbers drive sales professionals. How many cold calls did you make this week? How many contracts did buyers sign? How many customer contacts did you initiate? How many did you respond to? And perhaps the most important number of all—How much money did you make? As you and your colleagues move into the new millennium you'll want to consider all the possible ways to reward selling success in new and creative ways. You may not be a sales manager in a position to determine the sales compensation. However, the information on this list will help you understand how compensation systems evolve, and may even give you some ideas to suggest to your boss.

1. Establish strategic sales goals for your compensation plan.

Your primary goal is to increase revenue. However, this monetary goal is enabled by achieving certain strategic goals. Sales professionals may be rewarded for meeting one or more of these goals:

- To increase market share in a particular territory.
- To increase sales of a particular product line.
- To increase customer share.
- To decrease customer defections.
- To increase sales to former customers.

2. Establish strategic human resource goals for your compensation plan.

Your primary human resource goal is to attract and retain a motivated sales force. However, this primary goal will include a subset of strategic goals. For example:

- To ensure our compensation is competitive in the marketplace.
- To ensure our compensation is internally equitable.

- To ensure our sales force possesses state-of-the-art knowledge and skills.

3. **Establish strategic goals supporting corporate culture or philosophy.**

Your primary corporate culture goal is to create a "family of employees" whose performance is interdependent and who are committed to the long-term survival of the company. Employees might be rewarded for advancing strategic goals in this area as follows:

- Compensating any employee who refers a customer.
- Compensating any employee whose referral results in a sale.
- Compensating for sales team presentations.
- Compensating employees for overall company performance.
- Compensating production employees responsible for exceptional performance on a one-time order.

4. **Make sure the plan does not include contradictory goals.**

You may intend to increase teamwork in the sales force and increase total company sales. However, if two salespeople are paid strictly on a commission basis and if that commission is a major portion of total salary, they may sabotage one another while working the same territory.

5. **Provide a competitive fringe-benefit package.**

Health care, pension, vacation days, sick days, and educational benefits have become standard fare. To stand out and attract the best and the brightest, consider flashier carrots: dependent day care, 0% interest loans, free use of corporate retreats for family vacations, and so on.

6. **Don't forget "psychic income."**

Notes of appreciation, pats on the back, and sincere thank-yous will be remembered long after a bonus check is cashed.

7. **Provide family-oriented prizes for sales contests.**

Salespeople often sacrifice time with family to meet sales quotas. Consider these "pay-back" opportunities:

- Weekend getaways for the family.
- All-expenses-paid vacations.

- Free baby-sitting or dependent care for six months.
- Remodeling of a kitchen or bathroom.
- Maid service for six months (a WOW prize for two-paycheck families).

8. **Incorporate customer satisfaction data into the compensation plan.**

Salespeople responsible for measurably higher customer satisfaction should be rewarded. (100)

9. **Link a portion of individual compensation to team or company performance.**

Follow the model provided by professional sports teams: superstars receive a base salary with bonuses tied to team performance. Encourage team members to support each other by using team performance as one criterion for individual bonuses or merit increases. Never sign a huge bonus check to one or two people in the same year you file corporate bankruptcy.

▬ ▬ ▬

118 Ten Expectations to Have When Your Company Is Merged

> *Deceive not thyself by over-expecting happiness in the marriage state. Marriage is not like the hill of Olympus, wholly clear, without clouds.*
>
> —Thomas Fuller

What happens when your company is acquired or merged? This list takes a realistic look at that process. If—or perhaps we should say *when*—your employer experiences a takeover you'll know how to rise to the occasion. Internalize these ideas and you'll be more than a survivor. Help yourself and your colleagues thrive in the midst of a marriage with a firm whose culture may be totally unlike the one you know.

1. **Know that no company is immune to mergers or takeovers.**

They're happening everywhere, so don't waste the time it takes to say, "Why us?" And don't expect to understand the reason why your company has been targeted. Mergers and acquisitions don't always make sense to those who weren't part of negotiating them.

2. Expect your colleagues to get goofy.

There will be uncertainty and ambiguity. Decisions you "need" from others right away may not be made for months or even years. There will be mistrust and suspicion among employees who feel insecure and even betrayed by the decision. Self-preservation will rule. More than ever people will be looking out for #1.

3. Expect to get goofy yourself.

Allow yourself to grieve properly. When the announcement is made, expect to experience disbelief. You'll be shocked and even feel a certain amount of numbness. Next, you can expect to get angry, be bitter, and feel betrayed. You'll blame management for making the merger necessary, for letting it happen, or for botching it. Then the hurt sets in. You may brood, get depressed, and even feel some guilt. Part of your self-treatment will be to look on the past with fondness and the future with alarm.

4. Expect people to jump ship.

Those with other options are likely to see this as a good time to exercise them. Don't be shocked if your boss or best friend is in this number.

5. Expect communication to break down.

Don't count on timely, accurate, or sufficient information. People may be afraid to be totally honest, and especially to disagree with higher management. During mergers the rumor mill flourishes and exaggeration runs wild. (10)

6. Expect morale and productivity to suffer.

Employees see coworkers leaving the organization. People get frustrated. Poor communication leads to lowered productivity. People spend time talking and worrying about what's going to happen. They are afraid to take risks. They play it safe and go into holding patterns. You'll be tempted to let up yourself.

7. Expect teamwork and cooperation to go out the window.

People become self-centered. Organizational politics run high. Power struggles break out. The team becomes relatively less important than it once was. (112)

8. Don't expect the merger to work as well as promised.

Mergers achieve their full potential something less than half the time. In the other cases they either fail outright or achieve less than hoped for results in cost savings, productivity boosts, or market penetration. The decisions made by higher management, the cooperation provided by the rest of the company team, and unpredictable market conditions all factor into how your merger will turn out.

9. Expect to survive.

Not only will you survive; you'll probably *thrive*. Many people look back on their company's merger as the best thing that ever happened to them, despite the degree of success of the merger itself. Here's how to make this true for you.

- Manage your attitude and maintain a sense of humor. Even though you don't like everything about the merger, make a commitment to cooperate so fully with it that your superiors and your team will prize you. (22)
- Tolerate the inevitable mistakes management is going to make. They weren't perfect in the past; neither are they likely to be so now. \
- Make yourself more resilient to change. You became a success under the old way—learn and accept the new way. Decide to prosper even more under the new set of rules. (107)
- Get to know the other company. Meet and befriend as many people there as you can.
- Take advantage of the merger to grow by moving into a new job or learning a new set of skills.
- Create a plan to manage your stress. (24)
- Continue to do your job as well if not better than you do it now. (23, 107)

10. Expect to experience another merger.

Just because you've been mugged once, doesn't mean you've had your only mugging in life. Expect to live through a merger, or even a hostile takeover, at least once again before you retire.

━━ ━━ ━━

119   Ten Prescriptions for Staying Out of Legal Trouble

It ain't no sin if you crack a few laws now and then, just so long as you don't break any.

— Mae West

As a sales professional you walk a tightrope, balancing the competing demands of making the sale versus not doing something wrong to get the sale. Moreover, you perform this balancing act in an increasingly litigious society. Following these prescriptions will either keep you out of the courtroom, or put you on the right side of the case, as you practice your trade with zeal.

1.   Be truthful about the performance of your product or service.

Any claims you make to a buyer or customer must be accurate. If you state it as fact, it must be. (82)

2.   Be truthful about your competitors or their products.

Occasionally it pays to make yourself look good by making your competitors look bad. Just be sure that the shortcomings you highlight are real and current. (27)

3.   Direct attention to warnings and operating instructions.

Warnings are written to prevent accident, injury, and potential liability. Instructions tell the customers how to get the most value out of the product. Say nothing to trivialize the importance of warnings and instructions. In fact, where you feel written warnings don't go far enough or instructions are less than clear, add whatever is necessary to protect your customers.

4.   Counsel customers to use products for their intended purposes.

Misuse of a product that causes damage or injury makes you potentially liable. Don't hint at or imply misuse in any way.

5.   Make production and pricing decisions on your own.

Don't consult with competitors in making these decisions. You may be guilty of price fixing. (31)

6.   Submit bids independently.

Some companies conspire with competitors to submit low bids on a rotating basis to ensure equitable market share. This is another example of price fixing. What you call "informal discussion" the government may label "collusion."

7. Publish price lists independently.

Competitors sometimes agree to announce prices on the same day to avoid detrimental impact on stock prices or on customers. Again, this is potentially price fixing.

8. Use your attorney to keep you out of trouble, not just bail you out of trouble.

It's much easier to prevent legal problems than solve them. Use your attorney to:

- Check all your sales contracts.
- Advise you on issues of potential product liability.
- Provide the best-case and worst-case legal scenarios every time you consider a joint venture with another firm, especially if that firm is a competitor.

9. Keep in constant contact with customers.

You can prevent many legal problems by simply remaining accessible and clarifying issues before they become legal schisms. Remember that it is always preferable to discuss differences in a restaurant rather than litigate them in a courtroom. (98–100, 104, 105)

10. Make sure that anyone acting on your behalf communicates with clients ethically and legally.

More than one company has been sued because a sales rep or technician misrepresented company policy or product specifications. When an employee ("agent") of yours speaks, you speak. (21)

11 A Day in the Life of Wally Weakcloser

After reading the first 119 lists in this book, you're ready at last to meet Wally Weakcloser—a product-savvy salesperson from the Wilbur Widget Company. In this final list, your job is to help Wally do better with the advice in this book. It's up to you to turn Wally into a top-notch sales professional.

— — —

120 Forty-four Things Wally Did Wrong

Imagine you are Wally Weakcloser's new sales manager. You just called Wally on the phone to introduce yourself and to tell him that the next day you'd like to get to know him and his territory. The points that follow record Wally's words and actions. In each item on this list he either makes a mistake or passes up an opportunity. We've presented our advice for Wally at the end of the list; come up with your own answers before looking at ours.

Wally's Response to Your Call

1. "I'm glad you called. I would have called you first, but I've been worrying since I heard about your arrival that you wouldn't have the time for me."

You Arrive in Wally's Office the Next Morning

2. "Why don't you sit down for a minute and have a cup of coffee, and I'll explain my plans? I have all my prospects listed on this sheet of paper. It's a little difficult for me to keep them in order, so I bought this indexed Manila folder to keep them in."

3. "I've sorted them out, also. These on the yellow cards are the ones I consider good leads. These on the blue cards are not so good."

4. "I generally just call this other group—our present customers—on the phone for their orders. They've been buying for years."

5. "Have another cup of coffee. I need to go over my cards for today. Won't take me more than another twenty minutes."

Twenty Minutes Later Wally Makes a Cold Call on the Telephone

6. "Before we leave, I need a few more people to call on. Here's the yellow pages. Let's see if I can pick a good one. Ah! ABC Industries; that sounds good."

7. "Hello, ABC Industries? Let me talk to the gentleman in charge of widget buying."

8. "Mr. Jones, this is Wally Weakcloser from Wilbur Widget Works. We make [three minutes of explaining]. I'd like an appointment to see you to show you our product. [pause] Sure, I can tell you more over the phone: [three more minutes]. [pause] Sure, I'll call you back first of the week. Thanks!"

Wally Gets Ready to Make Personal Cold Calls

9. "OK, let's make some cold walk-ins. I wish the company had a better ad program to give me more backing on these calls."

10. "I hate to make these calls. I always wind up feeling so 'wiped-out' when I'm through. People can really get you where you live."

11. "I can't wait until I learn to like cold calling. This is the worst part of sales."

Wally Reaches the Site of His First Call

12. [To the receptionist] "Good morning, sweetheart."

13. "I'm Wally Weakcloser with the Wilbur Widget Works. This is my new boss. We sell custom widgets. And good ones too! Who buys widgets here?"

Secretary: "Do you have an appointment?"

14. "Well, no, but I'm sure as soon as you tell him what I have to sell, he'll see me."

   Secretary: "I'm afraid I can't do that, Mr. Weakcloser. Let me have your card. I'm sure he'll call you if he needs any. OK?"

15. "Sure, here it is. My company doesn't spare any expense to make a good impression."

At the Next Site the Buyer Comes Out to Meet Wally and You in the Lobby

16. "Ms. Smith, I'd like to have a few minutes to show you why the Wilber Widget Works is the #1 widget maker in the world. . . . Our widgets are [launches into a five-minute product seminar]."

   Ms. Smith: "Come back to my office."

17. "You're going to love this! I brought along several brochures and even a flip chart to show you how our widgets work. . . . Now, here is our model #435. It's automatic [a 10-minute demonstration follows]."

   Ms. Smith: "Interesting; how much are they?"

18. "The price is the best part about it. This group is only $287 a gross."

   Ms. Smith: "Too much, Wally, can't afford them."

19. "Wait! I think I can show you how you can afford them."

   Ms. Smith: "I'm sorry, Wally. Now, if you'll excuse me, I have work to do."

20. "I'm sorry you can't see the value in Wilbur widgets. Maybe we can help out in the future. Good-bye."

Outside Ms. Smith's Office

21. "I'm sick and tired of calling on these good-for-nothing buyers. This call wasn't worth the energy it took to push the elevator button."

At the Next Site, Wally Already Has an Appointment

22. "Hi, June, tell George good-old Wally is here."

A few minutes later George greets the two of you in his office and says, "Like I told Wally before, we're going to give your company every consideration before we make our decision."

23. "Thanks, we appreciate that. Why don't I show you some widgets?"

24. "Where can I set up the slide projector? [Wally has trouble setting up the equipment.] Darn! You never have a spare bulb when you need one. Well, I'll just pass these slides around and everyone can hold them up to the light."

   [Twenty-five minutes later] *George:* "That's fine, Wally. It really looks good. I'm enthusiastic about your widgets."

25. "Me too!"

   George: "How much are they?"

26. "I know you probably won't have budget problems with these. They're only $287 a gross."

   George: "Wow, Wally, I never had any idea they were that much!"

27. "These widgets have the highest quality on the market. The most talented and best-paid machinists in the industry produce them. If we priced them lower, we'd have to reduce our quality standards down to the level of our competition."

28. "I can understand your need to spend your money wisely, George, but don't you think $287 is fair?"

   George: "It's simply more than we can spend."

29. "Look, George, we don't usually make a practice of cutting

the price, but maybe since you're such a good customer, my boss here can do something about dropping it."

George: "Look, Wally, I'll tell you what. I'll arrange for my boss and the other purchasing agent to be here after lunch to look at your product. Maybe they can help you, although I can't promise. How's that?"

30. "Great!"

After Lunch Wally and You Return for the Group Meeting

31. "Gentlemen, we appreciate your seeing us." [Twenty minutes of demonstration follows.]

George's boss addresses you: "We'd like you to know that Wally is the best salesman your company has ever sent to call on us. He's a real hotshot. Must have written the book on selling."

32. "Thank you, Mr. Frank. Someone in my job doesn't hear that enough."

The purchasing agent: "OK, Wally, that certainly was a fine presentation, but we also understand you can't deliver them in the colors we need."

33. "That's right, we can't do that."

Mr. Frank: "Wally, we have to be careful how much we pay for widgets. This hasn't been a very good year for us."

34. "I understand. Things haven't been that good for me either. I was just telling my wife, Winnie, last night, we've just got to cut down."

35. "Gosh, there's one thing I forgot to mention. Our widgets are plastic coated for longer life! I didn't want to forget to tell you about that."

The purchasing agent: "Wally, if it weren't for price, you might be able to help us. But that price . . . I think you're out of our range. Why does your company always have such high prices?"

36. "They're not as bad as some of our competitors, and you only get what you pay for!"

37. "How about it, gentlemen, want to sign up?"

> *Mr. Frank:* "Wally, I think we need a little more time to think about your proposal, even though we told you we could make a decision today."

38. "I understand. You want to be sure you make a smart buy."

> *Mr. Frank:* "Let me ask you this, Wally. If we do decide to give you an order later in the week, can you get us product in ten days instead of the usual two weeks?"

39. "Sure. No problem."

> *Mr. Frank:* "OK, Wally, look for our call."

40. "Fine, looks like you guys are under a little pressure today, anyway."

> *Mr. Frank:* "Thanks, Wally, you certainly have a way of understanding."

On the Next Call, Wally Gets a Sale; You Question Why He Didn't Ask for a Referral

41. "Doesn't make sense asking her for referrals. She didn't seem too interested in helping me in her network."

You and Wally Part Company

> *You:* "Wally, it's been an interesting day. I need to get back to my office now, so we don't have time to talk. I'd like you to make arrangements to get into the home office early next week. We can debrief today's trip then, and I've got a selling system I'd like to show you."

42. "Actually, boss, I'm taking my family on vacation to the beach next week. That's what this big stack's all about—eight months of trade journals I need to catch up on."

43. "But, heck, vacation can wait—my family will understand. What day next week works best for you?"

You: "We can meet week after next. Meanwhile, I'll send you an e-mail in the morning with some ideas for you to be thinking about while you're away."

44. "E-mail? Gee, boss, I haven't had the time to get fancy with all that Internet stuff. Do you suppose you could overnight it to me?"

    You: "Wally, I have a better idea. Please go to your favorite bookstore tonight and get a copy of *Close the Deal*. The trade journals can wait. Give the book just an hour a day on the beach. When I see you week after next, come armed with three ideas you get from the book that you believe will increase your commissions."

▬ ▬ ▬
Wally's Mistakes

Did you find these mistakes in Wally's day? The comments that Wally's sales manager might make in the meeting week after next with Wally come out of the ideas presented in this book. Each one is keyed to the numbers in front of Wally's actions in the list above; many of them are cross-referenced to earlier lists. Do you spot other errors? Contact us via e-mail (see page 310) with a reference for each additional mistake you believe Wally made. Include your address and we'll send you a gift for your submission.

1. Worry is interest paid in advance on borrowed trouble. (9, 23)

2. No organization. No contact management system. No database. (13, 15, 25)

3. No priority rating system. (13–16)

4. Each day you keep a customer, you're one day closer to losing that customer. Connect with them, Wally! (104, 105)

5. Too much "no-pay-time" activity done during "pay time"— especially when you're with your manager! (14)

6. Don't you have any better sources for leads than the phone book? And, anyway, start at the back of the directory and work toward the front. ABC Industries gets all the cold calls.

Zygon Manufacturing never received a cold call from anyone. (36)

7. Only with incredible luck will you get through the receptionist with an opening like that. And don't settle for the buyer so easily; go for the top. (38)

8. That traditional approach got you nowhere. You really don't think the buyer will take your next call, do you? Where was your 30-second commercial? (37, 39, 83)

9. Accept responsibility for your successes and your failures. (5, 12)

10. Sales is no place to get your needs met—only a place to go to the bank. Wally, separate your "I" (your identity) from your "R" (your role as a salesperson). (43, 55)

11. You don't have to like cold calls—you just have to make them. (42)

12. Ugh! That kind of chauvinism and condescension should get you kicked right out of here. At best you've made an enemy. (3, 10, 38)

13. That receptionist hears this line every day. What makes you think it will work? (38)

14. Don't answer her question that way. Use a reverse, and keep reversing until she relents or kicks you out. (38, 71, 77)

15. You don't really think her boss will see that card, do you? And Wally, don't say anything unnecessary about yourself, your product, or your company. (38)

16. You're spilling your candy in the lobby. Give a 30-second commercial about what you help people do—not the features of your product—and start looking for pain. "We enabled Interweld Industries to cut their die manufacturing time an average of three days." (39)

17. People don't buy features and benefits. They buy ways to avoid or overcome pain. First learn Ms. Smith's pain. Then you can direct your presentation to helping her see the link between your widgets and pain reduction. (70, 75, 76)

18. Ms. Smith asked a question, which gave you an excellent opportunity for a reverse that may have revealed to you the importance of price versus value in her decision. (77)

19. Don't go positive when the buyer goes negative. You passed up a great chance to use negative reverse selling. (81)

20. Don't wimp out so easily. You had at least one more chance to probe for pain. (76)

21. You don't learn anything from getting a yes. You learn from your no's. What did you learn *here*, Wally? (79, 93)

22. You could have made that receptionist your ally with a respectful approach. This stuff is right out of the '50s. (38)

23. Find out exactly what he means by "every consideration before we make our decision." Don't worry about your presentation until you've gotten out all the pain. (75, 76)

24. Be prepared for disaster. Have a backup to whatever technology may let you down. (86, 109)

25. Don't be enthusiastic. According to the "pendulum theory" a buyer that is too positive too early will swing negative later on. Consider using negative reverse selling. (81, 102)

26. Again, Wally, you failed to answer a question with a question. And don't try to read the buyer's mind about his budget—find out what it is. (56, 58, 71–73, 77)

27. Never answer an unasked question. Because you didn't respond with a question, you enabled the buyer to put you under pressure. (71–73, 77, 78)

28. Wally, you're where you should never be—on the defensive. If you had used reverses instead of responses, you could have helped George resolve his own price objection. If you're feeling pressure during a sales call, you're doing something wrong. (77–79)

29. You ambushed your sales manager, Wally! Not good teamwork! And if you're going to give a price concession, you better get something of equal or greater value in return. (89–92, 112)

30. You should have asked, "What happens next?" (58, 59)

31. Have your contact person sum up the progress you've made before you talk—especially regarding how he sees your product eliminating pain. Add whatever George leaves out. Save the presentation for the kill. (86, 112)

32. You should be stroking the customer, not the other way around. (49, 53, 62)

33. Don't answer an unasked question. This was another great opportunity for a reverse that would have kept you in charge of the call. (72, 77)

34. There are no social calls in sales. Your meter's always running!

35. Don't paint "seagulls" in your buyer's picture. Frank may be allergic to birds. Rather than overload him with information, work on his pain! (70, 75, 76, 78, 80)

36. Price is never the issue. Reverse your way out of this dilemma and prove it. (77, 89)

37. Never ask for the order—make the buyer give up. (70–91)

38. There should have been an up-front contract that prohibited this response. If there was, don't sit still for a violation of it. (59)

39. Get an IOU for everything you do. (104)

40. Never help the buyer end the interview. (81)

41. No mind reading, Wally. *Always* ask for referrals. You may have to be creative to get them, but get them. (28)

42. Keep up with trends, rather than stockpile those journals. (26, 106–108)

43. Don't sacrifice this important time with your family for a meeting—even with the boss. (22)

44. Get on-line! (108, 110, 111)

About the Authors

Sam Deep is a trainer, motivational speaker, and organizational consultant who taught at the University of Pittsburgh and other colleges for more than twenty years. He is now Adjunct Professor of Management and Strategy in the Graduate School of Industrial Administration at Carnegie Mellon University.

Lyle Sussman is Professor of Management in the School of Business at the University of Louisville, as well as a consultant and speaker. He received his Ph.D. in Communications and Industrial Relations from Purdue University and serves on the faculties of several state and national banking schools.

Deep and Sussman's management advice has been featured in the *Chicago Tribune*, *Cosmopolitan*, *Working Woman*, and USAirways's *Inflight Audio Entertainment*, among many other publications. Their satisfied clients include Alcoa, Dean Witter, General Electric, KFC, Motorola, the Pittsburgh Symphony, Westinghouse, and Xerox.

The **Sandler Sales Institute** was founded by the late David Sandler to teach his revolutionary system of selling to organizations and individuals. With 180 affiliated offices across North America, the Institute is one of the business world's leading sources of sales training materials, including Sandler's book *You Can't Teach a Kid to Ride a Bike at a Seminar*. The Institute does not reveal its clients' names, but it has worked with some of the country's leading industrial, service, and financial firms.

✔ Does Your Sales Team Need Help?

Get greater value from your reading of this book by using Sam Deep or Lyle Sussman in one of these ways:

As Motivators

Call 800-526-5869 to see if the half-day program "Close the Deal" is coming to your city. Sam and Lyle also give customized presentations throughout the country on many of the topics covered by lists in this book. If you're planning an educational event for your company or sales team, either Sam or Lyle, or both, would be pleased to join the agenda.

As Management Trainers

Sam and Lyle lead a wide variety of seminars and workshops as well as motivational presentations in leadership, team building, conflict resolution, managing change, customer service, interpersonal skills, and effective presentations. These programs draw on expertly crafted workbooks and management guides to reinforce the learning experience.

As Team Doctors

Sam and Lyle can help you change the answer to any of these questions from yes to no.

- Do you have an executive team or sales team that needs better cohesiveness?
- Does your board or committee need to improve its effectiveness?
- Does your company suffer from interdepartmental conflict?
- Do you have two managers who don't cooperate with each other?

- Are too many of your employees less than loyal team players?
- Are your self-directed teams failing to live up to their promise?

Write to Sam and Lyle at Seminars by Sam Deep, 1920 Woodside Road, Glenshaw, PA 15116. Call 800-526-5869. Send e-mail to deepsam@aol.com. Visit the Web site: www.samdeep.com.

# Do You Have
Sales Smarts?

Would you and your sales team like to enhance your ability to apply the concepts in this book to your selling? Sandler Sales Institute has a wide variety of programs meeting the needs of selling professionals. With over 30 years as a sales skills training provider, SSI knows what it takes to sell successfully in today's world.

Sandler offers ongoing, comprehensive sales training, coaching, and professional networking opportunities, as well as one- and two-day seminars in relevant topics. Whatever your choice, you'll gain an arsenal of useful skills that will translate into growth and earnings.

If you're responsible for managing a sales force, you'll want to look into our Strategic Sales Management Program. It provides the next step in sales training, with a proven approach to the challenges faced by those in leadership positions.

For information on the Sandler Sales Institute and a trainer in your area, call 888-701-4993, or write to Sandler Systems, Inc., 10411 Stevenson Road, Stevenson, MD 21153. Mention that you saw us in *Close the Deal* and we'll send you a free copy of the booklet *Why Salespeople Fail*. You can also visit us on the Web at www.sandler.com. For information on SSI as a business opportunity, call 800-669-3537.